THE KING INCORPORATED

Neal Ascherson was born in Edinburgh. He reported from Asia, Africa and Central Europe for the *Observer*, where he later began his celebrated weekly column. Journalist of the Year in 1986, Ascherson's books include *Games with Shadows*, *The Polish August* and *Black Sea*.

THE KING INCORPORATED

Leopold the Second and the Congo

NEAL ASCHERSON

Granta Books
London

Granta Publications, 2–3 Hanover Yard, London N1 8BE

First published in Great Britain by
George Allen & Unwin Ltd 1963
This edition published by Granta Books 1999

A CIP catalogue record for this book
is available from the British Library.

5 7 9 10 8 6 4

Printed and bound in Great Britain
by Mackays of Chatham plc

CONTENTS

INTRODUCTION TO THE PAPERBACK EDITION

WHEN I WROTE THIS book, more than thirty years ago, the Congo was in its third year of independence, devastated by war, economic collapse and unscrupulous interference by European business interests which the 'international community' had failed to control. Belgium had abandoned its vast colony in 1960, with no real attempt to prepare the population for self-government or to educate or train a Congolese political class to take on the burdens of responsibility and nationhood. The attempted secession of Katanga, largely fomented and financed by multinational copper corporations, had cost the lives of Patrice Lumumba, the only potential African statesman to emerge in the Congo, and of Dag Hammarskjoeld, the UN Secretary-General. Backed by the Americans, Mobutu Sese Seko was embarking on what was to be an interminable and corrupt despotism that only ended in the 1990s.

Today, once more, the Democratic Republic of Congo, formerly Zaire, is a site of bloodshed. The fall of Mobutu and his replacement by Laurent Kabila did not bring peace and democracy, but what has been described as Africa's 'first continental war'. The aftermath of genocide in Rwanda continues to destabilize the whole region, and outside interference – this time, by other African states – continues to make a mockery of Congolese independence.

The term 'failed State' is often abused. It applies to the Congo, however. In the decades since independence, this huge territory has not been able to establish an agreed political identity acceptable to its peoples, to work through the curious but necessary process of 'inventing' its nationhood or to evolve a leadership whose authority is recognized by its main ethnic groupings. The causes of this failure go back beyond the short-sighted nature of Belgian colonialism. They lie, ultimately, in the trauma inflicted on the peoples of the Congo basin by Leopold II, King of the Belgians, and his so-called 'Congo Free State'. The brutalities and disruption brought about by that regime, in effect a private and personal colony whose single purpose was the extraction of wealth without regard to the human cost, were never overcome. The concept of politics has never risen above an image of plunder extorted by force, whether by a king, a European colonial system, a dictator or a regional warlord.

This book concentrates on the Belgian and European roots of Leopold's crime, and on the early international capitalism which Leopold marshalled to carry out the task of exploitation. It is about his unique and fortunately abortive attempt to establish a new form of kingship, a monarchy equipped with a private dynastic fortune so enormous that it could guide national political and economic development without interference from a democratic parliamentary system. It seemed to Leopold that only the 'colonial world', through its natural resources and the helplessness of its peoples, could return profit on investment on the scale and at the speed that he required. In that sense, this is a 'Eurocentric' book. Without understanding the dynamics of European and Belgian political change in the late nineteenth century, the catastrophe of the Congo Free State cannot be accounted for.

In the intervening years since the 1960s, the focus of historical interest has inevitably shifted. Most intelligent readers in Europe and North America today, asked to name the most significant event in the last century, would probably nominate the Jewish Holocaust. That would not have seemed so obvious when I was writing *The King Incorporated*. The answer then might well have been the outbreak of the First World War in 1914, the Bolshevik Revolution or the rise of Adolf Hitler. Since then, however, moral reflection on the details and implications of the Nazi 'Final Solution' – implications not only for Germany but for the entire human race – has come to overshadow all assessments of our times. And the discovery that genocide is still with us, in Cambodia or Rwanda, has only made that shadow darker.

This change of emphasis has altered perspectives on the history of the Congo Free State. What now seems most important is the sheer loss of life brought about by Leopold's policies, directly or indirectly; while not a case of genocide, in the strict sense, this was one of the most appalling slaughters known to have been brought about by human agency. Adam Hochschild was moved to write his book *King Leopold's Ghost* (Houghton Mifflin, 1998) by a sentence read on a transcontinental air journey, a footnote about Mark Twain which stated that he had campaigned against the 'slave labour' system in the Congo which had taken 'five to eight million lives'. He asked himself: 'Why were these deaths not mentioned in the standard litany of our century's horrors?' In the end, the brilliant book which he went on to write reckons an even higher death toll.

The population was calculated by several different sources to have been reduced by half during the period from 1880 to 1920. The first rough census carried out by the Belgian colonial author-ities in 1924 found some ten million people. The implication, if those figures are reliable, is that the victims numbered something like another ten million. Leopold's dominion over the Congo lasted from the early 1880s to 1908, when international protest and the Belgian parliament finally forced the King to surrender his colony. Most of those ten millions, accordingly, must be his responsibility. Roger Casement, whose consular report on the Congo did so much to energise the Congo Reform Association led by his friend E. D. Morel, guessed that three million people might have perished in a period of fifteen years. This was almost certainly an under-estimate. In this book, I cite Casement's figure with some scepticism, but I suggest that it is impossible to separate deaths caused by massacre and starvation from those due to the pandemic of sleeping-sickness (trypanosomiasis) which decimated central Africa at that time. As Hochschild says, these causes are closely related. The gigantic disruption of African rural society brought about by forced labour, punitive raiding to enforce wild rubber quotas, the destruction of villages and the abandonment of crops left a starving and often homeless population. The fugitives spread the disease as they wandered and in their weakened state made easy prey for infection. The responsibility for this disaster is no less Leopold's because it was a compound one.

It is good that the focus has moved to the Congo itself, to the sufferings of its people and the lonely struggle of those who denounced the system and eventually brought it down. Many more sources have been discovered, although – inevitably – very few of them are the narratives of Africans. But the European dimension still matters. A thread of continuity connects the methods of Leopold's ivory and rubber trusts to the way in which global corporations still disempower and shatter traditional societies in their greed for raw materials. And a tradition of bare-faced international hypocrisy also links Leopold to the present. This book describes how he was able to disguise one of the most brutal of all systems of exploitation as a high-minded crusade for the emancipation of backward peoples – and to get the rest of the world to applaud and even hold him up as a model. In our own time, summit conferences on the saving and healing powers of untrammelled free trade have the same Leopoldian quality.

In my 1963 introduction, I remarked that the Belgians had avoided any real reassessment of the Congolese past, and that Leopold II was still honoured as a national hero for his *mission civilisatrice*. It never occurred to me that this would remain the case more than thirty years later. But it is possible to visit the Africa museum at Tervuren without gathering a hint that the Congo was the site of one of the most atrocious and criminal regimes in history. The truth about Leopold and the Congo Free State is not complete until it is fully accepted, in Belgium as in the rest of the world.

Neil Ascherson, 1999

INTRODUCTION

I N THE EVOLUTION of monarchy, Leopold II of the Belgians
occupies a special position. Like one of those last dinosaurs
at the end of the saurian age whose very size or length of
fang or desperate elaboration of armour sought to postpone
the general decline of their race, Leopold developed in his own
person a most formidable type of King, designed for the environment of the late nineteenth century, which used the new forms
of economic growth to strengthen and extend royal authority.
Other monarchs watched the birth of modern trust capitalism
with mixed feelings of suspicion, incomprehension and contempt. Leopold understood that the private fortunes of a King
remained as much a measure of his power to act freely as they
had been in the Middle Ages.

New sources of money provided a new way of escape from the
control of Cabinets, now firmly in charge of the King's official
allowance through Civil Lists. The Belgian Constitution gave
the Kings considerable powers, but little freedom of action
beyond those specified duties; Leopold wanted to endow the
Belgian Coburgs with a great private fortune to be used for the
nation's good as they would see fit, and to liberate them from
the control of penny-conscious politicians. To achieve this, he
proposed that the King should himself become a grand financier,
a tycoon who could offer his creditors the incomparable security
of a Crown. Leopold had discovered a way to reverse the historical victory of the middle classes over their kings: a new path to
absolutism.

The attempt failed. Leopold made himself one of the richest
men in Europe, but he failed either to transmit the body of his
wealth to his descendants or to exercise freely the power it gave
him. With the rise of international trust capitalism came the
parallel growth of Socialism, and by the end of his reign the
Belgian Left, inside and outside Parliament, was strong enough
to block his way and even to strip him of his greatest private
acquisition—the Congo. After his death, the nation and his
disinherited daughters tore down the fabric of trusts and endow-
ments which he had created to last for centuries, and fought
over the fragments.

Leopold II is best known as the founder and owner of the ill-famed Congo Free State. To most English-speaking readers, his name evokes the phrase 'Red Rubber', and a world of plunder and atrocity: the Congo Reform Association in Britain and America which campaigned against his ruthless exploitation of the Free State has left behind it the notion of an aged, snow-bearded Satan who used black slavery to get money, and money to buy the favours of young girls. To many Belgian historians, on the other hand, Leopold II is still a Crusader, the carrier of Christianity and Belgian civilization into a dark land. The equestrian statue of him in the Place du Trône in Brussels makes an obvious reference to the statue of the Crusader Godfrey of Bouillon which stands on the other side of the Royal Palace. Godfrey's motives also have been somewhat unhorsed by research, but to the average Belgian Royalist, Leopold's critics remain mere jealous merchants or the hacks of greedy foreign Powers.

Belgian apologists for the old King are sometimes so truculent that they throw further discredit on the figure they profess to defend. As recently as 1950, a courtier could write of Leopold II: 'How tiny, how minute are those shadowy slanderers, carried away to eternal oblivion by the wind of destiny! They are crushed beneath the massive stone pedestal which bears the bronze image of our splendid sovereign.'[1] But with all his impatience at constitutional restriction, Leopold never sought the primitive flatteries suitable for a twentieth-century dictator.

Nor can the 'slanderers' be easily dismissed as 'shadowy'. In the King's lifetime, they came to include King Edward VII, President Theodore Roosevelt, Sir Roger Casement, Lord Cromer, Emile Vandervelde, Mark Twain, Joseph Conrad and many others. So prolonged, in fact, was the outcry against the labour and trading conditions in the Congo Free State, and so notorious the scandal of the King's private life, that when he died the topic of his crimes was dropped by the British and American Press as if from sheer exhaustion. Since then, no complete attempt has been made in English to detach Leopold's person from the garish exaggerations which both sides plastered over him in that old debate. A great deal of research on his African work has, however, been undertaken in Belgium. Between the wars, a number of rather servile biographies

[1] Count G. de Raymond; *Léopold II à Paris*; Brussels; 1950; p. 133.

appeared in French, but since 1945 there has been a growing volume of serious and detailed papers examining the acquisition of the Congo and Leopold's financial and administrative methods there. Most of these have been published by the Académie Royale des Sciences Coloniales, and are associated with the names of Professor Jean Stengers and of Father Roeykens.

It is now possible to escape from the 'saint or Satan' controversy, and to see Leopold as a statesman of exceptional skill and vision. Few men of his period could assess its possibilities with the logic that Leopold displayed, or emulate the brutal, subtle politics of deceit by which he herded parliaments and Powers down the lanes of his own purpose. Yet the very intensity with which Leopold could see the opportunities of the present seemed to blind him to the general movement of history towards the future. Everywhere, Leopold built fortifications against change which were beginning to crumble at their foundations by the time they were completed. Looking at people and at his times, the King saw only their weaknesses. He had no imagination, and could not feel the movement of change which is the strength of all confused things.

This book is not, except in a few very minor aspects, a work of original research. Its purpose is only to resume some of the work which has been done so far, to look at the way in which a cold, secret man dealt with his world, and to attempt a fairer picture of the greatest King of the Belgians.

CHAPTER I

BELGIUM IN 1865

ABELGIAN KING does not enter upon his reign by coronation. He is inaugurated, taking an oath before Parliament to observe the Constitution and to defend his country as if he were no more than a senior civil servant. Nor does he succeed immediately on the death of his predecessor: instead of the ancient arrogance of 'The King is dead—God save the King!', there ensues until the ceremony of inauguration an interval of power. For a moment, Belgium stands as a republic, considering whom to choose for her next guardian.

In practice, this interval is kept as short as possible. Leopold I, first King of the Belgians, died on the morning of December 10, 1865, when the enterprise of Belgium was only thirty-five years old, and while around her the major Powers of Europe were struggling through a new period of war, elbowing and straining at the neutral frontiers of Belgium as they manoeuvred for position. Without the King's austere protection, the country could not have survived even so long, and there was every reason not to linger over this dangerous transition from father to son. The dead man lay in state for a few days only and the inauguration of Leopold II took place the day after his father's burial, on the bright winter morning of December 17th.

He rode through the streets of Brussels to the Parliament on a black horse, a precise young man of thirty-five whom the generous crowds did not really know at all. His hair was parted in the middle, and much care had been spent on the culture of his soft chestnut beard; his nose was long and thin and his eyes were pale-blue, with heavy lids. When he read the oath, his speech was almost absurdly slow. His reputation, to those of the watchers who knew anything of him, was that of a bore, a lanky prince still retarded to the outlook of a first-year student who hung about government departments asking endless factual

questions in his dragging voice and noting down all the answers
without discrimination. The man seemed to combine this
adolescent taste for data with an interest in vague, vast, sentimental schemes for housing estates and colonial empires which
taxed the politeness of the Senators who had to listen to them.
With such reservations at the back of their mind, intelligent
Belgians welcomed a sovereign whose hidden abilities they did
not for a moment suspect. Nor did they suspect that Leopold
was looking back at them in the light of a compendious, perfectly
clear and unsparing knowledge of the strength and weakness of
Belgium.

In Belgium, as elsewhere, the family firms which had carried
out the industrialization of the country were now changing
themselves into public companies, strengthening their systems
of command and venturing out beyond local markets into the
outside world. Politically, Belgium herself had not yet under-
gone this sort of change, and remained—as in some ways she
still remains—a rich, parochial family business. Public opinion
was hostile to projects of expansion or public spending, while
successive governments had been inclined to leave foreign affairs
to the management of Leopold I. Patriotism, in other countries
a cloudy passion to unfurl 'national personality' to its broadest
limits of liberty and geography, was to Belgians a sensible
reckoning of their own interest in staying associated as an independent country.

The kingdom of Belgium appears on the map because of a
decision taken by the Catholic populations of the Low Countries.
In the sixteenth century, they had rejected the prospect of liberty
from Spanish domination because independence would have
associated them with the Protestant Dutch. Over two centuries
later, they fought twice for sovereign independence to save their
religion, first from the reforms of a free-thinking Austrian
Emperor, and finally from the rule of a Dutch Protestant King.
The two risings broke out in 1789 and in 1830, but the coincidence with Parisian revolutions was for the most part one of
timing only. The 1789 'Brabançonne' revolution degenerated
into the spectacle of monks leading lynch-mobs against the
minority of genuine radicals. These had taken up arms against
the despotism of Joseph II, not against his anti-clericalism, and
the victorious people of Brussels impaled on their pikes the heads

of freethinkers, not of aristocrats. In Liège, by contrast, the revolution took an enthusiastically French form, but the possibility of internal conflict was avoided by the annexation of all Belgium to France in 1795. A few years of modern legislation swept away the particularities of the past and integrated the various provinces into a uniform administrative system.

Napoleon forged this temporary alliance of Flemings and Walloons into a lasting solidarity. When the Treaty of Vienna plastered Belgium and Holland into a united kingdom under the Dutch Crown, the Belgians resented their subjection to alien Protestant authority with a new coherence, in spite of the tremendous industrial prosperity which they won through Dutch markets. Small grievances were magnified, and in reaction to unrest, the Dutch King was driven to take action against Belgian newspapers and conspirators. But the final revolution of 1830, when it came, was one of those unplanned, chaotic events which defy all searches for underlying purpose or inevitability.

It was a month after the July Revolution in Paris. From the Théâtre de la Monnaie, a well-dressed audience dispersed into the night singing a revolutionary song from the opera they had just seen. Their excitement spread to the crowds of unemployed hanging about the pavement, and an outburst of sentimental high spirits ended as a ferocious proletarian riot, in which raiding parties destroyed machinery in the factories and broke open the pawnshops to regain their pledges. The Dutch garrison shut itself up in its barracks, leaving the Brussels middle classes to organize their own emergency council and police force the following day to protect themselves and their property. The Dutch, endearingly anxious not to hurt anybody or to get hurt themselves, kept postponing military intervention; refugees and professional revolutionaries rushed to Brussels; and day by day the middle-class vigilante committee found itself being forced further towards the position of a permanent insurgents' congress dedicated to winning some degree of independence from Holland. As the affairs of this committee subsided into total confusion, the Dutch finally entered the city in force. The leaders of the insurgents bolted, but the citizens stayed to fight, and to the astonishment of the world, the Dutch were defeated and withdrew from Brussels. The leaders of the revolution emerged from hiding, and on the crest of a wave of triumph, demanded and were granted total independence.

The leaders of the revolution were young radicals. The Constitution they drew up for Belgium was republican and libertarian, fencing in the executive power and proclaiming that 'All powers emanate from the Nation'. Why then did they choose to head it with a King? They did so because the rest of Europe associated a Republic with social—not just political—revolution, and because not even Palmerston or Louis-Philippe, let alone the more conservative monarchies of Europe, could have tolerated such a challenge to the spirit of the Treaty of Vienna. And the middle-class revolutionaries themselves, though most of them were noisy young men in their twenties, were equally nervous about social change. Jean-Baptiste Nothomb, who was only twenty-five in the year of the revolution, told the congress: 'As a monarchy you will be a Power; as a republic, you will be a scarecrow . . . if you adopt monarchial institutions, you will put an end to the revolution; if you proclaim the Republic, you will begin a new one.' [1]

The final choice of King was Leopold of Coburg, the handsome, distant man who would have been Prince Consort of Great Britain if his wife Charlotte, daughter of the Prince Regent, had not died in childbirth. He had already, after hesitation, refused the throne of Greece. Everybody, including the Belgians, thought that the Constitution he was now accepting would tie him hand and foot, but Leopold, although he disliked the restrictions was at once able to find ways to make his influence felt without actually violating the terms of his inaugural oath. A Belgian King is commander-in-chief of the Army, a post he still holds and which is now something of a political embarrassment: Leopold I at once took direct charge of the nation's defence. When a Dutch counter-offensive in 1831 routed the Belgians and obliged them to call in French assistance, the King purged the high command and strengthened his control over the War Ministry. Defence being synonymous with survival, and survival depending entirely on Belgium's relations with the Powers which had guaranteed her existence and neutrality, Leopold easily extended his influence over the country's ministers in foreign capitals, and acted as Belgium's supreme

[1] Quoted in Emile Cammaerts; *The Keystone of Europe;* London 1939; p. 15.

ambassador. Preoccupied with internal politics, successive Belgian governments were content to let the King establish himself as director of foreign affairs. He was thus able to hand on to his son a set of executive powers which were not only wide enough to interest and satisfy most intelligent princes, but were actually protected by the very Constitution which had set out to limit the powers of a King. Leopold II, starting from there, was able steadily to increase his political influence throughout his reign at a time when the power of most constitutional monarchs was declining and it is one of the troubles of the Coburg dynasty in Belgium today that the executive powers acquired by the first King of the Belgians are now so well entrenched that they are very difficult to get rid of, even when their possession has become a liability.

In its first thirty years of independence, Belgium passed through several varieties of economic crisis. The severance from Holland had taken a market away from Belgian industry, and only gradually had other links been formed with Germany. The decline of the Flemish linen industry, the potato famine of the 'forties', and the general indifference of employers had degraded Belgian workers to brutal conditions from which they were only beginning to recover in 1865. Seventeen years before, one million people, almost a quarter of the whole population, had been receiving charity. By the year of Leopold II's accession, the economy was improving, expanding under conditions of almost total free trade, and although the average working day was not less than twelve hours long, wages were registering a slight rise. After 1873, they would begin a long and painful decline, only returning to the same level in 1898[1].

Industrially, Belgium in 1865 was still the workshop of continental Europe. The population had risen almost to five million, an increase of a quarter in thirty years, and well over a third of that population was employed in industry. More than a thousand miles of railway had been built in the country's confined area. The iron and steel industries whose precursor was the foundry set up at Seraing near Liège by the English workman Cockerill, were producing around half a million tons of metal annually, and the Scheldt had been opened to free navigation. In the main, Belgium owed this economic potential to two

See: Léon Delsinne; *le Parti Ouvrier Belge*; Brussels 1955.

things: to the tragically low price of labour whose tradition of mechanical skill went back to the medieval textile industry, and to Belgium's escape from the general wave of revolutions in the middle of the century.

As the Czechs were to behave in 1956, so did the Belgians behave in 1848. A speaker in Parliament observed: 'The ideas of the French revolution may go round the world. But in order to go round the world, they don't have to pass through Belgium!' A trainload of revolutionaries arriving from Paris was disarmed at the frontier station without difficulty, and Leopold I had the intense satisfaction of giving shelter to the fleeing Metternich, who had once regarded Belgium as the institutional embodiment of mob rule. Leopold's niece Victoria wrote in astonishment to congratulate him. The only sign of panic, in fact, was a disastrous run on the banks which followed the initial revolution in Paris, and which eventually obliged the government to set up a national bank with a monopoly of note issue.

The middle classes had been too prosperous to rebel and the workers too wretched and too far removed from the arena of Belgian political life. The original *pays légal*—the electorate— of Belgium consisted of only about 50,000 people, enfranchised on a stringent property qualification and although in 1848 these qualifications were lowered a little, they remained high enough to ensure that politics stayed a middle-class occupation.

The two political parties, the Catholics and the Liberals, had hitherto shared a complete loyalty to the constitution: more fortunate than France, Belgium had not been troubled by parties committed to a change of régime. Both parties supported the *régime censitaire*, or property qualification, and at the accession of Leopold II, they had only just abandoned a long tradition of unionism and coalition in the national interest, so that total opposition by a formally-organised party was still something new and rather shocking to most Belgians in 1865. Party differences were deep enough, but they were doctrinal rather than social.

One basic fact governed all Belgian politics at this time: the fact that the vast majority of Belgians were profoundly and incuriously Catholic. Universal suffrage would therefore have produced a Catholic landslide so powerful that it would have swept away the whole spirit of the Constitution, with its concern

for reasoned debate between men of substance, and the older
Catholics feared this as much as anybody. Only the property
qualification allowed the Liberal middle classes of the towns to
be a power in the land, and by keeping the Catholic masses out
of politics, restricted parliamentary proceedings to a dialogue
between country gentlemen and town worthies.

Only now was the Catholic party changing its nature. The
year before, on December 8, 1864, Pius IX had issued the
Encyclical *Quanta Cura,* which condemned secular education,
the separation of Church and State, and the very notion of a
secular State itself. At once, Belgian Catholics were forced to
choose between rejecting the Constitution which they had helped
to create, and disobedience to the Pope. Those who accepted the
papal view, as many did, had then to face the Liberal charge that
they had in effect declared themselves revolutionaries, dedicated
to destroying the legal institutions of the land. They were forced
towards the sterile position of 'ultras', whose political slogan
could only be that 'error has no rights' and whose loyalty could
only be confessional.

In response, the Liberals were also preparing for total conflict.
Main architects of the Constitution, the early Liberals liked to
trace their pedigree back to the Enlightenment and to the more
rational aspects of the first French Revolution. They were
enemies of gross superstition, even anticlericals, but at first they
were not anti-Catholic, and both sides fought only to define the
frontier at which Church and State should meet. For the most
part, it had been a matter of Catholic resistance to Liberal
measures intended to loosen the monopolistic hold of the
Church on national education. The Catholics had, however,
replaced the Liberals when they proposed a succession tax of
one per cent, and been in turn defeated by the Liberals in 1857
over a bill to free Church charities from State supervision.
Already there had begun the first stirrings of the solemn 'Question of the Cemeteries', to determine where the bodies of good
agnostics should lie. But from now on, these philosophical spar-
rings were to coarsen into desperate party warfare, irremediably
disrupting the old *censitaire* electorate which had once accepted
for Belgium the slogan that 'Unity is Strength'.

The Liberals were to remain in power from the victory of the
Charities Bill to 1870, a period of thirteen years. But within their

ranks two existing wings began to draw rapidly further apart, the enactment in a Belgian form of a contradiction which was affecting Liberalism everywhere. The party was still led by the stately old Freemasons who had founded it, personified in the glacial, handsome figure of Walthere Frère-Orban. He and his 'Doctrinaires', the governing right wing of the party, continued to believe in free trade, free thought, and a free internal labour market as the only necessary conditions for Belgian progress and prosperity. Any interference by the masses, whether by combination to raise wages or by extension of the franchise, could only upset these conditions: Frère-Orban warned the country against any pretext which might serve to awaken 'the coarse appetites of the mob'.

As long ago as 1845, however, other Liberals in his home town of Liège had called Frère-Orban and his friends a *coterie aristo-cratico-métallique*[1]. His beliefs formed a creed too suitable for rich manufacturers to be inspiring, and younger men turned in excitement to the company of the French intellectuals and revolutionaries who were chased across the frontier by the police after Louis-Napoleon's successful *coup d'état* in 1851. The 'Progressives', as these younger Liberals came to call themselves, were recruited from professional men rather than from the employer class. They looked towards universal suffrage as a remedy for the helplessness of the working classes, and they opposed the Catholic way of life with a fanaticism almost as bigoted as that of their enemies, even though they claimed to found their own beliefs on the reasonings of science. Societies pledged to abstain from the sacraments grew up in the larger towns: the impassioned quarrel which broke out in 1861 in the Brussels suburb of Uccle over where to bury the remains of an officer who had summoned up the originality to become an atheist on his death-bed was a warning of the extent to which Progressive opinions had permeated the middle class. A slight local incident on the religious front could now inflame the whole country, as the controversy over lay schools was soon to show.

Leopold II, as he addressed his parliament for the first time, looked into eyes already glittering with the fever of new and powerful ideas, and with anticipation of the struggles to put them into practice. But these were ideas, as Pirenne has put it,

[1] Paul Hymans; *Frère-Orban;* Brussels 1905; p. 87.

about human destiny; not so much about the nature of a social
policy and still less about the conduct of foreign affairs.
Indirectly, the coming party conflicts would make Leopold's
work difficult by the general turbulence they caused, and by the
preoccupation of ministers with internal affairs to the prejudice
of any schemes for Belgian expansion. But the only lasting feud
between the King and his governments occurred over the question of defence, where Leopold had to fight all his life against
the pacifism of the Catholics and the anti-militarism of the Left
to win for Belgium a modern military system and an adequate
chain of forts. His kingdom relied almost thoughtlessly on the
'scrap of paper', the Treaties of 1839 by which the Powers had
guaranteed her neutrality, and would not admit that a strong
defensive army was necessary to back those signatures with a
more positive deterrent to an aggressor.

Belgium could no longer remain safe and rich by merely being
passive. Alliances were changing in Europe, and in the tropics
new markets opened for European industry. To Leopold,
Belgium could only stay safe by becoming formidable, and
could only stay rich by seizing riches which lay unguarded.

CHAPTER II

THE FATHER AND THE SON

I N SPITE OF powerful lusts, the Coburgs were not generous with their affection. Nervous at first of their position and convinced that the best way for a family of small German princes to advance itself was by arranging good marriages for its members, they formed the habit of subordinating their emotions to their sense of duty. Only on their mistresses, in private, did they release the violence of strong and strongly inhibited feelings.

Leopold I had begun his life as the eighth child of a minor German ruler. By contriving to change sides at suitable moments, he emerged from the Napoleonic wars as a handsome young man reputed to harbour suitable ideas, and his marriage to Princess Charlotte of England in 1816 was a triumphant climax to his dynastic ambitions. Being young, he was able to find that he could love Charlotte as well as marry her; her death left him with only his arid matrimonial principles to guide him. He did not manage to love again. Instead, he arranged another fifteen royal marriages for suitable Coburgs and their supporters, including a second marriage for himself. Very few of these marriages were happy, with one shining exception for Albert and Victoria, and his own choice of Louise-Marie, daughter of Louis-Philippe, was a heavy honour for her to bear. When he married her in 1832 Leopold was forty-two and the French princess was a fair-haired, pathetically hopeful girl of twenty, who wrote to a friend a few days after the wedding: ' . . . my only compensation will be the hope of a happiness that I still do not feel or understand'[1].

Their life in Belgium together was grey and staid. Leopold was discreetly unfaithful as the years passed: Louise-Marie did her duty by supporting him in public and by bearing and loving

[1] Joanna Richardson; *My Dearest Uncle : Leopold I of the Belgians;* London 1961; p. 126.

his children but those who knew her were sorry for her. In suitably quick succession, the four children were born: a first son who died in infancy; Leopold, Duke of Brabant, born in 1835; Philip, Count of Flanders, born in 1837; and Princess Charlotte, future Empress of Mexico, born in 1840. The Queen hung anxiously over every detail of their upbringing and education, determined that they at least should not suffer from the loveless indifference she had found in the royal palace at Laeken, but although like the other two children Leopold remembered her with intense fondness, he was made aware that he was not her favourite.

From the outset, Louise-Marie found her eldest son withdrawn and apparently obtuse. She would preside each month while her children were examined on what they had learned, and it was Philip who generally won the prize of books from her own library. The Queen, who realized that Leopold was potentially very much more able than his brother, blamed him for idleness, but within a few years he was again outshone by the precocity of Charlotte, who at five was capable of reading the office for Holy Week. She received an education as intensive as that of her brothers, since she seemed to promise so well, and the Queen continued to regulate the life of her children hour by hour, maintaining her control when she was away from Laeken by a stream of worried notes about the clothes they should wear, the syllabus they should be finishing, the games they should be playing, and the food they should be eating, whose preparation she generally watched over in person. A letter written to her household from Paris, when Leopold was almost eleven, instructs: 'I forgot to tell you yesterday that the King allows the children to go down and see Charlotte if they have been good, on Thursdays and Sundays after their supper, and to pass part of their evening with her . . . (the meetings) should not be too noisy or in any way get out of control'[1].

It sounds fussy. But the Queen's intention was to mitigate as far as she could the harsh system which was then thought suitable for the education of princes, and which she knew their father would not spare them. Both were rather delicate boys, Leopold in particular suffering from a supposed weak chest and from a sciatic limp which stayed with him all his life, but this

[1] G. Freddy; *Léopold II Intime;* Paris 1905; p. 32.

did not save them from being put under military training when
Leopold was only ten. At first, he was taught only drill, and
allowed with the assistance of a sergeant-major to give orders to
squads of grenadier recruits sent up to the parade-ground at
Laeken. Then, at the age of eleven, he was commissioned Second
Lieutenant and placed under Colonel de Lannoy to begin a full
education with special emphasis on the military virtue of
discipline.

His father also felt that Leopold was mentally lazy and lacked
concentration. From Buckingham Palace, where he was staying
with his niece Victoria, he wrote instructions to the new tutor:

'My dear Lieutenant-Colonel;
Not having had time to give you instructions in person, I must
resort to writing to you.

'(1) It is desirable, above all for Leopold, to lay down a full
routine, covering even the small details of daily life;

'(2) Children notice everything that is said in front of them.
That means that one must be very prudent. Anything which
they are not meant to know must not be mentioned in their
presence;

'(3) As I wish to inculcate in them the sentiment of duty—a
sentiment which nowadays is growing weaker and only too often
giving way to considerations of utility and convenience—everything must be made relevant to this sentiment: you must take
pains to avoid any impression that you are consulting them on
their own education: it may be a good idea to explain to them
the usefulness of what they are studying, but to allow them
liberty to express an opinion would be disruptive . . . '[1]

But the heir to the throne continued to ignore what he did
not wish to learn. Only a year before she died, when Leopold was
fourteen, Louise-Marie wrote sadly to him from another visit to
London:

'I was very upset to read the Colonel's report and find that you
had again been so lazy and that your dictations had been so bad
and careless. This is not what you promised me . . . your father
was as grieved as I was to read your last report'[2].

Thin, weirdly tall, and domiciled apparently on another
planet, the adolescent Leopold was a sinister figure. At his first

[1] G. Freddy; *Léopold II Intime;* p 26
[2] *Ibid.,* p. 27.

ball, his mother reported to her parents, now in exile: 'Leopold is disfigured by his enormous nose which gives him a bird-like appearance . . . he resembles much the Duke of Coburg'. Philip, his younger brother, cut at this time a much more lively and attractive figure, although he was to live most of his life in contented retirement. Leopold, in contrast, had the typical Coburg characteristic of late mental development.

He enjoyed geography lessons, however, and it was afterwards assumed that Louise-Marie had encouraged this interest and given it direction by telling him the adventures of her brother, the Duke of Aumale, who was campaigning against Abd-el-Kader in Algeria. It is more certain that she supplemented his religious instruction with her own teaching, for although she was married to a Protestant, the Queen had remained a devoted Catholic, spending an hour or so each day in prayer and determined that her children should see their royal duty in a religious and charitable light as well as a military one. Charlotte was the most deeply influenced by her piety, but Leopold's tutor, Colonel de Lannoy, had a personal commitment to the Catholic party which provoked Liberal journalists to unfavourable comment. Under his supervision, eminent men called to instruct Leopold and his brother in modern languages, mathematics and Latin. The novelist Henri Conscience taught Leopold Flemish, which made a deeper impression on Flanders than on his pupil, for as King he practically never used the language except when he had to impress a Flemish audience and could think of no other way to do so. Glittering officers taught him to be a soldier, but although in later years he frequently wore uniform, it was usually creased and comfortably rumpled, and occasionally was observed to be lacking a button. Grooms and cavalrymen taught him to ride, but he fell off: nobody was more relieved to see the motor-car invented than the second King of the Belgians.

In spite of the pessimism of his instructors, their basic exhortation to systematize his life and to construct routines was absorbed. Leopold learned how to classify information, and he discovered that he enjoyed the accumulation of files, the noting down of chance scraps of statistical data. Yet even this taste could not persuade his father to give him the only sort of education which would really have been of practical use, by taking his son into his confidence and training him in the business of

government. The King was a lonely man, too accustomed to
keeping his own secrets, and there are few records of any
exchange of opinions on a matter of state between him and his
heir, even after the boy had achieved his legal majority at
eighteen and been installed as an honorary Senator. Instead,
Leopold resorted to winning the confidence of his father's secretary, Jules Van Praet, who admired his ability and allowed him
to go through old files and to ask the first of his innumerable
questions of fact. When Louise-Marie died, in 1850, Leopold
returned silently in his black clothes to Van Praet's office and
worked harder than before at his lonely documentation.

If they wanted to see their father, the sons were obliged to ask
formally for an audience as if they were ordinary clients on state
business. This the King considered to be 'English protocol':
wherever he had in fact learned it, such stiffness helped Leopold I
to impress on his subjects that he was a monarch beyond the
reach of the familiarity which he was sure would bring contempt. The dethronement of Louis-Philippe in 1848 had alarmed
him very much, and even before the explosion he had tried to
warn the French King that he should exert more authority. But
Leopold's advice, although generally wise, was often given with
a fussiness which made it unwelcome. 'Reassure my son-in-law,'
Louis-Philippe had told the Prince de Ligne; 'he is getting
worried over nothing. I'm not the man to be unhorsed by a lot
of cold-meat political banquets; I'm too firmly in the saddle'[1].
This remark, made in 1847, is one of the sadder exhibits in the
museum of famous last words, for it was the banning of a political banquet which ignited the 1848 rising in Paris.

The Second Empire was noisily hostile to Belgium. Personally,
Leopold looked down on Napoleon III as a parvenu with little
idea of how to run a Court or behave like a monarch, and the
formalities of Laeken grew more rigid in a reaction of distaste.
The Archduke Maximilian of Austria, contemplating marriage
to Charlotte, visited both countries in 1856 and found the French
Court 'absolutely lacking in tone'[2]. The Belgian palaces he
thought mean and comfortless, but at least the priceless,
indefinable quality of 'tone' was present. ' . . . a certain dignity
is to be noticed in everything, a *ton de bonne compagnie* and

[1] Freddy; *Léopold II Intime;* p. 22.
[2] H. Montgomery Hyde; *Mexican Empire;* London 1946; p. 53.

the accustomed formality of a Court, and by comparison with Paris I was impressed here with a comfortable sensation of being once again among my own kind, for Brussels has for me that pleasant feeling which I missed in France of well-bred existence and. of being at home'[1]. Not the least important reason for Maximilian's failure to stay alive as Emperor of Mexico was the lens of snobbery which distorted his understanding of the world around him.

The young Duke of Brabant was soon to be married, and through his marriage to become the centre of a minor skirmish between the Courts of Austria and France. His father had noticed that he was beginning to find his tongue—he had the unpleasant habit of putting people right about their own jobs, and the impression was spreading that he regarded most of the human race with scorn—and judged that he would now be capable of defending his own cause in the intricacies of a political marriage. The King had for some time been watching his heir with growing interest. He did not like him particularly, but he had to acknowledge that he was becoming formidable. In a surprisingly imaginative note, he recorded what he felt about his own son.

'Leopold is subtle and sly: he never takes a chance. The other day, when I was at Ardenne, I watched a fox which wanted to cross a stream unobserved: first of all he dipped a paw into the water to see how cold it was, then he lowered the paw carefully to see how deep it was, and then with a thousand precautions, very slowly made his way across. That is Leopold's way . . . '[2].

[1] *Ibid.*, p. 56.
[2] Pierre Daye; *Léopold II;* Paris 1934; p. 30.

CHAPTER III

FIRST STEPS IN DIPLOMACY:
LEOPOLD'S MARRIAGE

THE REST OF EUROPE had looked with suspicion, then with disquiet, on Louis-Napoleon's seizure of power and on his preparations to restore a Bonapartist Empire to France. Leopold I had kept up, all through his reign, a fond and frequent correspondence with his niece Victoria, and they exchanged many impressions on the events in France as they advanced from the *coup d'état* of December 1851 towards the proclamation of the Second Empire. Victoria wrote: 'With a man as extraordinary as Louis-Napoleon, one cannot feel oneself safe for a minute. Be assured that any attempt against Belgium would be for us a *casus belli*'[1]. But Leopold continued to bewail the danger to Belgian independence inherent in a new French Empire, in spite of Victoria's assurances. In March 1852, he wrote: 'We are here rather in the awkward position of persons in hot climates who find themselves in bed with a snake: *they must not move because that irritates the creature*, but they can hardly remain as they are, without a fair chance of being bitten'[2]. Such insistence was not a wise tactic of Leopold's, for British opinion was tiring of his interventions, and Palmerston, whose attempt to instruct his Ambassador in Paris to recognize the *coup d'état* had brought about his fall, had blamed his dismissal on 'foreign' influence. Liberal opinion in Britain at this stage was still impressed by Louis-Napoleon's claim to be the defender of the 1848 revolution, and suspected that the King of the Belgians was exaggerating his danger in order to cadge sympathy. This view was encouraged by the fact that in January 1852, a decree published in the French official gazette had confiscated all the French possessions of the Orleans dynasty, giving Leopold a personal and financial motive in his search for support

[1] Alfred de Ridder; *Le Mariage du Roi Léopold II;* Brussels 1925; p. 8.
[2] Quoted in Richardson; *My Dearest Uncle;* p. 186.

against France. In his view, this decree violated his marriage settlement, made on July 28, 1832, and deprived his children of their legal inheritance.

Elsewhere in Europe, Leopold worked to obtain assurances that the Powers would not permit French violation of Belgian sovereignty. It was believed at the time in the Belgian Foreign Office that a decree already signed by Louis-Napoleon existed in Paris, ready to be published at a suitable opportunity, which ran: 'Article I: the Kingdom of Belgium, Savoy, and the Rhenish provinces are reunited to France and become French departments once more. Article II: The Minister of War is charged with the execution of this Decree'[1].

But Leopold's diplomatic explorations were successful and by the time that the Empire was proclaimed in Paris in December 1852, he had received more or less clear pledges of military assistance in the event of a French invasion from Russia, Austria and Prussia, as well as from Britain. The way these assurances were given, however, showed that Belgium was not being humoured for her own sake. Nesselrode, the Russian Chancellor, explained to the British Ambassador in St Petersburg that 'I like Belgium; she keeps Britain in with us', and the Prussian Ambassador in the same city told his Belgian colleague: 'Providence gave us Belgium: without Belgium, England would leave the Continent to its own devices'[2]. The Austrians gave Leopold what he wanted because they considered that a violation of Belgian neutrality could only be part of a general French attack, across the Rhine in the north and against Austria's Italian dominions in the south. The coalition of 'the Northern Courts' against the new Bonaparte needed allies, and Britain might be conciliated through favours granted to her Belgian protégé.

French grievances against Belgium, on the other hand, continued to provide Paris with material for a campaign of diplomatic terrorism directed at Brussels. The pretext for most of these frights was the connected activity of French refugees in Belgium and of the Belgian Press. Ever since 1848, refugees of varying political views had made their way across the frontier, and after the *coup d'état*, the French police had taken to chasing

[1] Letter of Firmin Rogier, Belgian Minister in Paris, February 15, 1852. Quoted in de Ridder; *Le Mariage du Roi Léopold II*; p. 10.

[2] de Ridder; *Le Mariage du Roi Léopold II*; p. 39.

them deliberately into Belgium, perhaps to provide French diplomats with further reasons to complain. The first wave had included Louis Blanc and Ledru-Rollin, both leaders of the Second Republic, and after 1851, they were followed by Thiers, de Caussidière, Edgar Quinet, Alexandre Dumas and Victor Hugo, among the seven thousand fugitives who left within two months of the *coup d'état*.

The most defiant of Belgian liberties remained the liberty of the Belgian Press, which all through the century continued to speak its mind about foreign and even Belgian rulers with complete lack of inhibition. Taking advantage of this freedom, the refugees founded their own journals and launched attacks on the French dictator which were furiously resented. Two French refugees were expelled, but a Belgian government had no specific law at its disposal to suppress criticisms of foreign rulers made by Belgian journalists, and two prosecutions brought against newspapers at French insistence failed to obtain convictions. Finally, in order to spare the Belgian King and government future embarrassment, a procedure was established which made it an offence to calumniate foreign sovereigns but specified that prosecutions would only be made after a request had been lodged at the Belgian Foreign Office by the foreign government affected. But the French government was unwilling to use the new machinery, and continued to counter-attack by diplomatic protests.

After the formal declaration of the Empire, in December 1852, there was a temporary improvement in Franco-Belgian relations. In the New Year, however, the European situation deteriorated as Russian and French ambitions in the Near East came into conflict in the prelude to the Crimean War. Austria and Prussia seemed at first likely to take Russia's part and France threw herself into a dramatic posture of alarm. M. de Butenval, the French Minister in Brussels, thoroughly over-played this part, and declared on March 22, 1853 that 'the first shot fired will allow France full liberty of action. In her eyes the European balance will have ceased to exist'[1]. These words, which Drouyn de Lhuys, the French Foreign Minister, was obliged to disavow as far as he could, were at first taken in Brussels to imply that France would no longer recognize Belgian neutrality. Parlia-

[1] de Ridder; *Le Mariage du Roi Léopold II;* p. 130.

ment, usually reluctant to accord military credits, accepted an increase of the army to 100,000 men. Leopold felt that he must resume his campaign to strengthen the obligations of the Powers to Belgium, and he decided to do so by a marriage.

At first, it seems, Leopold contemplated a third marriage for himself. He considered approaching the Archduchess Elizabeth of Austria. Then he decided that it would be easier to use his son. The Duke of Brabant was eighteen in April, reaching his official majority, and in May his father set off with him on a tour of the German states which brought them in a few weeks to Vienna By now, the matter had been formally suggested: the Duke of Brabant should be married to Marie-Henriette, daughter of the Archduke Joseph, prince of Hungary and Bohemia. The Austrian Emperor agreed, and the young girl's parents approved of a sensible match. In ignorance and innocence, the two utterly unsuitable victims were laced into their best uniform and frock and paraded for inspection.

The Archduchess Marie-Henriette was sixteen. The conventional flatteries were recorded in official despatches by the Belgian Ambassador: ' . . . not tall, but well formed: her face expresses gentleness, her features are very pleasant, her complexion is remarkably fresh; her hair is ash-blonde and very pretty. Her Imperial Highness has received a brilliant education: she speaks very good French, Italian and English; she is a good musician; she paints flowers and fruit in oils with remarkable skill. She rides a horse with a grace only equalled by her boldness'[1].

Here for a moment the Ambassador spoke candidly. Marie-Henriette's father had thrown himself into his rôle of Hungarian prince with enthusiasm, learning the language and wearing national dress, and his daughter had learned for her part to ride like a young Magyar: stables and the great grass plains of the south were more her style than drawing-rooms, and the 'brilliant education' had gone for the most part in at one ear and out at the other. She was a pretty, fair-haired girl with a loud laugh, and a short, crude way of speech which was something of a puzzle to the grand Ladies who undertook to civilize her in Vienna. Countess Dolly de Ficquelmont wrote in a letter: 'I rely on good King Leopold's wisdom and tact to form her, for the

[1] de Ridder; *Le Mariage du Roi Léopold II*; p. 152, Note 2.

B

Palatine has brought her up more as a boy than as a girl.'
Neither did poor Marie-Henriette like what she saw of her future
husband. She was repelled by reports that he had 'a weak chest'
—generally a euphemism for tuberculosis—and by his pedantry.
The whole arrangement was viciously summed up by Madame
de Metternich, who observed that this was a marriage 'between
a stable-boy and a nun, and by nun I mean the Duke of Brabant'.

Lady Westmoreland (young Leopold was passing at this stage
in his life down a perfect corridor of lorgnettes) said that he
looked no older than sixteen himself, 'a stick of asparagus, with
a narrow chest and no suspicion of beard; he talks a good deal
and is not without wit, but he talk like an old man'. The geo-
grapher Humboldt, who had seen him earlier in the year at
Berlin, thought his nose threw a shadow like the shadow of
Mount Athos.

But the marriage was agreed by its organizers to be thoroughly
appropriate and delightful, and the engagement was announced
on May 18, 1853. A few slight problems remained to be smoothed
out. For one thing, it was only sixty years since Belgium had
risen in revolution against Austria : the Belgian Foreign Minister,
de Brouckère, therefore sent a circular to the diplomatic corps in
Brussels reminding them that 'this alliance . . . strengthens our
ties with one of the great Powers which signed the 1839 Treaties;
it has therefore a definitely political aspect'[1]. To his own staff of
Belgian diplomats abroad, he asserted in another circular that
when Belgium passed under the Austrian sceptre, she had gained
'what she had hardly experienced in the past : a government
paternal though foreign, an interval of peace, and a period of
intellectual development'. He added, rather defensively :
'Nobody could have supposed that the Princes of Belgium would
take a vow of celibacy and so imperil the very future of their
country.'

Another minor obstacle was a distant degree of relationship
between the Duke and the Archduchess, who were fourth cousins
through common descent from the Empress Maria Theresa.
This was easily surmounted by Papal dispensation, and preparations for the marriage went ahead. The first ceremony took place
in Vienna on August 10, but the Duke of Brabant was ill in
Brussels with scarlet fever and had to be proxied by the

[1] de Ridder; *Le Mariage du Roi Léopold II*; p. 153, Note 3.

Emperor's brother, Archduke Charles, who was notoriously frightened of women. The second marriage was to take place in Brussels on August 22. But before it could be celebrated, both parties were obliged to go through the extraordinary charade of 'fetching the bride home', a business which was meant to demonstrate the overwhelmingly political nature of royal marriage.

It was not possible for the Archduchess to do anything so simple as get into a train in Vienna and get out of it again in Brussels. That would have suggested a sort of Canossa, a marriage of unconditional surrender by Austria. Nor was it thinkable that the bridegroom could go to Vienna and escort her home: that would have presented a symbolic suggestion of victory by conquest. The thing had to be sorted out bilaterally, by the strong negotiating on absolutely equal terms with the strong, on neutral ground, very much as some mediaeval siege might have ended with a soldiers' agreement in the grounds of a nearby abbey. Obviously, neither Belgium nor Austria could be regarded as neutral ground, but neither were the German states along the railway-line between the two countries felt to be sufficiently uncommitted.

Finally, it was agreed that the Archduchess could be handed over to the Belgians on a piece of Belgian soil declared neutral for the occasion. The Countess de Biolley, a rich lady with a large house in the industrial town of Verviers, just across the border from Germany, offered her hospitality, and her house became for a moment the smallest of European enclaves. A special station was built nearby, and the road from the railway line to the Biolley palace was hung with flags and draped with purple velvet with gold fringes. An elaborate signal plan was drawn up, to keep everybody's nose in joint: a telegraph signal would be sent between the stations of Dolhain and Pepinster to set off the two royal trains at a moment which would ensure that they would arrive simultaneously in the temporary station in Verviers.

Unfortunately, these arrangements went wrong. The Belgian railways, the first on the Continent, had made their inaugural passenger run in the year of the Duke of Brabant's birth, and many hours of his reign as King were soured by their cheerful habit of running late on important occasions. Today was a foretaste of many later irritations. The Belgian train arrived at

Pepinster to await the signal: the minutes passed and nothing happened. Leopold I got out of the train and began to pace up and down the platform. The band on the station pooped and thumped on. Fifteen and then thirty minutes went by. Finally, the King sent an *aide-de-camp* to see what had happened, and the telegraph office was found to be empty: the boy who worked the machine had wandered off to listen to the band and the ringing of the signal-bell had been entirely drowned by the noise of the brass section. By the time that the Belgians finally steamed into Verviers, the Austrian train had been waiting there for half-an-hour[1].

The Archduchess was handed over in the end, but the wedding in the cathedral of St. Gudule in Brussels was delayed until a week later. Marie-Henriette had been upset by the parting with her Austrian suite, and the Duke of Brabant was still convalescing from scarlet fever. In the first few weeks after the ceremony, the Duke and Duchess toured Belgium, and were received with great enthusiasm, although it was noticed that Marie-Henriette had a tendency to burst out laughing at the solemnities of town hall receptions. It was wild laughter, perhaps, for the experience of marriage was already revolting her. The scornful Duke made it obvious that he thought her absurd and that her high spirits only annoyed him, and the sexual side of marriage to an indifferent stranger was a humiliation she never forgave. A month after the wedding, she wrote to a friend in Vienna: 'My poor mother, dear angel, is beginning to understand what she has done. She thought this marriage would make me happy, and sees that it has done the very opposite. If God hears my prayers, I shall not go on living much longer—unless everything changes'[2]. How could it change? Marie-Henriette lived for many years, slowly rebuilding her broken spirit into forms of Catholic self-discipline and humility, for she was a very religious woman with considerable energy. Grievance and estrangement from her husband finally rendered her indifferent to other people, and twenty years later Marie-Henriette helped to force her own wretched daughters into the beds of husbands as strange and unattractive as the husband who had been forced on her.

For the moment, she was young enough to fight back, to laugh

[1] Freddy; *Léopold II Intime*; p. 42.
[2] Quoted in Richardson; *My Dearest Uncle;* p. 188.

at times, and to organize distractions for herself. Her father-in-law liked her, and thought that she would be a good companion for his daughter Charlotte. By now, Charlotte and her brother Leopold had discovered a mutual dislike which would last all their lives, and it was natural that at first she should take the side of the latest victim of Leopold's arrogance and sarcasm. She was thirteen when she wrote to her grandmother, the exiled Queen Marie-Amélie: 'If Leopold is not happy with her, it's because he is determined not to be . . . ' Later, however, she became tired of Marie-Henriette's lack of intellect, and in 1856 she noted: 'Marie is very kind, but her education is so poor that she has not developed a taste for more serious things. I am being saturated with concerts. Marie has been arranging concerts with opera singers every two or three weeks. It is so dull: all day one hears nothing but "Mademoiselle Sforlanconi will be writing" or "Mademoiselle S. is coming"! Everything centres round these singers. I am bored to death. It seems frightful to me to have nothing in one's bones but music'[1].

The Duke of Brabant wrote a soulless letter of thanks to the Emperor for allowing his marriage to a member of the Imperial family. Then, at the King's suggestion, the couple went to Britain and stayed with Queen Victoria, his most precious diplomatic contact. They were well received, although Victoria never allowed the Duke to inherit the confidence which she had placed in his father. But the marriage had caused anger in France already, and Napoleon III was not happy to watch it being put to immediate political use.

Nesselrode, the Russian Chancellor, had commented to the Belgian Ambassador in St. Petersburg that one would hardly expect a man who had failed to find a wife in a reigning house to be gracious about a marriage between the Belgian and Austrian royal families. Napoleon had married Eugenie de Montijo that January, and the news of the Belgian marriage upset him badly, possibly for reasons of jealousy but more surely because he realized that it was another cord tied in the general anti-French coalition. In July, the Austrian Ambassador in Paris, Count Hübner, recorded: 'The Empress questioned me at length about the coming marriage of the Archduchess Marie-Henriette to the Duke of Brabant. The Emperor continues to

[1] H. Montgomery Hyde; *Mexican Empire;* London 1946; p. 63.

sulk at me, and I continue the pretence that I do not notice that he is sulking. Drouyn de Lhuys (the Foreign Minister) tries to make him understand the value of good relations with Austria at such a critical period'[1]

The French government resumed its complaints against the Belgian Press and the Brussels refugees, and an article which appeared in August in *Le Constitutionnel* claimed that the marriage was actually damaging to Belgian interests because it removed Belgium still further from Holland, did nothing to improve her relations with Germany or Prussia, and of course was a discourtesy to France. The French Minister at Brussels stayed away from the ceremony in St Gudule.

The King of the Belgians began to feel that he might perhaps have provoked Napoleon III too far, and in February 1854 he sent him the Grand Cordon of the Order of Leopold, enclosed in polite letters from himself and the Duke of Brabant. The Crimean War broke out in March, and Napoleon in his turn realized—as the 'Northern Courts' had realized—that he needed British support and that a good way to please London was to display some tenderness for Brussels: he sent Prince Napoleon on a visit to Belgium. He was kindly received by the Court, but the public was hostile. Leopold, taking note of this coldness, did not inform his government before in September he and the Duke of Brabant paid a call on the Emperor, who was with his troops in their base at Boulogne. A cabinet crisis followed, as his furious ministers offered their resignation, but Leopold felt that he was paying a cheap price for an important respite.

His son returned from Boulogne over-tired and coughing, and after an examination, the Court doctors recommended that he should take a journey to a warmer climate. It had been a long and hard year, which had introduced young Leopold to Emperors and Empresses and Queens, to the practices of diplomacy and formality and sex. He prepared to leave for the Mediterranean, taking with him his wife and a thick supply of notebooks.

[1] de Ridder; *Le Mariage du Roi Léopold II*; p. 159.

CHAPTER IV

FOREIGN JOURNEYS:
THE GERM OF IMPERIALISM

LEAVING BRUSSELS in November 1854, the Duke and the Duchess made their way slowly southwards through Vienna and Milan to Venice. Here they were seen by Countess Ficquelmont, who spread the news about Leopold's weak chest, and here they had an ugly quarrel in public. Marie-Henriette, who was now seventeen, wanted to have a second ride in a gondola: her husband the Duke, who was nineteen, forbade it and sent away the musicians and boats which had already been hired for the evening. The Duchess was seen to cry.

At Trieste, they were taken on board an Austrian warship which brought them to Egypt, and they landed at Alexandria on February 2, 1855. They were met by Blondeel, the Belgian consul, a remarkable man who stayed with Leopold for the rest of the voyage and who may have helped to form the Duke's interest in Africa, for in 1842 he had drawn up a plan for a Belgian trading establishment in Abyssinia which was intended gradually to extend its scope until it became the framework for something like a Belgian protectorate. From the moment he went ashore with Blondeel, Leopold's obsession with matters of trade and industry became apparent, to the boredom of his wife. The Khedive Said showed him the Nile dam under construction near Cairo, where he was received with gun salutes and an escort of five thousand soldiers. In Cairo, while Marie-Henriette rode on camels and visited bazaars, he continued to ask questions, and listened with particular excitement to the Khedive's talk about the projected Suez Canal. There is evidence that he was converted: the following year, when de Lesseps was trying to sell his idea to Great Britain, the engineer wrote in a letter: 'I was presented to the Queen and I also had a very long conversation with Prince Albert, who took me to his study and got me to inform him exactly what the proposed works of the Canal were. He told me that the Duke of Brabant, who was interested in the enterprise, had already recommended it to him'[1].

From Cairo, the Belgian party went upstream as far as Asswan, and on the way back made an excursion into the Fayum, protected by an escort against nomads and bandits. The Duke made a second visit to the Nile dam before leaving Egypt reluctantly, the party went on to Palestine, where they spent Holy Week, and to Damascus and Beirut. It was a pious interlude, but one project at least appealed to Leopold's imagination, already fascinated by the idea that Belgium might find a position for herself in these empty countries: the Belgian Ambassador in Constantinople had suggested that while in Jerusalem, Leopold might be allowed to mark the graves of Godfrey of Bouillon and of Baudouin, the two Belgian crusaders who became Kings of Jerusalem. The Turkish authorities, however, decided that the idea was improper.

Through the Aegean, the Duke and Marie-Henriette returned to Greece, then to Sicily and to Rome where they were received in the Vatican, and where the young Duchess made an excellent impression on Pius IX. Paying a visit to Victor-Emmanuel in Turin on their way home, they arrived back at Laeken on August 28th.

A few months later, they set out again on the Duke's first independent political mission. In October 1855, Leopold I sent him and the Duchess to Paris. The idea for the visit seems to have come from Palmerston, who was working to improve relations between France and the rest of Europe, but Leopold was worried enough by the persistent offences given to the Emperor by Belgian journalists. All his neighbours were now complaining. Even the Austrians supported a French suggestion that Leopold should muzzle his Press, or at least reduce its volume, by a stamp tax on newspapers, and the French foreign minister, Drouyn de Lhuys, wanted all political articles to be signed. The proposal of a stamp tax was too delicate, however, for a Belgian government to tackle in response to foreign protest: as the protesters well knew, the stamp duty on newspapers had been abolished in Belgium in May 1848, in a measure which had been an important gesture of appeasement to the Belgian Left in days

[1] Letter of May 6, 1856.

of revolution, and the abolition had allowed a whole new crop of journals to be founded. But Spain, Holland and the Vatican all added their voices to the general reproach, and in March 1855, the King had written to the Austrian Chancellor Buol: ' . . . our Press is still a catastrophe'.

Since the French refused to make use of the new Press law provided for their benefit, and since any further measure of control was not practical politics, a visit by the Belgian heir to Paris might help to soothe feelings. The Emperor himself was persuaded to invite the Duke of Brabant to the Exhibition of Arts and Industries, and to ask him to stay at St Cloud.

When the train arrived in Paris, there was nobody from the French Court to meet it. This was taken as an example of Napoleonic tonelessness, but it was in fact only an example of the invariable bungling of Prince Napoleon, who had been sent to the station to welcome the Belgians and escort them to St Cloud. When he arrived at the station, the Brabants had already set out, but by hard riding across Paris, he managed to catch them up in the Bois de Boulogne, almost at St Cloud, and to hoist himself puffing into their carriage before it drew up at the Imperial palace. Muddles with railway stations were something of a habit with 'Plon-Plon'. When the Archduke Maximilian arrived in Paris on a state visit the following year, the Prince managed to make the Gare de l'Est in time, but lost the carriages which were supposed to take him and the Emperor's guest through Paris: a very long, cold wait then ensued, while Maximilian studied the Prince's embarrassment: 'a strange, bearded figure' with 'absolutely the look of a worn-out basso from some obscure Italian opera-house'[1].

The visit was spend mostly in excursions and entertainments. Marie-Henriette was very much admired, and was allowed to enjoy herself in a way she understood. She taught her hosts a card game, a German amusement, which involved the winners of each trick blacking the face of the loser with burnt cork. Royalty was excused blackening, of course. The Belgian historian, Pierre Daye, records bitterly: *'Tout cela provoquait, paraît-il, des explosions de la plus folle gaîeté.'* They all went on playing it for a long time after Marie-Henriette had gone back to Belgium.

[1] H. Montgomery Hyde; *Mexican Empire;* p. 50.

The Duke of Brabant was not allowed to get into the kind of deep economic discussions he enjoyed, and was subjected to a series of receptions and concerts which obviously bored him. The Austrian Ambassador, Count Hübner, was specially charged to see whether Napoleon had reconciled himself to the Brabant marriage, and he kept a careful record of the visit in his diary. At a command theatre performance one evening, he noticed with approval that 'the Emperor, sitting beside the Duchess, was on his best behaviour with "the daughter of the Caesars" . . . ' The play, however, like most St Cloud entertainments, was too salacious for the old Austrian, who had unwisely brought along his young daughter, and he suspected that one of the short plays, *Les Premières Armes de Richelieu*, had been chosen maliciously by Napoleon III 'to take a dig at the Duke of Brabant, married young like Richelieu but in far less of a hurry to insist on his marital rights . . . I was appalled to watch poor Melanie obliged to listen to all the smutty jokes in these two shows. Luckily, she didn't understand any of them . . . ' Next day, Marie-Henriette, an experienced matron not yet twenty, came up to Count Hübner to commiserate about the threat to Melanie's innocence.

That evening, Hübner got a closer look at the pair. 'The prince resembles his father greatly, mentally and physically,' he wrote afterwards, 'except for his dislike of ballet. Like all the Coburgs, his nose is too long, his voice is a bit nasal, he is very tall and he talks very well—I would say almost too confidently—for a young man of twenty. The Duchess is charming. She does not say much, but her pretty face is eloquent, and in any case what she did say was just right. She has none of that forced banality, or the tediousness produced by it, which is the curse of Courts.'

The Duke was thirsty for serious conversation. He 'talked to me about Eastern affairs, wishing no hopes to be raised here, as at the Tuileries they were very inclined to laugh at people . . . I took refuge in generalities. The young couple are charming: or at least the Archduchess is charming in her simplicity, in her frank, childish little manners, in her bearing, and, when she talks, in her spontaneity. The Emperor is making a fuss of her, and does her the honours of Paris in person.'

Hübner saw them again a few nights later, at another reception. 'The Duke, who has the longest nose I ever saw, was deeply bewildered at being pushed around in the commotion, and talked politics to me—keeping to the views and presumably the instructions of the Prince de Chimay'[1]. This Prince de Chimay had been acting for the past year as Leopold's additional and unofficial envoy in Paris, and although he might now have been teaching the young Duke politics, he was soon to find himself taking orders from him over the 'Affair of the Horses', Prince Leopold's first scheme.

The 'Affair of the Horses' was a failure, but its technique was already that of the future King of the Belgians who was time and again to 'ring the changes' on less unscrupulous and more conventional opponents. This technique relied upon rapidly alternating appeals to motives of greed and to motives of accepted high principle, while the fact that its exponent was a King allowed him both a springboard into other people's confidence and a refuge from their recriminations.

The confiscation of the Orleans estates, known by untranslatable pun as *'le premier Vol de l'Aigle'* still preoccupied the Duke of Brabant, and on his return from Paris he determined to use the goodwill he might have accumulated there to start a fresh campaign for compensation. The Prince de Chimay was instructed to press for the release of the confiscated money in favour of the children of Leopold I. But the Duke of Brabant insisted that he should demand not only the whole sum, but the interest which had accumulated on it during the four years since it was sequestrated.

Meanwhile, he offered Napoleon III some horses. They were pure Arabs, which he had brought back from his journey to the Near East, and there had originally been five of them, but one had already died and the others were visibly losing the will to live in a Belgian climate. Two were offered to the Emperor, through the Prince de Chimay, and Napoleon accepted, politely hoping that he was not robbing the Duke in doing so. The bait was almost taken, but it remained to get the horses to Paris: another died, and there didn't seem to be much time left for the remaining three. On July 9, 1856, Prince Leopold wrote to Chimay, revealing fuller details of the plan. Once the horses had been delivered, then there would be no harm in letting Napoleon know that he *was* robbing the Duke in accepting them, because

[1] See, for above quotations, Count Hübner; *Neuf ans de souvenirs d'un ambassadeur;* Vol. I, p. 348 *et seq.*

they had cost more than 50,000 francs . . . The Duke added: 'If, however, there should be any bother about that, say that I am building or repairing a couple of palaces just now, and that I have no lack of ideas for decorating these residences with sets of porcelain or with Gobelin tapestries.'

The true vulgarity of this scheme lay in its assumption that Napoleon would not dare commit a breach of courtly manners, either by refusing to accept the horses or by ignoring the hint about the 'sacrifice' incurred by the giver. However, this plan to get by blackmail what could not be won by negotiation was overtaken by events: next day, on July 10th, Napoleon announced that he would concede to the children of the late Belgian Queen Louise-Marie, daughter of Louis Philippe, a yearly payment of 200,000 French francs. Prince Leopold dropped the project of the horses, and told Chimay to reject this rather generous compromise. The Belgian claimants continued to demand an annuity of 300,000 francs and the arrears of income on their share of the Orleans inheritance. But they never managed to make Napoleon improve his offer.

Leopold's motives in being so tenacious were not only personal. It was already apparent that he had developed the Coburg sense of dynastic loyalty even more strongly than his father. The episode of Charlotte's engagement to the Archduke Maximilian in the same year had demonstrated a rapid hardening of his opinions and of his self-confidence. Quite unnecessarily, he had insisted over this marriage that the national interest should take precedence over Charlotte's feelings, although even he, who, as his sister said, 'so readily belittles everyone and who is particularly zealous in the severity of his judgment on princes', had to admit that he approved of Maximilian and wrote Charlotte an intolerable letter to inform her that 'the Archduke is a superior person from every point of view. Had I a single thing to say against him, I would have done so, but you may be sure that there is absolutely nothing'[1]. In 1857, a memorandum attributed to him (but without any sure source) laid down a principle which he was to defend all his life, to the eventual disgust of his family and country: the principle that princesses should not have the same rights of inheritance as princes. By this, he meant to question the position of his own family which

[1] H. Montgomery Hyde; *Mexican Empire;* London 1946; p. 67.

was obliged by the Roman law governing Belgian inheritance to divide its possessions in specified proportions among the children of both sexes, and to suggest that such a system weakened the male line of the dynasty which would have to rule. The sons, the document argued, would divide the inheritance and the daughters, who after all would be exported as wives to strategic foreign capitals, would only receive a temporary allowance. 'My system would favour the male line of descent from the King, in other words, the Belgian dynasty. It seems to me unnecessary to put money into the pockets of Archdukes as yet unborn.' As Leopold II grew old, this search for ways to avoid Belgian law and to find ways to transmit his vast wealth only to male heirs became a major activity of his life.

Meanwhile, he became the father of a daughter, Princess Louise, who was born on February 18, 1858. In June the following year, however, Marie-Henriette produced a son, the ill-fated Count of Hainaut and the dynasty relaxed in the assumption that it was assured of two consecutive male successions. Prince Leopold, having done this service to his country escaped again in March 1860 to Eastern Europe, visiting Budapest and Bucharest and moving down the Danube on a Turkish warship, which aroused some Russian suspicion that he was playing an obscure game for French interests in the Balkans. The French, on the other hand, wondered if the Duke of Brabant was not up to some sinister design with the Turks which would counterbalance the French acquisition of Savoy the year before, and they speculated that he might be intending to buy the island of Crete off the Sultan. Everybody was by now aware of the Duke's interest in securing fresh outlets for Belgian trade, and his speeches in the Senate had made it clear that, in view of the government's obvious lack of interest, he felt himself personally qualified to do something about it.

He spent three weeks with the Sultan in Constantinople, and then sailed westwards along the Aegean coast to Athens, this time on board a British warship. Returning through Corfu, Dalmatia and Venice, he was back in Brussels by the end of May. For the next year he continued to speak on colonial themes in the Senate, to accumulate more information and more useful contacts abroad, and to produce large schemes for the improvement of Brussels. The capital annoyed him: its cheerful, dirty tangle of old streets and its almost complete lack of avenue or monument reminded him daily of the infuriating Belgian ability to be content with things as they were. He wanted to drive great boulevards through the national complacency, to clear parks which would let the citizens breathe and show them wider horizons, and to found model housing estates in which they could live more significant lives. Unfortunately, all these plans seemed to involve a large outlay of public money, and successive Belgian ministries, Liberal or Catholic, took care to avoid any suggestion that they sympathized with such economic madness.

His sister Charlotte had married Maximilian in 1857, and when four years later he heard of the plan to instal the Archduke as Emperor of Mexico, the Duke of Brabant was immensely excited. It was still believed by armchair colonizers in Europe that there was 'something to be done in Central America'—a belief which had managed for two centuries to ignore the evidence of repeated disaster and which later expressed its faith in the rush to buy shares in the first Panama Canal scheme—and even Leopold I had persuaded himself that the installation of an Austrian as Emperor of Mexico was the final achievement of that something. His eldest son wrote Charlotte an enthusiastic but typically ambiguous letter about it. 'It's a magnificent country, where there is plenty of good to be done,' he told her. 'If I had a son of the right age, I would try to get him made King of Mexico. Every brave heart must long to devote himself to that land. In America, there are so many great works to be done. I want the Coburgs to claim that task!'[1] Dynastic ambition and the lust to exploit fallow lands are concealed in the language of a school-book about missionaries.

The following year, in March 1862, the Duke of Brabant went to Spain. He avoided Madrid as far as possible, and concentrated on studying the archives preserved in Seville, writing home to his friend the soldier Brialmont: 'I am very busy here going through the Indies archives and calculating the profit which Spain made then and makes now out of her colonies'[2]. In October, he went back to the Mediterranean and moved eastwards from Algeria and Tunisia along the North African coast

[1] Count Louis de Lichtervelde; *Léopold II;* Brussels 1926; p. 49.
[2] *Ibid.,* p. 57.

to Egypt, where he at last met Ferdinand de Lesseps and watched the Canal being excavated. While he was there, Said was succeeded by Khedive Ismail, who up to the Egyptian bankruptcy of 1876 was to impress Europe with his programme of public works and industrialization, and the Duke, as a useful friend of Egypt, was treated to a long expedition to Mount Sinai, equipped with luxurious tents and a hundred servants. On his way back to Belgium, he again passed through Spain and paid a visit to the King of Portugal.

Nor was this the last of his journeys as Duke of Brabant. His health was still uncertain, even though he was suspected of encouraging his doctors to prescribe cruises in hot climates. Again he grew bored with Brussels, waited long enough to beget another child and to be disappointed at the birth of a second girl, Stephanie, and then made off to the south at the end of 1864. The ship took him straight to Egypt, where he inspected further progress on the Canal with de Lesseps, and then embarked at Suez for the Far East.

This was the most fruitful of all his voyages. From the plantations of Ceylon, from India, the Straits Settlements, Burma, Indo-China, the Dutch East Indies and from China herself, the Duke brought back trunks of notes and documents on the theory and practice of exploitation. Administration, the problems of colonial strategy, the proper relationship of metropolitan power to native ruler, did not attract him so much as the very limited science of using backward populations to produce wealth from the natural resources of their own country. That was the interest which had led him to present to Frère-Orban, then Finance Minister, a piece of marble from the Acropolis which is still in the possession of his descendants: cut into it is a relief portrait of the Duke of Brabant, and round the head runs an engraved sentence of startling directness: *Il faut à la Belgique une Colonie.* Those who took presents from Leopold were never left uncertain about how to express their gratitude.

CHAPTER V

THE ATTACK ON 'LITTLE BELGIUM'

SHUT OUT BY HIS FATHER from any share in the government of Belgium—even in the last months of intense pain before he died, Leopold I rejected any suggestion of a regency—the Duke of Brabant had to organize his own office and choose his own men to staff it. In the course of his continuous search for information about foreign trade, and through his alertness to any voice which seemed to share his interests, he acquired the services of two men whose work and loyalty laid the foundations of his own later achievements.

Auguste Lambermont and Alexis Brialmont had shared a hunger for violent experience when they were young, and as they grew older both men transformed their frustrations into belief in a strong 'forward' policy of Belgian expansion. They felt that they had been deprived of something by the experience of growing up in a peaceful, sceptical country, and they longed to see young Belgians united in some sort of wholehearted action, running some sort of risk for their country. Free trade, it seemed to them, had flung down the barriers separating Belgium from a world of huge promise, and yet their countrymen refused to enter that world. They longed to teach Belgium the healthy pleasures of adventure.

Lambermont, at the time that Prince Leopold encountered him, was working as Secretary-General of the Ministry of Foreign Affairs. Permanent head of the department, he was in his early forties; the son of a small Brabant farmer who had sent him to the village school. In 1838, a serious and romantic boy of nineteen, Lambermont had set off on his own to Spain, determined to defend the honour of Queen Isabella, and he fought bravely enough in the Carlist wars to be decorated. Returning in glory to Belgium, he had accepted a post in the Ministry of Foreign Affairs, and by the age of twenty-five, he had already made a considerable name as a Free Trade apostle in the Commercial Section. He had developed since then a specialized knowledge of waterway and navigational treaties, which was to be useful in negotiating the 1863 Treaty with Holland to redeem ships' dues on the Scheldt, and vital in the drafting of Leopold II's plans for the Congo.

He at least could look back on one adventure. Alexis Brialmont, who had been in correspondence with the Duke of Brabant since about 1853, was a soldier who passed a long and glorious career without ever seeing action. The omission gnawed at his self-respect: when the Théâtre Français burned down, he wrote to a lady who had been present: 'I envy you, Madame: luckier than I, you have seen fire!' From childhood, Brialmont had been goaded by the example of his magnificent father, a soldier who had fought in the Grand Army from Spain to Moscow and who lived on, telling his superb campaign anecdotes, until an onslaught of strawberries in champagne brought him down at the age of ninety-seven. Although Alexis Brialmont became, after Todleben of Russia, one of the best-known military engineers of his day, he was never able to feel that he had lived up to this example. He spent most of his life writing and planning—thirty-five books, seventy-four pamphlets, and twelve folio atlases issued from his study, to say nothing of countless fortification designs—but the work of his middle age was punctuated by pathetic efforts to get himself into range of a bullet travelling in unfeigned anger.

The government had stopped Brialmont going to the Crimea as an observer attached to the French army; in 1857, although he made a special journey to London, he failed to persuade the British to let him help put down the Indian Mutiny; and in 1860 he was denied command of the Belgian expeditionary force destined for China. Instead, apart from two years spent as a Liberal deputy campaigning against Catholic anti-militarism, he was kept to his work of designing Belgium's fortifications, around Antwerp and, later, on the Meuse. His own technical contribution was the design of overhead concrete protection for strongpoints against the new high-angle projectiles, but his Meuse forts, built against such bitter opposition, were not properly maintained. In August 1914, the Germans before Liège were able to pierce their roofs with bombs from their new 420 mm.

mortars and to slaughter the defenders without a frontal attack.

The pamphlet which first brought Brialmont to the attention of the Duke of Brabant was an argument for the enlarging of the Belgian navy. In his first Senate speech, made in December 1855, the Duke had called for the foundation of a permanent steamer service between Antwerp and the Levant, and had told his sceptical audience: 'Our resources are vast, and I am not afraid to say so: we can make immeasurably great use of them. To dare would be to succeed. That is one of the secrets of the power and splendour enjoyed for a century by our northern neighbour, the United Provinces'[1]. He and Brialmont were thinking at this period in terms of Belgian trading posts, established on the shores of foreign countries but supplied and defended by a Belgian merchant fleet and a Belgian navy. In this, they were looking back to the experience of Belgian merchant venturers in the seventeenth and eighteenth centuries, who had been at the mercy of English and Dutch warships in the competition for Eastern markets, and who had finally disappeared from the scene when the Emperor Charles VI had conciliated their rivals by suppressing the Ostend Company and ordering 'all trade and navigation with the East Indies to cease at once and for ever throughout the Austrian Low Countries'. It was agreed by both the Duke and Brialmont that the alternative notion of settling surplus Belgian population in tropical colonies was a futile one. They were referring here to the Guatemala episode, between 1841 and 1845, which had dumped 900 Belgians and their priests on to the shore of Santo Tomas de Castilla and left them to wither in poverty, disease and dispute[2]. The Flemish peasant, Brialmont concluded, would never settle down in a hot climate. And anyway, the fall of tariff barriers all over the world was making such a colony unnecessary: trading posts could now be set up on foreign soil and, he hoped, on foreign colonial territory too.

The separation of Belgium from Holland had deprived this highly industrialized little country of the great East Indies market. Now, in the new trading conditions, Belgium could regain what she had lost and more. But beyond these fairly obvious considerations, the Duke of Brabant was also calculating the

[1] Lichtervelde; *Léopold II*; p. 52.

[2] J. Fabri; *Les Belges au Guatemala*; Académie Royale des Sciences Coloniales; Brussels 1955.

effect which overseas expansion might be expected to have on Belgium politically. Now that the tradition of 'Unionism' in Belgian government was rapidly dying, he hoped that the acquisition of colonies would give the parties a new basis for unity, by entrusting the nation with a precious possession which violent party dispute might ruin. On February 17, 1860, he told the Senate: 'Before such an aim, let us hope that all shades of opinion will join hands: let us hope that our statesmen, who have for the most part been the fathers of useful legislation, will set about this new enterprise with determination'[1]. A few years later, just before his father died, Leopold drew up an open letter to be published over the signature of *un bon Belge* in which he presented this purpose of unification more emotionally: 'Only on the day when we possess an overseas policy will we be able to cauterize the appalling cancer of liberal-clerical conflict which is eating us away and wastefully diverting both our energy and the living strength of the nation'[2]. He added to the economic and political arguments for acquiring colonies a reasoning which was more crudely patriotic. 'Belgium, free only since 1830, suffered many amputations before and after that date: Picardy, Artois, Burgundy, Dutch Flanders, Limburg, Luxemburg, etc. In the East we must win for our fatherland what we cannot reconquer for her in Europe'[3]. Only his accession prevented this significantly anti-political document from appearing in the Press, where everybody would have been able to deduce its real author.

The politicians, who disliked what they understood of the Duke's views on their functions, tried to avoid the trap he was setting for them by retorting that in a free-trading world there was no longer any need for governments to take responsibility for the colonies their citizens chose to found. Ruthlessly, Prince Leopold walled off this path of escape. 'I had yesterday,' he wrote to Brialmont, 'a rather serious brush with the Finance Minister. M. Frère-Orban argued that the American colonies, founded by the English and others, were founded by free enterprise without any government intervention. Same assertion about Australia.

[1] Fr. A. Roeykens; *Les Débuts de l'Oeuvre Africaine de Léopold II*; Académie Royale des Sciences Coloniales; Brussels 1955; p. 35.
[2] L. le Febve de Vivy; *Documents d'Histoire précoloniale belge*; Académie Royale des Sciences Coloniales; Brussels 1955; p. 34.
[3] *Ibid.*, p. 34.

I answered that he was speaking out of ignorance and in error. The discussion was broken off till Christmas. I would be most grateful to you if you would produce for me a little table, very concise, showing that the beginnings of what M. Frère-Orban calls the "new-type free colonies" were all in fact subsidized . . . I am sorry to give you so much bother, but reflect that you are doing it to make our country great'[1].

Where were these Belgian colonies to be? Brialmont favoured the West African coast, as long as the establishment was understood to be a trading factory and not a tropical workhouse for the unemployed Flemish masses. An anonymous pamphlet by a naval officer known to Brialmont had suggested in 1855 that the coast between St Louis de Sénégal and Cape Masuradi would be most suitable; Belgian trading voyages to Sierra Leone, the Gambia, and other places in that region had been unable to establish themselves because of the presence of British or French armed forces. The Duke at first, seemed to agree with Brialmont that West Africa was the most suitable field for search. In 1859, Brialmont published his most famous colonial pamphlet, *Le Complément de l'Oeuvre de 1830,* which was almost certainly written with the approval, if not the assistance, of the Duke of Brabant and which once more suggested that with the backing of an adequate navy, West Africa was ready to be exploited by Belgian traders. Peel, Brialmont wrote, had launched the standard of free trade on the march to complete victory. Overseas colonies should soon open their territories to foreign traders: the development of industry in the metropolitan countries no longer depended on protected tropical markets.

Here Brialmont, whose faith in the new economic doctrines was clear and childlike, went beyond the opinions of his master. Prince Leopold already had his reservations about the prospect of free competition and a free labour market within any colony that Belgium might acquire. Carried to extremes, he suspected that such doctrines would not pay—or at least, would pay very much more slowly than certain older and less fashionable practices; and Leopold was always a man who insisted on quick results. The author, however, ended his booklet with a song of praise to 'a man with wide views, active, intelligent, energetic, devoted; enjoying enough influence or authority to force the

[1] P. Crokaert; *Le Général Brialmont;* Brussels 1928; p. 417.

country and the legislature to busy themselves in these important schemes . . .'[1]

After 1860, and in particular after his journey to the Far East in 1864-5, Leopold's interest in West Africa as a possible site for a Belgian commercial outlet began to wane. Brialmont had already argued with him over a map in favour of the Gulf of Guinea, and at one moment had even let his finger rest on the mouth of the Congo itself, but his master's ideas were turning away from the original suggestion of trading posts on foreign shores and fastening increasingly on the idea of sovereign concessions of territory. This, in turn, led the search towards areas in which old-fashioned political units were crumbling and surrendering their possessions to stronger nations. For the Duke of Brabant, such loot was most easily to be found in the East.

A note written on March 17, 1861, addressed to Lambermont, ran: 'It is time to put the efforts made in various parts of the world to win a colony for Belgium on to a practical footing . . . The Chinese and Japanese question has been in the public eye for three years, and nothing has been done about it. But it would none the less be useful if without further delay we could win some right to take an interest in Far Eastern affairs.

'We must try to form in Belgium a company for the exploration of the Far East, which can study on the spot practical ways to open outlets for Belgian industry in China, Japan and Cochin China.' The Duke then went into an elaborate description of the sort of company he meant, hinting broadly that he himself would put forward nearly half the initial capital required. But the company's trading and fact-finding would be only half the total scheme. A typical Leopoldian strategy had already been developed: the company's ultimate rôle was to acquire a political influence and to become owner or concessionaire of lands made over to it by some helpless local ruler. It would end by resembling the East India Company. 'The day when Cavour was able to speak for Italy to the rest of the world, he was halfway to victory. The day that the Belgians can speak with authority to the rest of the world about the Far East, they will have gained for their country a chance to take her share of the wreckage of the empires which are about to collapse out there.' In another place in the same memorandum, he said explicitly: ' . . . we

[1] Roeykens; *Débuts de l'Oeuvre;* p. 22.

shall involve ourselves, first by publishing information and later, if we can, in a more serious fashion, in the overthrow of the East'[1].

In detail, the way Leopold's thoughts were running now is made clear in another memorandum to Lambermont, dated June 11th of the same year. 'I am specially interested in the Argentine Province of Entre Rios and the little island of Martin-Garcia at the confluence of the Uruguay and the Parana. Who owns this island? Could one buy it, and set up there a free port under the moral protection of the King of the Belgians? . . . In 1832, on November 5th, Bolivia gave one Manuel Luis de Olinden full proprietary rights, with right of resale, over the vast province of Otuquis, 900 leagues square, an area equal to Hanover and Saxony combined. This superb concession on the upper Paraguay in the gold and diamond regions was designed to commit Citizen Olinden to establishing a port at the confluence of the Otuquis and the Paraguay. Port revenues for fifty years were made over to him. It would be interesting to know what happened to this deal. Is Olinden still alive? Is his business flourishing, or would he like to sell?

'You can see by this example that nothing would be easier than to become the owner of lands three or four times as big as Belgium in the Argentine states. I would like to offer my country an estate like that . . . '[2]. This was a policy far more aggressive than anything contemplated, for example, by a British government of the period. It amounted to deliberate use of the Chartered Company technique to cover a national raid on the possessions of states too senile or too inexperienced to hold on to them. It was nearly an invitation to piracy as a form of national expression.

Writing to Brialmont on July 26, 1863, the Duke tried to clarify further his own thoughts about the theory of colonization. He discarded the arguments of the Manchester School against the possession of colonies by retorting that the failure of cotton supplies from the United States, due to the Civil War, had put 'half a million' workers out of work in the Manchester region itself, driving the manufacturers to appeal to the government for increased Indian cotton production. Then he suggested

[1] Daye; *Léopold II;* pp. 72-4.
[2] Roeykens; *Débuts de l'Oeuvre;* p. 413, Note 1.

that three categories of colony could be defined. First, there was the Slave Colony, and he cited Cuba as an example. Secondly, there were colonies containing large native populations under European administration, like Java, the Philippines, Cochin China, or India. Thirdly, there were colonies of white emigration.

The first and the last types did not interest him. The second did. In Java, he noted, wealth was produced by a system of forced labour: 'the only way to civilize and moralize these idle and corrupted populations of the Far East. The day will come,' he added with perhaps rather less conviction, 'when this kind of work can be abolished without danger to public security and without financial loss to the colonial power'[1]. The negatives here are more important than the positives: forced labour is to Leopold both the best method of producing wealth from a backward population and the best insurance against organized rebellion. Considerations of civilization and morality might incidentally be satisfied by a system necessary for other ends.

What should Belgium do? He suggested the setting up of an 'Overseas Fund', an earmarked sum out of budget surplus to be augmented by gifts and legacies which would eventually 'undertake the exploitation of some fine country, following the best available examples'. Beginnings would be small: China, Japan, Borneo, Central America and even Africa were possible sites, and he quoted the example of Sarawak as a private concession company which had already achieved sovereignty. Leopold had for years been enviously following the doings of the Brooke dynasty, who had won the concession of Sarawak from the local Sultans in 1842 and installed themselves as Rajahs, and he had even managed to interest his father in a plan to buy the rest of Borneo off the Dutch. When in 1861 Sir James Brooke had announced that he intended to abandon his independence, the Duke of Brabant had rushed out to him an invitation to visit Brussels and discuss matters, all expenses paid. Brooke did come to Europe, possibly on the Belgian steamer ticket, but he went to London first and was persuaded there to offer Sarawak to Britain. In spite of this snub, the Duke's interest in North Borneo survived, although he probably exaggerated to himself the wealth which the Brookes had made out of their kingdom.

[1] le Febve de Vivy; *Documents d'Historie précoloniale belge*; p. 20.

Leopold had already departed a long way from the free-trading
views of his contemporaries. But he knew perfectly well that
openly to advocate protectionism or state monopoly would
scandalize the very Belgians he wanted to impress. Perhaps this
explains a contradiction in some notes dictated by Leopold to
his secretary Le Jeune; a generalization which is rapidly under-
mined by the reflections which follow. Leopold reflects conven-
tionally: 'The principles of the mercantile system recommended
especially a form of colonization by monopoly and by prohibition . . . today the principles of the mercantile system have been
condemned and abandoned.' Or have they? Leopold goes on to
remark that the problem today is not so much one of exchange
as of production. 'Exchange between the Old World and these
territories has to be organized, but the really important thing is
to increase and organize production in those territories, and
while organizing production to create outlets for Europe. Free
trade for exchange of goods, but: *query*: free labour for production?'[1] The direction of his thoughts lay towards the institution of forced labour organized by a European colonial
administration, but what private trader could compete easily
with the State under such conditions?

The authors of *Africa and the Victorians*[2] consider that 'the
imperialism of Free Trade' as practised by Palmerston aimed to
'protect strategic interests in the Near East by trade and
influence'. The Victorian British looked first for a 'collaborating
class', to accept another of the authors' definitions: where such
a class could be found, the logic of Free Trade ran against occupation. Leopold seldom bothered even to look for such a class,
although he occasionally invented one for purposes of propaganda. For his view of colonial trade and colonial purposes was
an entirely different one. British imperialism, especially in
Africa, responded to strategic motives or to the attractions of
the market offered by a large native population. It followed that
the richer and freer these populations could become, the better
British commercial purposes would be served. Leopold, on the
other hand, was obsessed by the productive, not the consump-
tive, capacity of colonial territories: he intended that their
natural resources should be immediately realized to the profit of

[1] le Febve de Vivy; *Documents d'Histoire précoloniale belge;* pp. 130-131.
[2] R. Robinson, J. Gallagher, and A. Denny; London 1961, p. 78.

the colonial power by the use of a tax in labour. Obviously, the logic of this kind of exploitation ran in favour of occupation, not against it.

In reality, Leopold's idea was that a colony should become a department of the metropolitan economy: a national investment. The most significant, perhaps, of all reforms in colonial thinking was the growth of the belief that a colony should have its own budget, and that the surplus of a colony's revenue should be used in the interests of the territory concerned rather than be shipped home and marked to the credit of a metropolitan Treasury. Leopold turned his back irrevocably on such enlightened ideas. His model remained the brutal old régime of the Dutch East Indies: State imperialism designed to make a profit for Holland.

He wrote: 'If Belgium, which already possesses its railways, could add to them some new Java, one might be able to hope for a reduction in the salt duty, the suppression of customs dues, etc., etc., etc., all achieved without the slightest call on our own resources or on our current expenditure . . . '[1] A colony, in other words, was as directly State property as a State-owned railway: it was as absolutely a possession as if it were a single, enormous crate containing gold and rubber, paid for and delivered to the buyer. For Leopold, the human beings who lived in such a territory were no more than convenient tools provided to help in the unpacking.

He went on amassing information and widening his ring of contacts, studying the technique of exploitation and prospecting for the right place to install its apparatus. 'My intention,' he wrote to Brialmont in 1861 (November 6th), 'is to extract from history and from statistical returns everything which justifies our notions and discredits those of the "Little Belgium" advocates'[2]. His staff was kept hard at work. In November 1863, Brialmont complained to Lambermont: 'My dear Baron, the Duke of Brabant takes me for a statistics office: His Royal Highness is asking me for "a little table showing on one side the balance of French trade and on the other side the balance of Belgian trade for the first eight months of 1863 . . . " ' The Duke planned that Brialmont should write a book on the subject of

[1] le Febve de Vivy; *Documents d'Histoire précoloniale belge;* p. 31.
[2] Crokaert; *Brialmont;* p. 416.

colonies, and for a time collected material for him. A little later, he decided that he ought to write or at least edit the book himself. He told Brialmont in 1863 that 'in order to make it (the book) known to the public, the Prince intends to find some eloquent speakers and writers worthy of the subject'. A big dossier entitled *Belgians Abroad*, found among official papers and dating from 1863, was examined by the historian le Febve de Vivy and found to contain a vast mass of historical material collected and annotated by Leopold, dealing mostly with the old Belgian merchant venturers, but also with the mediaeval and subsequent migrations of Flemish weavers to Britain, the activities of Belgian missionaries in China, South America, India and the Pacific, and the voyages of Belgian trawlers to foreign fisheries. All this was evidently material for such a book, left uncompleted when Leopold became King in 1865.

And yet all Leopold's activities and speeches, and the pamphlets of his assistants, did not manage to arouse Belgian enthusiasm for a colonial venture. He began to realize that it was not enough merely to hold out a financial bait, and that even the appeal to patriotism was failing to lure his comfortable people out of doors. If Belgium were to get a colony, she would have to be given it, or even be tricked into taking it. 'Belgium doesn't exploit the world,' he had written in 1863 to Brialmont, 'it's a taste we have got to make her learn'[1]. Now he was beginning to feel that Belgium might never acquire that taste unless her mouth were held open and the stuff poured down her throat. He came to the throne already experienced and embittered with his own subjects, having lost the first round of his struggle to make Belgium great, but determined to win the next one. The vision was so clear to him: why would his people not follow his lead? 'We shall point out the domains which the State will acquire, where there are people to be civilized and led towards every kind of progress, and which will guarantee for Us new revenues, for our middle classes the new occupations they are looking for, for our Army a little action, and for all Belgians a chance to show the world that they also are an imperial people capable of dominating and teaching others'[2].

[1] le Febve de Vivy; *Documents d'Histoire précoloniale belge;* p. 23.
[2] Roeykens; *Débuts de l'Oeuvre;* p. 23.

CHAPTER VI

THE NEW KING AND THE PARTIES

IF HE DID NOT TRUST his elder son, the old King continued to trust his daughter-in-law. Marie-Henriette could at least speak German to him, and they shared a passion for hunting and an interest in music. Perhaps, too, he thought that she brought him luck: there is a legend that Leopold I sent an equerry to buy a sweepstake ticket when he came to Vienna for her engagement, and had won the jackpot of the Austrian State Lottery. Whatever the reasons, he made Marie-Henriette promise that she would tell him when he was about to die.

His mistress, Madame Meyer von Eppinghoven, looked after him in the last weeks of his life, and he would allow nobody else into his presence until the very last days. On December 9th, indifferent to the presence of the royal mistress, Marie-Henriette came to him and gave her warning.

Leopold probably realized that she would inevitably try to use her position of trust to persuade him into a deathbed conversion to Catholicism, and he resisted her with patience. He allowed her to hold his hand, he was even persuaded to confess in German to her and to make an Act of Contrition to a crucifix, but when she dared to suggest that he should formally enter her Church, his kindness could no longer be maintained. To her deep distress, he sent instead for a Protestant minister, and died in his own faith at 11.45 on the morning of December 10, 1865, grasping Marie-Henriette's hand and repeating dimly the name 'Charlotte'. His family and the Cabinet ministers standing round the bed could not tell if he was talking of his own first wife or of his daughter.

Marie-Henriette was rapidly put back in her place by her husband. At the ceremony of his inauguration in the Parliament building, he insisted, much to the embarrassment of his ministers, that she and the rest of the Royal Family should sit at the side of the Chamber of Representatives, well separated from the royal throne installed for the occasion on the tribune. The ministers had wanted to present a conventional group of father, mother and children all clustered together round the throne, but the new King refused even to let the Queen enter the Chamber in his own procession. He was nervous and very much on his dignity; the State guests for the occasion included the British Prince of Wales, King Luis of Portugal, the Crown Prince of Prussia, the Dukes of Connaught and Cambridge, a host of German princes, and Archduke Joseph of Austria, his own father-in-law. Leopold obviously feared that a ceremony with no crown, no sceptre, no Swords of Justice and no moth-eaten nobles in ermine, already threatened him with the contempt of his guests. The ministers' idea would have lowered the occasion to the level of a family pose before a beach photographer.

After taking the oath, Leopold II made his speech, sitting on his throne and reading it from a text. Everybody was very pleased with it. Combining dignified grief for his father with an attractive humility about his own achievements, Leopold managed also to introduce a hint of defiance to the great Powers already planning war around the Belgian frontiers. 'If I cannot promise Belgium a great reign like that which laid the foundations of her independence, or a great king like the man whom we mourn today,' he said, 'I can at least promise her a King who is Belgian in heart and soul, whose whole life belongs to her.' With modesty he had drawn notice to the fact that he was a Catholic born in Belgium, not a royal mercenary who might in his time occupy several thrones before he found one to fit him. After a few more sentences, he rose with deliberate theatricality to his feet and went on in a louder voice: 'In my thoughts, the future of Belgium is inextricable from my own, and I always think of it with a confidence inspired by the rights of a free, honest and courageous nation which insists on its independence, which knew how to conquer it, and to show itself worthy of it, and which will know how to hold on to it.' All eyes went to the Prussian and French representatives, and the Belgian Parliament shouted approval.

A little later, the King remarked, 'The edifice whose foundations were laid by the Congress can and will be built higher still.' It was the only warning in his speech of his own plans for Belgium, but few of the audience drew its full implications. The

King had paid compliments to the Constitution, and he had defied the threats of the great Powers: that was enough[1].

Leopold continued to move very softly, as he picked up the reigns of power and felt for the first time the answering resistance of ministers and departments of State. Frère-Orban, Finance Minister and effective leader of the government, was an old enemy. The others were perhaps softer, and might be ingratiated. Much the best account of these first encounters comes from the recollections of Auguste Vandenpeereboom, the elderly Minister of the Interior, and a moderate Liberal who still dared to go to Mass. Initially, he was flattered by the King's pose of candid ignorance, which also disarmed the Cabinet at its first meeting with Leopold a few days after the inauguration. Shyly, the King confessed to them: 'I have kept out of matters of state, and I don't know how anything works. I want to be a constitutional monarch because I am sure that Belgium's prosperity and security are both due to the constitutional regime which she runs so well.'

After a few weeks, however, Vandenpeereboom and his colleagues began to suspect that their condescension to the 'childish naïveté' of Leopold had been misplaced. 'Little by little, the King is revealing and displaying himself; I am certain that he means well; he has talent, tact and good judgment; he is experienced and he knows a lot—but I feel that he is sly. He is devious, cunning: I dare not call him treacherous. He hides his thoughts, and advocates what he does not believe in order to protect his inner reflections from attack. It is often going to be difficult to tell at once the goal towards which His Majesty is setting his course, but will the King have the qualities of perseverance and will-power? The future will tell.'

Vandenpeereboom seemed to realize, as he wrote, how dangerously he had been underestimating Leopold, and the memoir became more alarmed as it ran on: 'Leopold II continues to show himself mild, insinuating and modest, but this is another example of his skill: he realizes that a King can get nothing done by his own will, but has to gain his ends through the influence he exercises, and this is why he is trying to win himself influence: later . . . perhaps . . . he may try to set up an

[1] Lichtervelde; *Léopold II*; pp. 64-6.

autocracy or at least to exercise a great control over the conduct of policy'[1].

In July, Leopold set off on the first of a long series of cere-monial visits to the towns of Belgium, re-enacting the old *Joyeuse Entrée* of the Dukes of Brabant, who were obliged to guarantee certain liberties before they could be welcomed into their inheritance. Almost everywhere, he was magnificently received. Each city was showing its traditional independence by conducting its own royal inauguration: all summer the speeches blared on, the carillons rang and the little decorations were dis-tributed. In his campaign to please everybody, Leopold even proposed that all the bishops should be decorated, and when the Liberal Cabinet recoiled, threatened that he would give a personal present to those whom the Government refused to honour with an Order.

There was, in fact, only one exception to the generally warm reception he encountered, and that was the attitude of Antwerp. Through most of his reign, and in spite of the great financial gain it was to draw from Leopold's Congo, the great port remained truculently Catholic in politics and, in particular, strongly pacifist. This pacifism arose from Antwerp's violent objection to being fortified: the citizens considered that this would make them only more likely to be bombarded, and, worse, would add enormously to the rates. Their obstinacy brought them into direct conflict with both Leopold I and his son.

The original plan, as described in 1853, had been to make Antwerp into a vast fortified camp, a sort of tribal earthwork into which the whole nation might retreat from an invader. In 1859, young Captain Brialmont had submitted a design for these forts, with the backing of Leopold I, and had been awarded the prize by the Russian engineer Todleben against the competition of more experienced men. However, the city of Antwerp con-tinued to create scenes at every proposal to enlarge the existing defence works, especially after an unlucky muddle over compen-sation for land taken for entrenchments. In November 1862, a deputation from the Antwerp Council had called on Leopold I to petition against any further work on the fortifications. Leopold, frozen with rage, confronted them in full-dress uni-form, read through the burgomaster's petition, thrust it back to

[1] Daye; *Léopold II;* p. 98

him and left the room without having uttered a word. For this snub, Antwerp did not forgive him. The middle classes and the city fathers carried on their resistance, and called into their struggles the voteless Flemish masses of the streets, in a campaign of public agitation which was the first deliberate extension of political life beyond the narrow circle of the *censitaires*. Out of this campaign and its huge public rallies grew the movement known from its technique as *Meetinguisme*. On the right wing of the Catholic party, *Meetinguisme* came into confluence with more philosophical streams of Catholic pacifism and with the traditional Belgian dislike of military budgets, and founded an extreme Catholic hostility to all suggestions for Army reform or national defence by fortification. Leopold II never made his *Joyeuse Entrée* into Antwerp: the town council, provided with a statue of his father, had refused to put it up, and it remained in storage of one kind or another until a Liberal council won power in 1873.

While Leopold was touring his country, the parties observed an uneasy truce. Both sides, though reserving judgment about the personality of the new King, had been genuinely moved by the inauguration's brave renewal of the Revolution, and they had been impressed by congratulatory messages from abroad which showed how important Belgium's internal unity seemed to her guarantors. Lord Clarendon had told the Belgian Minister in London that he considered the demonstrations of popular loyalty to the Crown not only as a new consecration of the achievement of 1830, but 'as the strongest assurance that peace will be maintained. Looked at in this way, it was a European occasion'[1]. The unspoken hint that a divided Belgium could not be protected was easily to be drawn from these words. In a mood of conscious self-restraint, the 1866 budget went through Parliament after three days of polite conversation: the first to be given such an easy passage for some years.

Frère-Orban was now at the height of his powers. His first period of office (1847-52), as Minister of Works and then of Finance, had rescued the Société Générale from commitments it could not fulfil and had set up the Banque Nationale de Belgique, to take care of note issue: he had moved the country far towards free trade with its neighbours, but had helped to

[1] Quoted in Daye; *Léopold II;* p. 95.

bring defeat on his own Government in 1852 by proposing a death duty of one per cent. Now he was back in office, dominating the elderly Rogier who nominally led the administration and impatient to introduce a full programme of Liberal legislation which would permanently lay down the frontiers between Church and State, evict the Church from the areas of power which Liberals considered to belong by right to the lay authority, and erect a solid defence of statute and regulation against Catholic counter-attack. He would not hear of a proposal from the Progressives of his own party that the franchise for provincial and communal elections should be widened, warning them openly that to introduce a worker element into the electorate would endanger the dominance of the middle classes, and a bill to add those with three years middle schooling to the *censitaires* lay before Parliament until 1870.

Meanwhile, the general elections of June 1866 increased the Liberal majority. The Right was in confusion, and a handy financial scandal helped Frère-Orban to useful anti-Catholic ammunition for several years. The financier Langrand-Dumonceau had for ten years been involving the clergy and members of the Catholic party in a well-publicized scheme to 'Christianize capitalism'. This huge aim was to be achieved by the investment of 'Catholic' money in the Langrand-Dumonceau companies, and nunnery savings and parish collections flowed obediently into his 'Société Générale Allemande', his 'Banque de Credit Foncier', and his 'Austro-Hungarian Railway Company'. Langrand-Dumonceau was made a Papal Count, and settled senior members of the Catholic party on his various Boards. Then his bubble exploded.

By the time that Langrand-Dumonceau was finally sentenced in 1872 to ten years imprisonment for several degrees of fraud, including even fraudulent bankruptcy, the Liberal Press had wrung from the affair every available drop of anti-Catholic propaganda. But the noisy gloatings of the Liberal party could not divert attention from threatening transformations under way both in its own attitude towards the general public and within its own parliamentary strength.

At the top, Frère-Orban was taking the party towards a more rigidly anti-religious position, and the Freemasons were being allowed to increase their hold over the branches. More significantly, the local Liberal associations were now being encouraged by party headquarters to nominate teams of Liberal supporters to man posts in local government. The Liberal party was deliberately extending political commitment and the operation of a 'spoils system' over the whole surface of Belgian life. Down at the grass-roots, in the communes, party affiliation was being forced on stationmasters and postmen and, above all, on school-teachers. Communities and even families were finding that the politics of their members were dividing them, segregating friends and relations from each other as if in the first act of a civil war.

In the parliamentary party, the Progressives continued to bewilder Frère-Orban and the *aristocratico-métalliques* by clamouring for further extension of the franchise, sawing away the very branch on which as Liberals they sat. Already, earlier in the year, they had accepted some Catholic support in their demand for a lowering of the *cens*. In 1867, the mine strikes and the shooting of workers by troops alienated them still further from their own leaders, who seemed to them to embody a funda-mental hypocrisy by at once preaching *laissez-faire* and defend-ing this gospel with bullets against hungry men. The agitation for universal suffrage spilled over, like *Meetinguisme,* into mass rallies. In January 1868, Frère-Orban managed at last to dislodge Rogier and to take command of the government, but at the commune elections in October 1869, his own left wing joined with Catholics to defeat some of his 'Doctrinaire' Liberal candi-dates. It was a fair warning. At the general elections of June 1870, the Progressive radicals under Paul Janson threw their support behind Catholic candidates, and after thirteen years in power, the Liberal administration was defeated.

Under the surface, beneath the artificial waterline drawn across Belgian political life by the *cens,* the doctrines of Socialism were making intermittent progress. All through the century, French revolutionaries had cultivated Belgian disciples. A few had been taught by Buonarotti, the disciple of Babeuf; St-Simon had sent a team of socialists in 1831; Considérant, the follower of Fourier, had paid two visits to Brussels and attracted a slight following among intellectuals. Karl Marx had lived in Brussels between 1845 and 1848, working on the *Communist Manifesto* and in 1847 helping to found the *Association Democratique,* a group

C

composed largely of foreign revolutionaries in exile, which sent Marx with a fraternal delegation to the London congress at which the 'Communist League' was founded. Marx was expelled after the 1848 revolution, however, and his works were not translated in Belgium for another twelve or fifteen years. A much more immediate influential event was the founding of the group known as *Le Peuple*, or the 'Association of Militant Democracy', which set up its own newspaper in 1860 and enrolled not only 'pure' socialists like César de Paepe, but young radicals like Paul Janson whose target was universal suffrage rather than common ownership of the means of production. In 1864, the year before Leopold II was inaugurated, *Le Peuple* appointed itself the Belgian Section of the First International, formed in London on September 28th that year, and set up branches in the industrial areas. The economic crisis and strikes of 1868 brought a rapid but temporary surge of popular support. Ten miners were killed by security forces in Charleroi, and troops dispersed the metal-workers who struck at the Cockerill works in Seraing: eight more men died as troops opened fire among the collieries of the Borinage. In the ensuing year, Belgian socialists worked hard to build on foundations of anger and insecurity, and were able to establish unions, co-operatives and some local newspapers. Even in the Catholic party, these years saw an awakening of minds to social problems. The 'Social Catholics' brought their party to face these questions at the Malines congresses during the 'sixties, and the socialist Ducpetiaux even tried to get the 1864 congress to accept a twelve hour day, inspection of working conditions, and the principle of an adequate living wage.

But none of these things detained the King's attention. While at home the truce declared for his investiture wore away and his subjects renewed their clamour over religion and the franchise, he looked beyond the frontiers and watched the approach of a European crisis which was to explode around Belgium and threaten her existence, as France and Germany manoeuvred for the advantage on their northern flank.

CHAPTER VII

NEUTRALITY THROUGH STRENGTH

THE BEST WAY for Belgium to please her guarantors was to show them that she could defend herself without their help. The less heavily Belgium leaned on their promises, the more stoutly the Powers declared that they would fight to preserve Belgian integrity. The making of the Treaties themselves in 1831 had demonstrated the price of Belgian military weakness. In 1831, the Dutch counter-attack had routed the Belgian army, and had only been repelled by French troops. This impressed the Powers, and the three great reactionaries, Prussia, Russia and Austria, supported some of the Dutch King's claims for territorial concessions in 'rebel' Belgium: why should they commit themselves to apparently endless police work in the disputed tracts of a country unable to hold its own borders? The final Treaty of Twenty-Four Articles, which bound the Five Powers 'jointly and severally' to maintain Belgium's integrity in return for her neutrality, returned to Holland North Limburg and the strip of Zeeland Flanders on the Belgian bank of the Scheldt estuary and gave back to the Dutch King as a member of the German Confederation the German part of Luxemburg. King William I of Holland haggled on for another seven years in the hope of improving the bargain still further, while the deputies of North Limburg and Zeeland Flanders and Luxemburg continued to sit in the Belgian Parliament in attitudes of piteous valediction. By the time that William I at last decided to accept the Twenty-Four Articles, in 1838, the Belgians were emotionally inclined to defy him. The probable consequence of defiance, however, would have been the obliteration of Belgium from the political map, and with tears and resentment the nation accepted the Treaties after their final signature in London on April 19, 1839.

The sacrifice left a deep scar across Belgian national consciousness. Leopold II never abandoned the hope that he might win back the Grand Duchy of Luxemburg. He often presented the acquisition of Belgian colonies as a just recompense for the amputations of 1839, but in practice he did not see why Belgium should not have both the Congo and Luxemburg. Many other Belgians, some of them in office, felt as he did about the Duchy. In the Luxemburg crisis of 1867, Leopold led his country into serious danger by encouraging such wild men to fish in the waters of Franco-German relations.

This was the more foolish because Franco-Prussian relations were at this time fundamentally rather good. Bismarck and Napoleon were both determined that there should be no war between them; they were personally on cordial terms, and Napoleon's lack of control over his own Bonapartists was not yet apparent to Bismarck. Particularly dangerous, France and Prussia were in a measure of agreement about Belgium: subject to prudence and the right opportunity turning up, they were willing to divide Belgium between them as a bond to preserve their good relations. Leopold, who in later life showed himself perfectly aware that Belgian security was often best served by the mutual suspicion of her guarantors, did not at first understand this situation.

The Austro-Prussian War of 1866, culminating in the battle of Sadowa on July 3rd, had left Prussia dominant in Central Europe. France, which had rejected territorial baits offered by Bismarck to get her into the war, now looked sullenly at the results of Prussian victory. Leopold assumed at once that Bismarck intended to fulfil something of his pre-war suggestions by offering France compensation in the shape of Belgian territory, and tried to sound a general alarm. But Frère-Orban was not to be moved. During the war, Leopold had appealed to him to fortify the left bank of the Scheldt: Frère-Orban had answered briefly that such a plan was politically impractical. Leopold then suggested the construction of 'a little fleet of iron-clads', but got the same reply. After Sadowa, Frère-Orban decided with relief that the danger was over. He refused to take seriously the possibility that Napoleon might be bought off Germany at Belgian expense, and set about reducing the exceptional military budget which had been most unwillingly voted by parliament at the outset of the Austro-Prussian War. There was little that Leopold could do with him. The fact that the King won over the nominal leader of the government, Charles Rogier, was of little use to him; Rogier, a man of the 1830 revolution who had retained into old age a fervent and romantic liberalism which was entirely out of fashion, was no longer on speaking terms with his lieutenant. When Leopold tried to suggest that Sadowa made the defence of the Scheldt more, not less, important, Frère-Orban threatened to resign if he did not let the topic drop. He had already told Napoleon III in person that, whatever the King might want, the Belgian government would oppose the fortifying of the river against a French advance.

In July, interrupting his *Joyeuses Entrées,* Leopold went to England to lobby a firm statement of support out of London or Windsor. He saw his cousin Victoria, and he met Gladstone, Disraeli and the Duke of Edinburgh. Little was achieved. The new Tory government encouraged Leopold to suppose that France was not as dangerous as she seemed and discouraged Belgian rearmament. About the guarantee British ministers were evasive, although the Belgian Ambassador, at Rogier's orders, was pressing for a declaration that Belgium would be defended by Britain 'as if she were as much British territory as the Principality of Wales . . . ' The British hesitated; meanwhile the Belgian Foreign Office was very much alarmed by a remark of the British Ambassador in Paris to the effect that, in his personal view, Britain would not stir to help Belgium. Leopold continued to believe that Bismarck was actively preparing to suggest a partition of Belgium, and in August 1866 it was reported that he had done so in the course of meetings with Benedetti, the French Ambassador in Berlin.

He wrote a characteristic begging letter to Queen Victoria on September 10th, suggesting that she should use British officials as Belgian catspaws. 'The French Emperor is all right from our point of view. I hope his health improves again. As for Bismarck, we know for a fact that he keeps on offering us to France. If Lord Loftus could find an opening one day to tell Bismarck that England hopes that Prussia will stay on good terms with Belgium, that might be a good thing. I do realize that it is a most delicate topic to bring up in Berlin, because the initiative must seem to come from the British Ambassador and nobody else . . . '[1].

[1] Quoted in Daye; *Léopold II;* p. 114-5.

Here Leopold's interpretation of events was quite wrong. Bismarck was not frightened of France, and although he wished to keep on good terms with Napoleon, he did not yet feel it necessary to give him quite such expensive presents. Napoleon, on the other hand, was under increasing pressure to develop a forward Imperial policy from his own supporters: the fact that he dreaded the consequences of such a policy explained the alternation of hostile Note and personal reassurance which so much puzzled the Belgians in their relations with the Emperor in this period.

The truth about the meetings with Bismarck was that Benedetti had been instructed to offer him a double treaty: a public one ceding Luxemburg to France and a secret one for an offensive-defensive alliance permitting France to annex Belgium with Prussian support when she thought fit. Bismarck put these wild documents away, saying he would have to consult his King. He had no intention of accepting them, because there was no need to accept them: instead, he kept the draft treaty as a surety against France and in 1870, with a shattering effect on British and Belgian opinion, he fished it out of its drawer and sent it to *The Times*.

But Bismarck had at least realized the strength of the forces that were shoving Napoleon towards French aggrandisement against his inclinations. At the end of the year, he suggested that if France were to make the King of Holland a cash bid for the Grand Duchy of Luxemburg, Prussia would not object. The fortress and its Prussian garrison were not very valuable to him, and Bismarck hoped that the deal would go through quickly and quietly. Unluckily the French hesitated, and did not make their offer to the Dutch King until early 1867: by then the sort of situation which Bismarck had been trying by speed and secrecy to avoid had become inevitable. The German Federal Parliament, which had been designed after the Austro-Prussian War, came into being in 1867 and accused the Chancellor of abandoning 'Germanic' lands to occupation by alien nations. The King of Prussia, Bismarck's Old Man of the Sea, suggested that there should be no cession to France but that the signatories of the 1839 Treaties should be summoned to discuss the Grand Duchy's future. The situation stiffened abruptly: Prussia told London that she would not make any concession over Luxemburg, and asked to know British intentions in the matter. The Foreign Office returned that Britain remained neutral over Luxemburg, but would regard any attack on Belgium as a *casus belli.*

Napoleon had made his offer to the King of Holland in March. The Belgian parliament was persuaded to vote a large supplementary defence credit. Meanwhile, the King gave encouragement to an imprudent campaign for the return of Luxemburg to Belgium. Its senior advocate was old Charles Rogier, who remembered that in the fifteenth century Luxemburg had been attached to the Burgundian states and had passed with the Belgians under Spanish, Austrian and finally French rule. Detached in 1815 and made a Grand Duchy under the House of Orange-Nassau, all Luxemburg except the city itself had risen with the Belgians in 1830. Rogier, as an old revolutionary liberal, wanted to buy the Luxemburgers back into liberty, and he ordered the Belgian ministers in London and Vienna to test reactions in their capitals to such an idea. Leopold, however, had for a long time considered that Rogier was senile, and he reserved his personal support for the schemes of a remarkable man whose talents were to enrich Leopold's resources of propaganda for the next thirty years. This was Emile Banning, a young man with a limp like his master's, who was now rising to prominence as a romantic Imperialist of the most dangerously sentimental breed. Born in Liège in 1836, Banning had written a long and lugubrious poem called 'The Slave Trade' at the age of twenty, and as a journalist on the liberal *Echo du Parlement,* had taken a special interest in the anti-slavery issues of the American Civil War. His talents came to official notice in 1863, when he wrote a legal study of river navigation, and Charles Rogier had appointed him archivist in the Ministry of Foreign Affairs. This, of course, made him the direct source of most of the data which the Duke of Brabant was accumulating, and in 1865, Leopold had asked him to prepare a study of the commercial possibilities for Belgium in Formosa.

Banning's Liberalism was of the variety which sought to define 'races' among men and to assign to each race its true historical destiny, a belief already declining into a compost which was to nourish the growth of racialist fascism in Europe. He was easily induced to see in the Luxemburg dispute an example of a minority oppressed by Germanic aliens, and he fought for reunification through articles published in the Belgian and, possibly, in the Luxemburg Press which were read and revised by Leopold before they were sent to the printers[1]. Banning seems also to have made a secret journey into Luxemburg, carrying a load of proclamations and Belgian flags.

The Press campaign was carried on by Banning for several years after the Luxemburg question had been settled by treaty. For his part, the King soon realized that the attitude of the Powers made reunification with Luxemburg impractical for the moment. Frère-Orban, who thought Rogier's plan to buy back the Grand Duchy ridiculous, pointed out that at best the purchase would be intolerably provocative to France, and at worst might encourage Belgium's neighbours to extort a territorial 'compensation' from her. Austria had already replied to Rogier's soundings by suggesting that if Belgium was going to extend its frontiers to what Banning called a 'natural' frontier down on the Moselle, then France might be pacified by the return of her 1814 frontier, which would have taken from Belgium large districts south of Namur, on the left bank of the Meuse. It seems possible that Beust, the Austrian Chancellor, had in fact shown Rogier's suggestions to Napoleon's Ambassador in Vienna and asked for his comments. For whatever cause, the French Press increased its hostility towards Belgium, and by early April, Leopold felt that national safety demanded that he should go to France in person. As usual, Napoleon seemed delighted to see him, as if he were relieved to be able to play down the effect of his own officially-inspired Press. Leopold sent a message to Rogier, ordering him to do nothing rash.

The opportunity to regain Luxemburg, if one ever existed, had passed and Leopold knew it. On April 19th, he was back in Brussels to preside over a Cabinet meeting, silent and gloomy, with a streaming cold. A few days later, he set off for Germany to repair the damage done by Rogier's imprudence, and to attend the marriage of his brother Philip, Count of Flanders, to Princess

[1] Lichtervelde; *Léopold II;* p. 90.

Mary of Hohenzollern-Sigmaringen[1]. From Berlin, his old secretary Van Praet wrote home on April 14th to the Government, opening blandly: 'The King has discovered that we are considered to be intriguing at The Hague and in Berlin for the possession of Luxemburg, and His Majesty would consider it useful if a circular were sent to our legations authorizing them to declare that it is quite wrong to assert that the government has involved itself in the Luxemburg question.' Leopold met Bismarck, but the two found little to talk about beyond the exchange of a few bored jokes. They had annoyed each other, and now the Luxemburg crisis was subsiding with no benefit to either of them. In May, the London Conference proclaimed and guaranteed Luxemburg's independence in neutrality, ordered out the Prussian garrison, and had the fortress pulled down. Later, Leopold was to say that 'only fear prevented us from getting Luxemburg in 1867'[2]. It was a fear which, luckily for Belgium, he came to share, and it was well-founded.

That month, Leopold and Marie-Henriette went in state to Paris for the Universal Exhibition. The town was full of Princes and Emperors, and alive with rumours about their intentions. Leopold did his best to live up to more absolute colleagues, with larger kingdoms, and was seen at a reception by Marshal Canrobert, conspicuous 'by his great height, his great nose and his great beard; with his sword, which banged about among his legs, he looked like an official who had put on his uniform without knowing how it should be worn'[3]. In spite of a warm official welcome, however, Belgium was not yet out of danger from France. Bismarck and Napoleon met at the Exhibition and were perfectly friendly, but the Emperor's rabidly excitable advisers now considered that Bismarck had led France into a deliberate trap over Luxemburg, and they persisted with their policy of taking experimental knocks at Belgium for signs of weakness. France, in their view, needed a triumph more than ever.

[1] This marriage, which was happy as well as strategic, was arranged by Queen Victoria and Queen Augusta of Prussia. Princess Mary's eldest brother was Leopold, the subject of the 'Hohenzollern Candidature' for the Spanish throne which was the occasion of the Franco-Prussian War: her youngest brother became Carol I of Rumania. The second son of the marriage, Albert, was to become successor to Leopold II on the Belgian throne, after the death of his elder brother.

[2] Lichtervelde; *Léopold II*; p. 92.

[3] Daye; *Léopold II*; p. 130.

Towards the end of 1868, the Belgian Government discovered
that a French railway company, the 'Compagnie Française du
Chemin de Fer de l'Est', was engaged on a share raid against
two Belgian railway companies, one of them operating the line
between Liège and the city of Luxemburg and the other serving
the Belgian province of Luxemburg. The strategic value of this
deal to France was obvious, but to the Belgians it also smelt
of previous French suggestions that commercial unions should
precede a political merger between France and Belgium. Frère-
Orban, who had ousted Rogier and taken full leadership of the
Cabinet a year before, now rose above his free-trading prejudices
and forbade the sale. Napoleon III wrote an unconvincingly
fierce letter to his Minister of War in which he treated this
refusal as a provocation and argued (more perhaps to convince
himself than his Ministers) that this was a safe moment to
launch an attack on Belgium. Frère-Orban went to Paris to con-
front him, but it was ultimately a reluctant British warning
which persuaded the French to sign a compromise agreement
sharing out the traffic on the disputed lines.

The truth was that Belgium, although now thoroughly
alarmed, was rather safer than she had been two years before.
For one thing, the growing hostility between France and Germany was playing on Napoleon's underlying dread of war: it
seemed less likely that Belgium could be either amicably parti-
tioned or unilaterally grabbed without a violent German
reaction. For another, the British guarantee had at last been
reaffirmed, in a vague enough way. After the London treaty on
Luxemburg, Lord Derby's Conservative government had suggested in debate that, while the Powers were bound to defend
Luxemburg 'jointly', the 1839 Treaties bound them to defend
Belgium 'jointly and severally', implying that even if one of the
guarantors attacked Belgium, the other guarantors would still
be obliged to oppose their colleague. Lord Stanley, the Foreign
Minister, did not go into details of how this was to be done, but
at least the intention was finally clear.

Leopold's own life in these years was barren and disastrous.
In the summer of 1868, the Count of Hainaut, a gay little boy
whose life centred on a Shetland pony called 'Kiss-Me-Quick',
fell into a pond on holiday and caught pneumonia. A heart
complication developed, and he was unable to recover. On

January 22, 1869, his incredulous father watched him die in a big room full of sobbing women and muttering priests. Leopold never recovered from this moment. At the funeral, for the only time in his life, he broke down in public: the loud and terrible noise of his crying was heard by all the congregation above the music as he collapsed on his knees beside the coffin. For the rest of his life, he seems to have regarded himself as a man under a curse: the great dynast had lost his only legitimate son. Marie-Henriette was somehow to blame. He brought himself to approach her again in 1871: the result was another daughter, Clémentine, born in 1872, a failure for which the Queen was not forgiven.

Marie-Henriette herself had found a number of distractions which helped her to survive the bleak years at Laeken. She bred her own horses, rode with a wildness which puzzled Leopold, and formed a close friendship with General Felix Chazal, the Minister for War in several cabinets. They kept up a warm correspondence, and Chazal used to take the young Queen out to manoeuvres, where she drilled troops and joined cavalry charges, unworried by the noise of the guns.

In 1865, a son of Chazal's was killed on active service in Mexico, ambushed by the partisans of Juarez who were soon to bring down in ruins the whole pathetic wedding-cake of Maximilian's empire. A year later, Charlotte herself arrived back in Europe to plead for support for her husband, and terrified the courts she visited by signs of paranoid insanity. In the Vatican, the Pope's inability to help her brought on a general crisis, and the Empress, who was still only twenty-six, was taken away under the persistent delusion that she was being poisoned. She was shut up in her own villa of Miramar, outside Trieste, but Marie-Henriette determined to get her back to Belgium. Maximilian was shot at the stake on June 19, 1867, at Queretaro: Marie-Henriette, with her usual busy interest in detail, turned up at Miramar in a coloured dress to conceal his death from Charlotte, and persuaded her to make the move to Brussels. There Marie-Henriette nursed her in hope of a recovery. Her repressed energy found fresh outlets in the struggle to make poor Charlotte go to confession, for the Empress was now tortured by guilt for apparently delusive sins and by fear of God's judgment on them. In January 1868, Marie-Henriette finally broke down Charlotte's resistance, and after calming a midnight failure of her courage, brought her next morning before a priest to confess and be absolved. For a time after this, Charlotte's mental state appeared to improve: she talked fairly rationally, and was even given a room at Laeken. But in 1869, when the young Count of Hainaut died, she was moved to the Chateau de Tervueren, a few miles away from Laeken, and began to show delusive symptoms again. Charlotte never fully recovered, and lived on as a helpless ward of the Belgian Royal Family until her death in 1927, at the age of eighty-six.

Marie-Henriette continued for the rest of her own life to look after her sister-in-law and to pay her regular visits. But the death of her son had broken her spirit, and her attitude towards the survivors of her own family began to change. In spite of the severe Germanic discipline to which she had subjected her daughters, which relied more upon riding and painting and the corrective effects of shutting small girls up in confined dark places than on lessons, she had allowed herself to show them evidence of her underlying tenderness out of school hours. Now she went suddenly cold on them: a betrayal which was to have the worst possible effects on the personality of eleven-year-old Louise, the eldest child. Nor could they find refuge in the affection of their father. Leopold watched his daughters grow up with silent but damaging contempt. In the year of her brother's death, Louise took a pear without permission from one of the trees in the famous glass-houses of Laeken, on which the King had already spent many millions of francs: caught, she had to face an almost judicial enquiry which pronounced sharp punishment. Once, Leopold did give her a flower from the Laeken hot-houses: she remembered that because it was the only time, and she did not understand it.

CHAPTER VIII

WAR AND PACIFISM

WITHOUT REALIZING IT, Leopold had sentenced the Liberal government to death. The incessant, harrying pressure to rearm and to fortify which he had been putting on Frère-Orban must have seemed to him almost without result. To the Liberals, on the other hand, Frère-Orban seemed to be betraying his principles further every time he made a compromise with the King. They drew away from him, and he in turn was forced to rely more heavily on Leopold. Particular offence had been given by his success in getting parliament to accept an increase in army intake to 13,000 a year, even though he had left intact the old system of *remplacement* which allowed a young man who drew an unlucky number in the conscription lottery to buy himself a substitute—if he could afford it. Even moderate anti-militarists had come to regard this system as a pillar of the subject's liberty, but pacifist extremists of both parties wanted to sweep away the whole system, *remplacement* and all, and rely on an entirely voluntary army. Their position was at least more consistent.

As Leopold thanked Frère-Orban for his grudging support— the Minister knew perfectly well that the middle-class electorate would not forgive him for it—the Catholic *Meetinguists*, the Progressives in his own party and the Socialists were combining to bring him down. At the elections of June 1870, Frère-Orban was narrowly defeated. After a long haggle, Leopold managed to extract from the moderate Catholic d'Anethan an assurance that he would not tamper with the last government's defence legislation and allowed him to form a government.

It was a curious moment in history for a small nation to vote for disarmament. Two weeks later, the French government discovered that Leopold of Hohenzollern was about to be elected King of Spain by the Cortes, and the fatal Franco-Prussian crisis began. At the instigation of the King of Belgium, the Count of

Flanders urged his brother-in-law to withdraw his candidature, which he was only too willing to do when he understood the use to which the French meant to put their discovery, but it was already too late. The French insisted on a full apology from King William of Prussia for the episode; Bismarck edited his master's answering telegram from Ems to make it quite clear that William had no apology to make; and war was declared on July 19, 1870.

With a characteristic sense of priorities, Belgium set about hiding her money before bothering to mobilize her armies. Unfortunately the news that the Banque Nationale was moving its bullion from Brussels to the 'national redoubt' of Antwerp leaked out, and there was an alarm in Brussels which turned into a panic when the Bank tried to save its bullion from the public clawing around the counters by devaluing the bank notes they were clamouring to change. Then, on July 25th, as the government worked to restore public confidence, *The Times* ran the text of the Benedetti draft treaty which Bismarck had put away so carefully four years before.

Up to this moment, Leopold and his people had assumed that in spite of all the Imperial growls of the past few years, the racial and cultural and historical ties which bound so many of them to France still meant something, and that alien Germany was the more dangerous neighbour. Now, as Prussian and French armies manoeuvred against the Belgian border in a war whose issue was far from clear, they saw the full extent of their danger. In terrible disorder, the national army stumbled up to its frontiers and prepared to do what it could against a sudden flanking drive into Belgium by either combatant. Leopold, who as their commander-in-chief had his doubts about the efficiency of his men, stayed in Brussels and used his energies in shoring up his country's diplomatic defences.

London was horrified by the 'Treaty of Spoliation', which the Prussians had in fact been hawking around Whitehall for some days before *The Times* used it. The Belgian Ambassador wrote home: 'This publication has revealed to England all the prestige she has lost as a Great Power. The revelation that other governments disposed of nations without consulting her and against her wishes has deeply aroused her and she feels the need of asserting herself anew. No better occasion could be found than in reminding the other Powers of the sanctity of treaties from which no war could release them . . . Add to this the interest of England not to see Antwerp fall into the hands of the French, and her real sympathy for Belgium, and you have all the motives which are prompting these splendid Englishmen to help us'[1]. He was perfectly right in his prediction, if rather cynical in his interpretation: at the end of July, Britain asked Prussia and France to agree that if the armies of either violated Belgian territory, British troops should help the other to expel the intruder. The treaty was at once signed by Prussia, and France reluctantly agreed on August 9th. Gladstone, in his first period of office as Prime Minister, was not easily comforted in his scrupulous soul for this engagement of his country to an eventual use of force: John Bright was even less happy, and Gladstone wrote to him on August 4th: 'I add for myself this confession of faith. If the Belgian people desire, on their own account, to join France or any other country, I for one will be no party to taking up arms to prevent it. But that the Belgians, whether they would or not, should go "plump" down the maw of another country to satisfy dynastic greed, is another matter. The accomplishment of such a crime as this implies, would come near to an extinction of public right in Europe, and I do not think we could look on while the sacrifice of freedom and independence was in course of consummation'[2].

In the first days of September, the Prussians brought Napoleon to bay at Sedan, just south of the Belgian frontier, and Leopold's army listened anxiously to the guns. Late on September 1st, a thickening stream of French wounded and fugitives began to cross the border. The next day, the Emperor and his army surrended, and on September 3rd, Napoleon appeared at the frontier followed by an escort of Uhlans, asking to be allowed to cross Belgium on his way to Germany as a prisoner of war. He was given leave, a sick, docile man in pain from his kidney-stones who passed two nights in obscure commercial hotels, inspected a guard of Belgian troops, and slipped away again over the German border beyond Verviers into captivity. When he had gone, General Chazal rode into France with two squadrons of Belgian cavalry to describe his journey to King William of Prussia.

[1] Daye; *Léopold II;* p. 148.
[2] John Morley; *Life of Gladstone;* London 1903; Vol. II, p. 342.

Paris still held out, and a partisan, republican France was to go on resisting, but the danger for Belgium was over. Fresh elections in August had given the Catholic ministry under d'Anethan an increased majority, and the anti-militarist movement which had shown its strength earlier in the year renewed its pressure. Even in the middle of August, at the height of the fighting in eastern France, the government had tried to send home on leave a part of the reservists called up to man the frontiers, and Leopold's impression of the incompetence revealed by the emergency call-up resolved him to demand further reforms. A new commission on the Army recommended raising the annual draft to 14,000 men, increasing the artillery, establishing an adequate reserve system, and abolishing the practice of *remplacement*. But Frère-Orban, now in opposition, united with the extreme Catholics and the Progressive Liberals in demanding that *remplacement* should stay. A wave of self-confidence swept through Belgian politics, as the frightening events of the war faded into the past. For the Catholics, the point that neutrality was its own defence seemed proved by the fact that neither belligerent had violated the frontiers. When Leopold insisted that *remplacement* must go, the Catholics outside the government and the *Meetinguist* Victor Jacobs inside it retorted by calling for the demolition of the North Citadel of Antwerp; d'Anethan himself could not indefinitely go on standing out against the feelings of his own party and, to a lesser extent, against his own electoral promises. The young Charles Woeste, the most formidable of all Belgian ultramontanes, was already making a name for himself as a journalist on his *Revue Générale* by his reckless attacks on Government defence policy, and Leopold began to suspect that the Prime Minister himself was not altogether out of sympathy with them.

On May 6, 1871, he wrote to d'Anethan in angry warning: ' . . . I know that we live in a country which enjoys complete liberty of the Press, but I also know who writes these articles and I know that they can be checked. Otherwise this would be the first time that a Cabinet has been unable to control its own party Press . . . I call on the Cabinet, on each individual minister and on the leaders of the Right, to give me a formal promise that they will grapple with this specious and anti-national movement . . . We do not live on an island; we cannot escape the repercussions of the events which are taking place on our doorstep and which have not nearly concluded, and you must know that for my part, I am determined to do anything rather than to govern in conditions which would endanger our national security'[1].

But Leopold did not get the promise he demanded. The Cabinet, squeezed between the King and the threats of their own party, continued to haver miserably over carrying out the recommendations of the Army report. To a letter of excuses from d'Anethan, Leopold replied furiously on May 9th: 'You talk to me about my popularity: that is not the point now, and anyway, my dear Prime Minister, I declare that between my popularity and my duty I will not hesitate, and that a popularity bought by deceiving the country about its true interests would be a weight on my conscience which I do not intend to bear. Who dares to say, after the crisis which we are going through now, that my father who was also thought by some to have risked his popularity more than once was wrong, any more than the cabinets which helped him were wrong, in tirelessly insisting that Belgium should be provided with a proper system of defence?'[2]

In November the government agreed to set up yet another defence commission, but d'Anethan's administration was already doomed by one of the last eruptions of the Langrand-Dumonceau affair. Leopold and the government had agreed to nominate the ex-minister Pierre de Decker as Governor of Limburg province, and the opposition seized on the fact that de Decker had been involved—not in fact to his discredit—in the Langrand projects to launch a parliamentary attack which was violent enough to provoke street rioting. It was assumed by the crowds that Leopold had acted as d'Anethan's rubber stamp for the appointment of Catholic placemen, and squads of rioters stood under the windows of the Brussels Palace shouting: 'Roi de carton! Au balcon!' To d'Anethan, the idea that Leopold was a 'cardboad king' must have seemed a sour joke indeed. But Leopold was infuriated, and to the horror of the Catholics he formally withdrew his confidence from the Government on the well-justified grounds that it had failed to keep order in the streets of Brussels. Reproaches that he had betrayed his ministers and allied the

[1] Lichtervelde; *Léopold II;* p. 120.
[2] *Ibid.*, p. 126.

Crown to the mob failed to move him in the slightest, and in early December 1871, he accepted a new Catholic cabinet led by the old Count de Theux and by Jules Malou, an able political organizer and a hardy and experienced man of finance.

The Catholic party took many years to forgive Leopold for this stroke. For his part, the King withdrew a little distance from the political scene and concentrated on his own plans. He visited Britain, Austria and France, evaded a wild plan that he should accept the French crown, which had been dreamed up by Thiers before the final surrender to the German Empire, and two years later allowed his government to refuse permanent asylum in Belgium to the Count of Chambord, Legitimist heir to the French throne. Meanwhile, political life in Belgium intensified its conflicts to a point close to the absurd.

Small-town life doubled its manifestations like a reproducing amoeba. There were Catholic butchers, bakers, chemists and doctors and there were Liberal butchers, bakers, chemists and doctors: the customer shopped with his own sort. Liberal processions went through the streets with blue flags and cornflowers in the buttonhole, while Catholic processions used pink flags and poppies. The priests on one side and the Freemasons on the other roused this football-crowd clamour to a frenzy at local and national elections. In the towns, where Liberals were strong, resolute atheists with walking sticks attacked religious processions, and in the villages the faithful broke up civil funerals and desecrated coffins. Polling-days became signing-on ceremonies in a petty spoils system, as vote-papers were marked and registration lists altered.

It looked terrifying, but it meant little. The historian Henri Pirenne considers that the institution of the *cens* kept Belgium from revolution in this period by keeping this agitation to the middle-class issues which interested middle-class voters[1]. Since the vast event of the Paris Commune in 1871 had dazzled and terrified the European Left, the Progressive wing of the Belgian Liberals had dropped its campaign for extension of the franchise and had to some degree renewed its interest in the issues of secularization which still obsessed its elders. As in Britain, there was a tendency to seek a Liberal teleology in history, and to identify Protestantism and the Reformation with anti-

[1] H. Pirenne; *Histoire de Belgique;* Vol. VII, pp. 225-6.

monarchical and libertarian ideas. The Dutch must have been amused to watch certain Belgian Liberals forcing themselves through the spiritual experience of 'conversion' to Calvinism, and to hear them rechristening their associations *Les Gueux,* after the Protestant partisans who fought both the Spanish and those 'collaborators' of the sixteenth-century Netherlands who were to become in the fullness of time the Belgians themselves. The Belgian Catholics, for their part, were becoming increasingly Ultramontane, committed by the anti-secular Encyclicals and by the doctrine of Papal Infallibility to a position of outright hostility to any constitution which drew a frontier to the proper activities of the Church.

Malou steered his government as far towards moderation as he dared, loyal to the constitution and to the ideal of a balanced budget, and even tried to draw some of the sting out of politics by legislating for secrecy of voting. But the gestures and the processions stormed on, choppy waves on the surface of an ocean. In 1871, the widened communal franchise for local elections gave the vote to only 350,000 out of a population of 5,000,000. At general elections, a mere 100,000 men were allowed to decide the composition of parliament. By 1873, wages had reached a high point and were about to decline, and the price of bread was beginning to rise. Far-sighted men in both main parties were wondering how long the political segregation of the middle classes could endure.

Meanwhile, Malou had been anxiously watching his King as he wove his way through one of his most characteristic intrigues. In 1840, a group of Belgian financiers had managed to get a draft agreement drawn up with the Spanish government which offered them a fifty-year concession of the Philippines in return for a loan of 50,000,000 francs. The Cortes had never ratified this, but Leopold must have unearthed and studied the records of the transaction. In 1869, he discussed it with Lambermont, veteran of the Carlist Wars; his idea was to profit from the financial troubles of Spain by offering her a lump sum in exchange for a ninety-year concession with sovereignty over the Philippines, granted to a Belgian company with an official charter. He observed that he would like to be a helper in the hour of Spanish need. Worried advisers told him that he should aim only at a Belgian tobacco monopoly, without sovereign rights, but when

the succession crisis of 1870 opened in Spain, Leopold thought
that he should reveal his plans to Jules Malou, at that time
Governor of the Société Générale. Malou discouraged him at
once. He did not think that the revolutionary Spanish government would accept the idea: even if it did, the thousands of
Spaniards settled in the Philippines would probably resist. Going
into detail, Malou gave his opinion that Spain would take care
to keep the profits made by any Belgian operation, and that no
international concession run by Belgians stood much chance of
attracting investment[1].

Leopold was not at all put off by this depressing opinion, which
he probably expected from the chief of the Bank which would
be expected to subscribe a large slice of the enterprise's capital.
He continued secret negotiations for some years with shadowy
people in Spain. Even after the Spanish Restoration in 1874, he
was still persisting: papers studied by Fr. Roeykens reveal that
a M. de Montenaken of Antwerp was reporting in August 1875
that negotiations with a 'Count X.' in the Spanish diplomatic
corps had collapsed. Some months earlier, another envoy had
warned that the Germans were turning their interests towards
the acquisition of rights in Polynesia, now that their own
approaches to Spain over the Philippines had fallen through,
and this letter may have encouraged Leopold to make a final
offer where the Germans had left off. But even this last bid failed,
and Leopold shelved his Philippine schemes until the Spanish-
American War of 1898 gave him a fresh opening.

Meanwhile, he wrote to Lambermont, on August 22, 1875, a
letter whose last paragraph forms the first clear warning of the
new direction in which his thoughts were moving. 'Please thank
M. de Montenaken, and accept for yourself . . . all my thanks
for the trouble which once again you have been good enough to
take. The soundings are not promising, and I do not see any
purpose in pressing the matter further. For the moment, neither
the Spanish nor the Portuguese nor the Dutch have anything
to sell.

'I intend to find out discreetly whether there may not be anything to be done in Africa'[2].

[1] Daye; *Léopold II*; p. 146.
[2] Roeykens; *Débuts de l'Oeuvre*; p. 95.

CHAPTER IX

THE AFRICAN PLAN

B Y 1875, THE INHABITANTS of Western Europe still knew more about the physical geography of the moon than of the interior of Africa. A map presented to Leopold II in 1876 by Sir Henry Rawlinson, President of the Royal Geographical Society, has to modern eyes a blank and tentative appearance, although to contemporaries it recorded an astonishing increase of knowledge achieved in a very short space of time[1]. The southern cape of the continent is fairly well covered by the names of tribes and of physical features: the Sahara and the Eastern Sudan are filled in with the imposingly shaded caterpillars which represent mountain ranges and depressions. The great Lakes of east-central Africa are in their correct position, although their drainage system is not quite clear yet. But to the west of the Lakes there stretches to the coast an enormous patch of white uncertainty, inadequately filled by the insertion of a Key to 'Recent Explorations Accomplished, In Progress, Projected . . . ' This blank is the basin of the Congo.

Leopold's own experience of African matters was not large. He had visited the Suez Canal project three times, and almost certainly invested in it very boldly indeed. Portuguese East Africa is mentioned in an otherwise unexplained note found among his papers: '1873. Plan to found an East Africa Company with capital of 110 million francs in the Portuguese colony of Mozambique and later in other Portuguese colonies *to take over with full sovereign rights*. As Portugal is obviously not prepared to sacrifice her sovereignty, the plan founders'[2]. In his study of archives, he had read about the voyage of the *Louise-Marie* to West Africa in 1847, an attempt to lease a foothold on the Guinea coast which failed after war with the local King. Undiscouraged by such records of Belgian failure in the tropics,

[1] Map reproduced in Lichtervelde, *Léopold II*, facing p. 154.
[2] Roeykens; *Débuts de l'Oeuvre;* p. 46.

Leopold had taken out subscriptions to various journals of exploration, and as their news from Africa became more promising and definite, his interest was re-awakened.

Most explorers were now turning their efforts towards the central blank of the Congo basin, while the problem of the Nile sources was reduced to mere detail. In 1862, Speke had stood at the Ripon Falls and watched the Nile running out of Lake Victoria towards the north, but the question of other sources was kept open, especially after Baker's discovery of Lake Albert and the Albert Nile in 1864. Sir Richard Burton continued to insist that other sources would yet be found to provide the true origin of the river, and far to the south, David Livingstone was moving up the Lualaba in 1871, convinced as he followed its northward course that he must be following some headwater of the Nile.

This Lualaba question brought the problems of the Congo and the Nile together. Although the Portuguese had been in touch with the Bakongo people of the Lower Congo since the sixteenth century, and had enabled them to set up a Catholic-African kingdom of considerable attainments with its capital at what is now San Salvador in northern Angola, navigation further up the river had been blocked by the rapids and cataracts which let the Congo down from the 3,000 foot plateau of Central Africa to the level of the Atlantic. It remained, therefore, for the course of the Congo to be discovered by travellers moving downstream from the East. Here lay the importance of the Lualaba, the long and powerful river which is in effect the continuation of the upper Congo and which runs northward, parallel to Lake Tanganyika, for the first part of its course before curving slowly round to the west to modern Stanleyville.

In 1872, the Royal Geographical Society had organized two expeditions to find Livingstone. Neither had succeeded in that purpose, for Stanley had already discovered him at Ujiji on Lake Tanganyika in 1871; Livingstone himself had then gone south to Lake Banweolo, to die in the wilderness in May 1873. But one at least of them had great consequences. The Grandy expedition, starting from the mouth of the Congo in 1873, was defeated by the physical difficulties even before the news of Livingstone's death, but the Cameron expedition, setting out in March 1873 from the East Coast at Bagamoyo, eventually traversed the con-

tinent. Although he had met the bearers carrying David Livingstone's body at Tabora, Cameron decided to go on to Ujiji to
collect what might remain of Livingstone's papers there, and
once at Ujiji, he decided to investigate the Lualaba problem
himself. He sailed round Lake Tanganyika until he found what
he thought was an outlet flowing west. At home, a new subscription was opened to pay the expenses of Cameron's plan to push
further into the interior, towards which Leopold II offered
100,000 francs.

For some reason, his offer was not accepted. But as Lovett
Cameron disappeared into the unknown, Leopold could see for
himself that he was entering the back door of the region which
was increasingly interesting officially-sponsored exploration
societies in Europe. From 1873 onwards, the French Marquis de
Compiègne and the German Lenz were probing up the Ogowe
from Gaboon on the west coast, along a route which came to be
known as 'La Ligne Française', and which in fact offered a way
of approaching the middle Congo from the north, evading the
cataracts. In 1875, the French Admiralty gave support to the
brilliant Italian, Count Savorgnan de Brazza, for a plan to push
further along Compiègne's route up the Ogowe, and it became
clear to everybody that something like a race to the upper
reaches of the Congo was developing. The same year, a German
expedition led by Dr Güssfeldt tried a direct march eastward
from close to the Congo mouth but bogged down in disease and
mutiny within days. Meanwhile, Stanley and his backers on the
New York Herald were preparing to finish Livingstone's work
for him and to solve the Congo problem for ever by a march
from the Indian Ocean. But somewhere between Lake Tanganyika and the Atlantic was Cameron, perhaps already in possession of the answer. Leopold watched intently, read the papers,
wrote letters to learned societies, and kept his slanting, illegible
notes.

In 1867, he had joined the Société Geographique de Paris, and
given 1,000 francs towards the expenses of an international conference to be held under the society's auspices. For such a small
outlay, he was to receive an invaluable return. From the International Geographical Congress which took place in Paris in
August 1875, Leopold seems to have drawn many of the ideas

and tactics which, once mastered, he used in the campaign to set up the Congo Free State.

Leopold sent a reliable man to the Congress, charged to take notes and to report to his master in full. He was to pay special attention to the proceedings of two subcommittees, Section V (Economic), and Section VII (Problems of Travel), and as Leopold expected, these proceedings turned out to be interesting. The Economic Section talked over techniques of tropical colonization, prompted by the questions of a well-primed Belgian delegate, and in their Plenary Session its members produced a remarkable recipe. The colonizer, they said, should regroup the native population into communities which each contained a few Europeans. This tiny group of Westerners would form a *noyau dirigeant*, a controlling nucleus, employing modern productive techniques and civilizing the mass 'mainly by setting a good example'[1].

The suggestion cannot have convinced Leopold for an instant. No such system could ever produce wealth on the scale which Leopold would have regarded as acceptable. Yet there were interesting points about it. In the first place, it was highly idealistic: it even suggested the decentralized, co-operative units of production which had been described by the early French socialists, as if the colonists were to establish multi-racial *phalanstères* in the Guinea bush. And secondly the plan assumed direct rule. It did not suggest the usual process of trading within an existing social framework which was characteristic of European posts in West Africa at the time, and which was to develop into the 'Indirect Rule' policy consummated in Lugard's Northern Nigeria: it did not assume that the colonists had to find a 'collaborating class' on which to rest their influence. Instead, it suggested that native society would have to be entirely remodelled. The juxtaposition of these two points, the connection of highly respectable and even missionary idealism with the suggestion that a colonial power ought to carry out a fundamental reform of local society, was later to be a most powerful tactic in Leopold's campaign to make his Congo enterprise sound fit for international recognition. The power he took from this scheme was real: the high end to which this power was to be used existed only in Leopoldian propaganda. And when the

[1] Roeykens; *Débuts de l'Oeuvre*; p. 83.

propaganda had secured international recognition for the Congo State, nothing more was heard of the plan at all.

The Problems of Travel subcommittee, whose members included most of the well-known French and German explorers, heard Savorgnan de Brazza address them the day before he left for the Ogowe. It had already been agreed that it was better to travel light and fast (in the Brazza manner) than with a big force like Stanley's: now Brazza pleaded for an end to national rivalries and a pooling of information. Leopold evidently noted that de Brazza was in effect suggesting the formation of some standing international body, and that the 'travel light' recommendation would involve the setting-up of small stations along the main routes, to provide supplies and rest for small travelling parties, which could be permanently manned by such a body.

Leopold's emissary, Baron de Borchgrave, came back from Paris to report, and was sent off again almost at once to Berlin, where he was to take soundings for the formation of the international body to co-ordinate African exploration and development. Already the King seems to have known what he intended to do. Only the question of just where he intended to do it remained to be settled.

It was at this moment, on November 22, 1875, that Lovett Cameron emerged at Luanda after his two-and-a-half year journey from the east coast. He claimed to have established the identity of the Lualaba with the Congo, although he had not followed the stream down its full course to the sea, and in January 1876 his letters describing the lands he had passed through arrived in Europe. They were ecstatic, even, it was felt, exaggerated. He spoke of healthy climates, beautiful scenery, and of deposits of coal, iron, gold, and copper (he had passed through what is now the Katanga and across the Lunda country on his way towards Portuguese territory). He had seen rich crops of sugar, grain and fruit, and harvests of wild rubber, and was full of a scheme for a canal to connect the Congo and the Zambezi. To temper these rich prospects, he described the Arab slavers he had seen taking their long caravans to the coast with ivory, and the scenes of misery and depopulation left behind them.

Leopold knew that it would be difficult to interest his countrymen in the economic attractions of Africa, but he calculated that even a nation as hard-headed as the Belgians might respond to

humanitarian appeals to suppress the slave trade, which would
involve their religion in demands for an extension of missionary
influence. Already he was planning to convene a Geographical
Conference of his own in Brussels, and the slave trade was
obviously an indispensable addition to its agenda. In May 1876,
while Borchgrave carried out his spadework in Berlin, Leopold
left quietly for London.

'Keeping strict incognito', as innocent Belgians have put it,
Leopold settled in at Claridges. He had arrived on May 29th,
intending to work fast, and on May 30th he interviewed Lovett
Cameron and had dinner with the Prince of Wales and Princess
Alexandra. Next day, he had lunch with Lady Burdett-Coutts,
patroness of missionaries. (Like most Belgians to this day, Leopold believed that British missionaries were directly the agents
of the Foreign Office and even *agents provocateurs* who
deliberately created difficulties for themselves from which only
a declaration of British Protectorate could extract them.) In the
ensuing week, Leopold saw many prominent geographers and
soldiers, dined yet again with the Prince of Wales, and paid a
rapid visit to the Queen at Balmoral, arriving back in Brussels
on June 11th. He had found in Britain a number of encouraging
signs. In the first place, Britain apparently did not want the
Congo basin, which Cameron had actually annexed in the
Queen's name on December 28, 1874, only to hear his deed
crossly repudiated by the Government when he returned home.
Secondly, the proud tradition of British anti-slavery, revived by
the terrible reports of Livingstone from the Lualaba country,
had been further roused by Cameron's experiences and public
opinion was ready to listen to any plan of action. Thirdly, the
British were currently blaming much of the Congo basin slave
trade on the indifference of the Portuguese; this, too, favoured
Leopold's design, for the Portuguese, with footholds all around
the outfall of the Congo, held it in their power to cut off trade
on the upper river from its outlet to the sea.

In Germany Borchgrave made contacts with leading explorers
and secured their promise to attend the forthcoming Brussels
conference. He got himself elected a fellow of the Berlin Geographical Society, collected information about German travellers
currently in Africa, and made frequent trips back to Brussels
for fresh instructions. On July 28th, he was warned that the

Conference would meet in September, and the King asked him for potted biographies of the Germans likely to attend. Leopold was making preparations in unprecedented detail, adjusting his secret plans to every development of popular feeling in the countries he wished to influence, and among the wilder schemes for penetrating Africa which were reported to him by his foreign agents, he was often able to find an underlying idea which would be useful to him. Typical of such projects was the 'Inland Lake' plan, canvassed in France and in Britain in 1875-6, which proposed to dig a canal inland from Gabès in Tunisia in order to flood the low-lying desert with seawater and provide a vast lake across the Sahara which would be easily navigable. This fantastic plan seems to have been taken quite seriously for a time, and some British businessmen thought that it might provide an inland waterway to Central Africa. The French, whose idea it originally was, hoped that an inland lake forty or fifty feet deep would form behind the coastal ranges of Tunisia and Algeria, and feared that the British, by laying hold of the island of Djerba, off Gabès, might block this 'new Mediterranean' with a new Gibraltar. All this was absurdity. But in commenting on it, *The Times* of September 2, 1875, wrote: 'It is admitted on all hands that the only practical way to redeem the African continent from the slave trade and other evils is to open a direct highway into the interior and establish depots with easy access to each other . . . ' Here, Leopold saw, was a significant development on the 'travel light' premises established the month before by the Paris Geographical Conference.

The ground was prepared both administratively and emotionally. Borchgrave showed a rough agenda of the Conference to the President of the Berlin Geographical Society, Baron von Richthofen, well before the delegates had assembled in Brussels. Meanwhile, Leopold put his own thoughts in final order. Out of his Conference, he intended a standing international body to arise. What was its purpose to be? He had his own ideas which he must not let the other delegates guess: instead, he must produce a structure of feinting arguments which would persuade them to the act he wanted of them. A draft note in his handwriting seems to be a guide to trains of thought which he must appear to follow.

'The aim of the conference is to found if possible the international work of the rest-houses and scientific posts in Africa. Before the horrible evil of the slave-trade, which in the interior of Africa claims over 100,000 victims yearly (sic), the citizens of civilized countries must come to an agreement to heal the sore. The headquarters of this humane undertaking might well be situated on Belgian soil. But we do not aspire to the direction of it, nor can we lay down for it any absolute form. The organization must be managed by an international committee with a permanent executive. It would be desirable that the conference agree to appoint this committee, staff it with one or two representatives from each nation, and designate Brussels as its base . . . '[1] The posts set up in Africa by the new body would be ultimately controlled by this committee, but the work and form of the posts ought to be left to the choice of the national exploration-societies which manned and paid for them. This suggestion was seriously meant, for Leopold intended it to free the hands of the Belgian posts for his own purposes. The rest of the memorandum was pure humbug.

On the eve of the conference, Emile Banning showed the King his draft for a pamphlet about the meeting. He was suggesting that European governments ought to subsidize the central authority which was to be founded, and that the African posts ought to be specifically 'national' foundations belonging to the European state which built them. Some of the Belgian delegates who heard of Banning's idea were horrified at its assumption that Leopold meant the 'international' nature of this scientific conference to act as a basis for a share-out of sovereignty over Central Africa. Leopold was equally horrified and made Banning alter his draft, because that was only too nearly what he did mean.

[1] Quoted in H. M. Stanley; *Unpublished Letters;* London 1956; p. 3.

CHAPTER X

THE BRUSSELS CONFERENCE OF 1876, AND THE FOUNDING OF THE INTERNATIONAL AFRICAN ASSOCIATION

B Y THE TIME that the eminent explorers and geographers took their places in the conference chamber prepared in the Brussels Palace, they could feel both that they knew what was going to be asked of them, and that they should agree with it. Like all good men of science, they detested the interference of nationalism in matters of research, and dreaded to see their fascinating Africa ruined under their eyes by a European scramble for colonies. Now the King of the Belgians, an innocuous and thoughtful man, was suggesting that Central Africa ought to pass under some sort of international authority which would set about the suppression of the slave trade, the process of civilization by normal commerce, and the systematic exploration and survey of the continent under conditions which could not easily be violated by the rapacity of European governments. The local branches of the central authority would be private learned bodies, prepared to accept any subsidy which their own national government might offer but not directly committed to its foreign policy.

It all sounded magnificent. The delegates who came from Britain included men like Cameron and Grant, for exploration; Sir Bartle Frere and Sir Rutherford Alcock, for geography; Sir Thomas Fowell Buxton and Sir John Kennaway, for the missionaries[1]; and William Mackinnon, chief of the British India Line, for the business interest. The Germans sent Baron von Richthofen, and the explorers Rohlfs and Nachtigal. The French delegation included the Marquis de Compiègne. Other delegations came from Austria, Italy and Russia.

---

[1] *Sir Thomas Fowell Buxton* (1865-1919); President of the Anti-Slavery and Aborigines Protection Society; Treasurer of Church Missionary Society. *Sir John Kennaway* (1837-1919); President of Church Missionary Society.

Leopold opened the Conference himself, on September 12, 1876, with a politely idealistic speech which in effect laid down the agenda he wanted the delegates to follow. 'The subject which brings us together today,' he observed, 'is one of those which must be a supreme preoccupation to all friends of humanity. To open to civilization the only area of our globe to which it has not yet penetrated, to pierce the gloom which hangs over entire races, constitutes, if I may dare to put it in this way, a Crusade worthy of this century of progress, and I am delighted to note how deeply public opinion approves its accomplishment: the tide is running our way.

'Gentlemen, many of those who have made the closest study of Africa have come to the conclusion that their common purpose would be well served by a meeting and a conference designed to get their work in step, to concert efforts, to share all resources, and to avoid covering the same ground twice.

'It seemed to me that Belgium, a neutral and centrally-placed country, would be a suitable place for such a meeting . . . Need I say that in bringing you to Brussels I was guided by no motives of egoism? No, gentlemen, Belgium may be a small country, but she is happy and contented with her lot; I have no other ambition than to serve her well . . . '

He concluded by laying down a suitable agenda. 'Among the questions still to be examined, the following have been mentioned:

'(1) Precise location of the bases for operations to be acquired, among other places, on the coast of Zanzibar and near the Congo mouth, either by treaties with chiefs or by purchases or leases arranged with private individuals;

'(2) Location of routes to be successively opened towards the interior, setting-up of medical and scientific posts and of 'pacifying' bases from which to abolish the slave trade, establishment of peace among the chiefs and provision of just and impartial arbitration, etc.;

'(3) Establishment, once the project has been fully worked out, of a central international committee and of national committees to carry out its orders, each as best it may; putting across the aims to the public of all countries and making to their instinct of charity the sort of appeal which has never been made in vain'[1].

[1] Lichtervelde; *Léopold II*; p. 155-8.

The proposal to set up medical and scientific stations was at once agreed. On the question of where to set to work, the conference divided into two working parties. Sir Henry Rawlinson's group put forward a vast scheme for an operation setting out from the East Coast and radiating routes from Lake Tanganyika towards the Congo mouth, the Zambezi, and the sources of the Nile. The group under the Russian Semenov preferred to assign different task areas to individual explorers, on a more fragmentary plan. These two views were rapidly stewed into one in the course of a forty-minute meeting which recommended that the work should be done by individual explorers, that initial stations should be set up at Luanda and Bagamoyo, and that subsequent posts connected by tracks should be established at Ujiji on Lake Tanganyika, at Nyangwe on the Lualaba, and in western Katanga. The emphasis lay heavily on an approach to the Congo basin from the east.

The next business was the foundation of the international authority itself, the 'Association Internationale pour reprimer la traite et ouvrir l'Afrique centrale', generally known as the 'Association Internationale Africaine', or more shortly still, as the 'AIA'. At its head was placed an 'International Committee': Leopold was elected its first chairman on the understanding that the chairmanship would pass annually to the representative of a different country. Then came an Executive Committee of four. Finally, there were to be National Committees, adjured to keep in close touch with the central authority in Brussels.

This imposing superstructure withered and fell to pieces with all the planned rapidity of the husk around a hidden seed. The International Committee met once more in 1877, violated its own rules by re-electing Leopold as chairman, and was never heard of again. The Executive Committee survived, in a somnambulous way, until 1880, when its bulletins on the AIA's operations in East Africa broke off. In 1883 a Swiss delegate to the Executive Committee, one Gustave Moynier, asked pathetically what had happened to it, but his voice died away on emptiness. As for the National Committees, the only one to survive to any effect was none other than the Belgian Committee.

The collapse of the National Committees took place, in fact, so precipitately that it actually outstripped Leopold's intentions. Hindsight suggests that he would have let them die sooner or later, but he had hoped that they would first justify their creation by raising money and passing at least some of it to the AIA headquarters in Brussels. The British Committee, however, on the return of the delegates to London, showed immediate signs of what might be called 'nationalist deviationism'. At a speech in Glasgow, Sir Bartle Frere announced that the Prince of Wales would become chairman of the British Committee, and roused the members of the Glasgow Chamber of Commerce to such enthusiasm that they at once set about raising money for a route of their own between Buganda and Mozambique. Leopold must have feared all along that the British would see no reason why they should subordinate their immense commercial and anti-slavery experience to a committee of foreign do-gooders: hoping to get his money before this mood of reaction broke over the country, he despatched Lambermont across the Channel in November 1876 to lobby influential figures in London for contributions. Lambermont, whose English was not good, did his best. He asked Alcock and Frere for money, but it was autumn, and many of the people he was supposed to see were shooting birds and animals in the north of this intimidating island. Where he called in vain, Lambermont left a card with the sinister superscription: 'Baron Lambermont, whose stays in London was infortunately shortened . . . '[1]

Even in their transient mood of approval, the British evolved curious misconceptions of the nature of the AIA. The *Daily Telegraph* welcomed the foundation of the AIA on the grounds that it would resemble the Red Cross, as an international philanthropic society. The Glasgow businessmen assumed that Britain would be allowed a sphere of influence extending across east-central Africa and, incidentally, cutting Leopold off from the only proved route to the Congo basin[2]. But presently the hostile reaction set in, as the Foreign Office came to the conclusion that the suppression of the slave-trade in Africa would amount, in the circumstances, to a political act which in the British view was unsuitable for an international body. By the end of the year the Prince of Wales had been persuaded to withdraw his chair-

[1] Roeykens; *Débuts de l'Oeuvre;* p. 193.

[2] The Glasgow committee later dissolved itself when it was clear that Scottish money would be spent at the discretion of the Catholic majority on the AIA. See R. T. Anstey; *Britain and the Congo in the Nineteenth Century;* Oxford 1962; p. 63.

manship of what was now felt to be a committed political association. In March 1877 the Royal Geographical Society opened an 'African Exploration Fund', patently for British purposes only, and on July 19th, a meeting at the Mansion House refused to endanger the British campaign against slavery by sharing its direction with any other authority or nation. All that Leopold seems directly to have received through his apparatus was a cheque for £250 from the African Exploration Fund, a 'first contribution' which had no successors.

The French Committee was chaired by Ferdinand de Lesseps, but also suffered from suspicious tendencies to favour patriotic aggrandisement. Neither did it provide Leopold with any money: grants totalling 122,000 francs made to the French Committee in 1879 by various government departments failed to cover even the publicity expenses incurred by the Committee at the 1878 Exhibition in Paris. The German committee started promisingly and went so far as to found stations in the region of Lake Tanganyika, but gradually a specifically German interest began to dominate its activity, and within a few years the existence of the stations was being adduced as proof of German territorial possession. The Dutch Committee was the most generous, contributing £560 to Brussels, but by the end of 1879, according to Father Roeykens' calculations, the AIA had received a total of only 44,000 francs or about £1,780. Fine words had cost the national committees nothing.

It is now time to consider what Leopold, in all these elaborate preparations, was really up to. The monster which finally grew out of the Brussels Geographical Conference is familiar enough to posterity in the form of the Congo Free State, but as its sovereign burned most of his Congo papers before he surrendered his colony to Belgium, Leopold's original intentions must remain uncertain until some lucky haul of documents reveals his basic plan of action in 1876-7. However, some papers which have survived are able to throw a partial light, qualified always by the fact that Leopold never showed his whole mind to anybody, and dosed his correspondents with the truth in proportions varying according to the effect it would have on them in given circumstances. Except at the very end of his life, Leopold had no consistent *confidantes*.

Less than a month after the end of the conference, on October

D

4, 1876, the King issued a restricted circular to his diplomatic corps and consular agents. 'It is advisable that you should avoid intervening (in AIA affairs) in your official capacity, but . . . if an appeal was made for your co-operation or if your own personal inclinations prompted you to support the views of the Conference, you would naturally remain free to evince for the impending institution the favour which the government shares . . .'[1]

Here already is a strong hint that Belgium might ultimately expect to gain from the AIA. Clearer evidence emerges from the correspondence between Greindl, Belgian Minister in Madrid, and Lambermont, who on Leopold's instructions was trying to persuade Greindl to accept the post of Secretary-General of the AIA. Greindl was not only a diplomat, but a sculptor, and an orientalist with an academic reputation. No fool, he was certain that his King was not setting up this structure purely out of respect for knowledge and pity for the African condition. On October 14, 1876, he wrote a deliberately coarse reply to Lambermont: 'By the way, with all due respect to the scientific and humane ends in view, the scheme no doubt answers to some entirely national purpose: what is it?'[2]

Lambermont now realized that wide-eyed assurances would not do for Greindl. He confided to him that 'it was only for the sake of politeness to foreigners that the King on his own initiative suggested a one-year term for his chairmanship; but everyone realizes that His Majesty will not abandon his task . . .' Then he went on warily: 'There is no entirely national purpose in this. The project will be to the profit of science and philanthropy and therefore must be in the interests of everybody, but Belgium and her King will indirectly get out of it both honour and a large moral profit: in this sense, it is true that there is a purpose which is truly and usefully Belgian. We are not thinking about procuring a colony, but, in time, trade will draw due benefit from this'[3].

Excited and dissatisfied with this answer, Greindl found the audacity to send a cable to Leopold himself asking him why, if Belgian nationality was so unimportant in all this, he could not

[1] H. M. Stanley; *Unpublished Letters;* p. 8.
[2] Roeykens; *Débuts de l'Ouevre;* p. 165.
[3] *Ibid.,* p. 167.

appoint some foreign African explorer to the job of Secretary-General instead. He was determined to call the King's bluff and to discover what ends he was really being asked to serve: the reactions evoked by his impertinent cable have been put together carefully by Father Roeykens[1], who has made them reveal more of the truth than was revealed to Greindl himself.

The cable was sent from Madrid on October 23rd. A memorandum from Leopold to his secretary, Jules Devaux, seems to represent the King's first reactions on opening it: 'Can't imagine what brought him to suppose that Belgian nationality would not be necessary: on the contrary, it is an essential condition . . .'

The next document in order is the draft of a telegram to Madrid. ' . . . Belgian nationality essential for secretary-general . . . possibility of serving under foreigner not seriously to be feared above all at the outset.' This was dangerously candid, and the final version, sent on the 24th, had been watered down by the King, with the addition: 'Essentially international affair. Based on Brussels and will fly its flag there. No fear of serving under foreign power.' The possibility of Belgian predominance, displayed for a moment, had been discreetly covered up again.

Leopold already intended, it is clear, to use the international nature of the AIA as a Trojan horse for Belgian aggrandisement in Central Africa: to this end, he made sure that the organs of the AIA which he dominated had no life of their own. Suggestions for practical methods of establishing the AIA in Central Africa may well have come to him from Cameron's account of his journey, published late in 1876, which urged the exploitation of the Congo and Zambezi river systems by chartered companies with powers to administrate their concessions. Visualizing the movement of steamers on the Upper Congo, Cameron also threw out the suggestion that a 'tramway' might be built round the falls, to link the inaccessible upper river to the Atlantic.

There remained the problem of Belgium herself. Leopold intended the Belgian Committee of the AIA to remain active and perhaps to form the nucleus of a Chartered Company which would slide its concessions gradually under Belgian sovereignty. But it soon became clear that Belgium might not accept the present. The project of the AIA was no sooner published than it

[1] *Ibid.*, p. 168.

was melted down for use as political ammunition in the columns of the Belgian Press. The Ultras argued that the organization, if it had sincerely humanitarian aims, should immediately be handed over to the charge of the Congregation de Propaganda Fidei, in Rome. The Liberals, much alarmed, retorted that the AIA must act as the lance-head of 'free thought' in Africa. Efforts by Leopold and even by the Queen to conciliate both sides only made Liberal suspicion worse. On October 14th, the Liberal *La Chronique* wrote: 'If Leopold II has decided to use the money entrusted to him to carry out his civilizing plan for greasing the palm of missionaries, then I hope that the entire Liberal Party will raise powerful protests.'

So far, the hostility had come mostly from the anticlerical Left. In July 1877, however, some minutes from the sessions of the expiring International Committee leaked to the Catholic Press, and the editorial staff of *L'Indépendence Belge* construed them to mean that a Masonic Empire was about to be proclaimed over the jungles of Africa. The AIA stations, they told their readers, would give shelter only to those approved by the organization, preference being of course given to anti-slavery officers over missionaries, and the local post commanders would have power to expel missionaries whose work was considered to create unrest among the natives. The worst of this leak and the resultant outcry, from Leopold's point of view, was that the writer was in fact a member of the Belgian Committee of the AIA, which now lost any chance of remaining outside the commitments of Belgian politics. Meanwhile, the rest of the Catholic Press fulminated on about the 'Masonic, anti-Christian' features of the AIA, and a rumour went round that Cameron had told the King at the time of the Brussels Conference that 'missionaries are the plague!' It became almost impossible for Leopold to persuade Belgian religious houses to send out missions to central Africa, in spite of reassurances from the Pope and Cardinal Dechamps[1]. The Liberal victory of 1878, and the hysterical fervour of lay-clerical conflict which followed, put a Catholic reconciliation to the Central African project temporarily out of

---

[1] *Dechamps, Victor* (1810-83); Archbishop of Malines from 1867, Cardinal from 1875. Acted as religious tutor to Leopold I's children 1851-3, with lasting effects on the mind of Charlotte, Empress of Mexico. Among the stiffest supporters of Papal Infallibility at the Vatican Council in 1870.

the question, and even provoked the boycott of Court invitations by some prominent Catholic families.

Even if he had planned to do so, it was now quite impossible for Leopold to work on the assumption that an African dominion, once carved out, could then be handed over to the Belgian government. Belgium was not only unwilling but in his view unfit to receive it. There remained the alternative of somehow placing this unborn dominion under his own personal trusteeship until the day when Belgium and its colony were ready for each other. Two years later, Greindl was to write to Leopold: ' . . . with time, the enterprise will become, by the force of circumstances, as Belgian in name as in fact. It is advisable, especially at the outset, that the business should shelter under the international flag. The colonial concept still rouses sharp antipathy in Belgium, where the memory of our unfortunate attempts is not yet obliterated. In the preliminary conferences of 1876, strong opposition broke out against anything that might lead to isolated action. A project advanced in too exclusively Belgian a light would rouse almost certain resistance, whereas it would have a much better chance of being well received by public opinion if it presented itself under an international flag'[1].

This much was now clear: that Leopold had founded the Association Internationale Africaine with the ostensible purposes of furthering exploration and repressing the slave trade, but with the real purpose of using it as a smokescreen to confuse stronger nations while he laid the foundations of a colony in Central Africa. He had further decided that this colony would have to be his personal possession, until Belgium was ready to accept it. It would be located in the Congo basin, and if a 'tramway' really could be built, it would open on to the Atlantic with an ocean port at the river mouth. It remained for Leopold to set his men to work on the chosen ground, and to find a man to lead them.

[1] H. M. Stanley; *Unpublished Letters;* p. 8.

CHAPTER XI

LEOPOLD AND STANLEY: THE CONGO

HENRY MORTON STANLEY WAS THE MAN. Hardy, experienced, and as idealistic at heart as he was ruthless in his outward behaviour, Stanley was still fighting his way down the Lualaba and the Congo at the head of the biggest expedition ever to head west from the Indian Ocean coast of Africa. In 1877, at the age of thirty-six, Stanley was at the height of his career. He was a grizzled, anxious-looking man with an almost invincible constitution; content to use his talents as a mercenary, his genuine desire to lighten the 'darkness' of Africa never fettered his choice of means of illumination, and his equally genuine hope that the Congo basin would one day pass under British influence did not prevent him from laying the massive foundations of a Belgian Congo. His ambition, simply, was to perform great works for 'progress', and to be allowed to write a book about them afterwards.

This was the sort of man Leopold needed for the work ahead. Stanley had a bad reputation among his exploring colleagues and among philanthropists for his addiction to gunfire as a method of bargaining and for the inelegant scale of his expeditions, but the founding of permanent stations and the construction of a route round the Congo cataracts would require qualities of dictatorial energy which a wandering solitary was unlikely to possess. It was also true, though Leopold could hardly know it yet, that Stanley's own brand of self-reliance contained elements which made him an easy dupe for a clever master. Like almost all nineteenth-century explorers, Stanley had developed a chronic self-pity which expressed itself in that familiar irascibility towards native staff on the march and armchair critics at home which makes so many travel diaries of the time such wretched reading. In Stanley, this self-obsession produced not only indifference towards the sufferings of his colleagues (tempered by a rather horrible sentimentality when they perished), but a certain blindness towards the purposes of his European sponsors. He often assumed that opinion would be hostile to what he was doing : Leopold later realized that Stanley would be impervious not only to criticism of the work he undertook for the AIA, but equally to suggestions that he should suspect Leopold's motives in Central Africa. Moreover, the job which Leopold planned for Stanley was not simply the accomplishment of yet another journey; it was a work of exploitation, of opening-up, which because it was more demanding and less productive of applause would engage his self-respect at an even deeper level. And so it turned out. From the Congo, Stanley was to shower Brussels with complaints and with scornful commentaries on Leopold's detailed suggestions, but from the beginning of his first contract to the end of his association with the Congo, he seems to have discounted automatically the criticisms levelled by others against the undertaking he served[1].

Leopold's interest in Stanley awoke, not when he emerged at Boma on August 10, 1877, at the end of his three-and-a-half year journey, but when news arrived in Europe that Stanley planned to attempt that journey down the Lualaba from Lake Tanganyika. Cameron had made out his case for the identity of the Lualaba and the Congo, and Leopold had accepted it : believing, therefore, that Stanley would indeed come out on the Atlantic sooner or later, to the applause of the whole world, Leopold took the chance of making plans in advance.

The news of Stanley's feat broke in Europe in the *Daily Telegraph* of September 17, 1877. In spite of the glory which promptly descended on Stanley, Leopold and his collaborators were fairly sure that the ultimate reaction of the British Government and of British explorers and geographers would be qualified by moral doubt and political caution. It was true that there were certain grounds for alarm in Brussels : that July, the Baptists in Britain had announced that they would be sending a mission to the San Salvador region of the lower Congo in 1878, and no doubt Stanley's accounts of the rich land he had crossed and the benighted heathen he had encountered would encourage the British public to finance more of such independent settlements in the Congo. But on November 7th, Greindl wrote to

[1] See H. M. Stanley; *Unpublished Letters; passim.*

Baron Solvyns, the Belgian Ambassador in London, to say that he expected that there would be a reaction against the 'scrapping instincts' which had led Stanley into thirty-two fights on his journey, and a feeling that he had made the route unsafe for later travellers. One should wait and see if Britain found a job for him.

On November 17th, Leopold himself wrote to Solvyns one of the most revelatory letters he ever allowed himself to send to a subordinate. The plans which were in vague embryo at the time of the Brussels Geographical Conference are now seen developed in startling detail, already equipped with limbs and claws.

He opened by unfolding his plan to hire Stanley to explore the Congo basin and report on its potentialities, referring to him as 'The great traveller whom I dream of making the Belgian Gordon Pasha'.

The letter went on : 'Greindl has spoken to me of an idea you gave him for the Congo : it is something like that I'd like to attempt, if the English do not forestall our efforts by getting hold of all Central Africa. We should be at once prudent, skilful and rapid in the way we set about this. I do not want to risk either offending the English or losing a fine chance to secure for us a slice of this magnificent African cake . . .

'To sum up : (1) I want to see Stanley when he has received due congratulation in London;

(2) If I like Stanley, I will raise money for him to arrange the thorough exploration of some of the territories on the Congo and its tributaries, and to found posts there.

(3) As circumstances allow, I shall try to transform these posts into something like Belgian establishments, or into water or land stations which will be ours . . .

'I think that if I entrusted Stanley publicly with the job of taking over part of Africa in my own name, the English would stop me. If I consult them, they will again try to stop me. So I think that at first I shall give Stanley an exploring job which will not offend anybody, and will provide us with some posts down in that region and with a high command for them which we can develop when Europe and Africa have got used to our "pretensions" on the Congo. The Stanley posts will be put freely at the disposal of the International Association which I hope to see developing.'

This remarkable letter[1] is self-explanatory. It is both a candid appreciation of the immediate opportunities and difficulties, and an outline of the programme which the King in fact followed in the ensuing years. A moment had been reached in the advance of Leopold's Trojan Horse at which Solvyns could no longer serve his master adequately without knowing the full extent of his plans. He had to understand that British ambitions in Central Africa were especially dangerous, because the interests they endangered were ultimately Belgian.

But London was not the only point at which Leopold planned to make contact with Stanley; nor was Solvyns the only agent with this charge. On his way to London from Boma, the explorer would stop at Marseille, and the King laid plans for a platform welcome on the territory of the Third Republic. Leopold's emissaries were to buttonhole Stanley as soon as his legs touched the ground and make him an offer of employment on behalf of their master. All this was fixed up through a characteristic Leopoldian contact. Throughout the gestation and life of the Congo Free State, Leopold's most useful allies for international lobbying and propaganda were provincial shipping magnates with African interests, and in Marseille he was already in close co-operation with Alfred Rabaud, a partner in the shipping firm of Roux-de Fraissinet & Cie.[2] Rabaud was the first President of the Marseille Geographical Society, founded in February 1877, and an enthusiastic admirer of Leopold's Association Internationale Africaine; his company's interests in Zanzibar added to his humanitarian motives for supporting the Association, the baser need to oppose the establishment of British commercial monopolies in the interior, and he was already helping Leopold to fit out the East African expeditions allotted to the Belgian Committee of the AIA. For his services in the netting of Stanley, he was to be awarded the Order of Leopold two months later. But even Rabaud was not as important to Leopold as another of the emissaries who met Stanley at Marseille, the American

[1] Baron Zuylen; *L'Echiquier Congolaise;* 1959; p. 44.
[2] The Fraissinet dynasty is still a major force in the Marseille shipping world, and leads the city's right wing in politics. A de Fraissinet owns the daily paper *le Méridional*, which was fiercely anti-Republican in 1958 and came close to the policies of the OAS in 1962. The Fraissinet interests in African trade nourish the clan's long vendetta with the present Mayor of Marseille, the Socialist Gaston Defferre, who prepared the original *loi-cadre* bringing the French colonies in tropical Africa to internal self-government.

Henry S. Sanford, who had been u.s. Consul in Brussels and who for the next seven years was to act as one of Leopold's most useful tools in the long propaganda campaign to secure diplomatic recognition for his nascent state in Central Africa.

In the evening of January 13, 1878, Stanley stepped down off the express from Italy. '. . . Two commissioners from His Majesty the King of the Belgians met me, and before I was two hours older I was made aware that the King intended to do something substantial for Africa, and that I was expected to assist him'[1]. But the two emissaries, Sanford and Greindl, could extract no definite promises from Stanley, who was a tired man and in any case preoccupied with the reception his discoveries might be accorded in Great Britain.

He went on to London, and embarked on a programme of interviews and lectures which ultimately failed to persuade British chambers of commerce that his discoveries were as financially promising as they were geographically instructive. But by May, the manuscript of *Through the Dark Continent* was in the publisher's hands: a best-seller whose countless translations fixed for a century in the Western mind the myth of a barbaric Africa to be rescued from itself only by force.

In Brussels, these were months of uneasy waiting and of frayed nerves. Leopold's propagandists, writing in geographical journals, urged that the Congo should be neutralized by the Powers, and a name found for it at an international geographical conference (Stanley had frightened Leopold by a suggestion to the British that the Lualaba might be rechristened the 'Livingstone'). Meanwhile, Greindl underwent another attack of misgivings. How, he asked the King in May, could Stanley be signed up to lead an expedition nominally under the standard of the AIA without full information being given in advance to the Executive Committee of the AIA? How could the complete secrecy of Leopold's preparations be reconciled with the international and philanthropic nature of the Association—or was the AIA to act as no more than a flag of convenience?

Greindl was one of those souls whose conscience could only be soothed by forcing his colleagues to admit that they were as aware of their own double-dealings as he. He was not really

[1] H. M. Stanley; *The Congo and the Founding of its Free State;* London 1885; p. 21.

hostile to Leopold's plans—which he understood perfectly well—but the sanctimoniousness of his fellows upset him. From Lambermont, he extracted a lame declaration of purpose, which suggested that the Executive Committee could be safely told about the plans for Stanley to found posts on the Congo 'and (informed) in a more general way about the developments which would follow'.

In June 1878, whether as a result of further needling by Greindl or not, Lambermont produced an enormous, unhappy memorandum for his master in which he attempted the absurd task of explaining to Leopold that his motives were not what both of them knew quite well that they were. Greindl alone wanted to hear the other courtiers whisper that the Emperor was naked before he joined in the applause for the imperial robes: Lambermont, a less complex man, preferred to play the farce through consistently. There was no reason, he wrote, why Belgium should not undertake African operations on her own, outside the AIA framework. 'The fact that the Association's resources have been almost entirely provided by the King of the Belgians and by Belgium naturally means that the freedom of action allowed to our country is increased rather than reduced. But this conclusion ought perhaps to bow to considerations of a higher order, and it would no doubt express a certain august will accurately to predict that there will be no grounds to suppose that the African Association has been set up only to serve as a cloak for schemes serving one particular interest . . . '

Moving out of this thicket of verbiage, Lambermont tried again to define the labels to be attached to each stage of the impending operation. The line of posts up the Congo would be established in co-operation with the AIA: but 'a co-operation which would be nominal rather than effective, in view of the state of the central treasury'. The commercial stations would be paid for by Belgium, but Stanley would use the 'international' posts as bases from which to found them[1].

In other words, Stanley would officially be working for two masters. The first chain of posts would be founded for the Executive of the AIA, while the trading stations would be set up for some commercial body based in Belgium. In reality, and assuming that the moribund councils of the AIA raised no objec-

[1] Roeykens; *Débuts de l'Oeuvre*, pp. 319-26

tion, all the posts would slide under Leopold's control. Greindl, now apparently reconciled with his conscience, wrote to his King: ' . . . with time, the enterprise will become, by the force of circumstances, as Belgian in name as in fact. It is advisable, especially at the outset, that the business should shelter under the international flag . . . a project advanced in too exclusively Belgian a light would rouse almost certain resistance . . . '[1] It was all the more annoying for Greindl and Leopold that Emile Banning chose this moment to point out the very possibilities they were hoping to conceal. Banning, in a memorandum on colonial possibilities in the Cameroons which he presented in May 1878, observed that the two sorts of stations were liable to fuse into one, and asked naïvely: 'Is it possible to find grounds for such posts in declarations of the 1876 conference, without violating either its spirit or its letter?'[2] Could the same bases legally undertake both the original scientific projects and the work of *centres coloniaux*?

On June 10th, Stanley came to Brussels, disappointed with British inertia and interested to hear more of Leopold's plan, which, he assured the King, would be hopeless without the construction of Cameron's 'tramway' or railway round the cataracts. A first effort to raise money for a railway company did not succeed. In August Stanley met Greindl and Rabaud in Paris, and they all went into greater detail on the costing of a trade project and of 200 miles of track. Dutch capitalists, already established at the Congo mouth, suggested a 'syndicate' to study the railway project, under the chairmanship of Leopold, but Stanley insisted that the first task must be the construction of posts up the river, to support whatever was to follow. Sanford advised Leopold that Stanley's approach fitted in better with the ostensible purposes of the AIA. The King appears to have agreed, but the Dutch suggestion for a 'Study Syndicate' attracted him also as a device.

In 1873, when British and foreign steelmasters had met at Liège to discuss trade and the expansion of their markets, Leopold had distributed to the Belgian delegates a handout proposing a concerted Anglo-Belgian approach to the vast market for railway equipment apparently opening in China, and he had suggested

[1] See p. 164 above.
[2] Roeykens; *Débuts de l'Oeuvre;* p. 334.

the formation of just such a syndicate as the Dutch were now proposing for the Congo. A joint *Comité d'Etudes* would plan exploration of the ground and the establishment of bases, would gather information and would ultimately apply for concessions from the Chinese government, whose suspicions would be allayed by 'placing the study group under a neutral flag. That would be achieved if it was founded in Belgium'.

Early in November, Stanley was again summoned to the Royal Palace in Brussels: 'I there discovered various persons of more or less note in the commercial and monetary world, from England, Germany, France, Belgium and Holland . . . ' This preliminary and unofficial syndicate questioned Stanley about Congolese conditions. 'Some of the above questions were answerable even then, others were not. It was therefore resolved that a fund should be subscribed to equip an expedition to obtain accurate information, the subscribers to the fund assuming the name of 'Comité d'Etudes du Haut-Congo'. A portion of the capital amounting to £20,000 was then and there subscribed for immediate use'[1].

On November 25th, the commercial and monetary gentlemen and Stanley met again in the Palace, and voted the Comité d'Etudes into being. Stanley's formal instructions for the organization of an expedition were drawn up in writing. Whether or not the executive of the AIA had given permission for the forming of the Comité d'Etudes remains a mystery to this day, but the significance of this moment was the entrance of the Leopoldian project to its second stage. The philanthropic body had acquired the powers of a great commercial undertaking. Now it only remained for it to add to itself the rights of sovereign territorial dominion.

[1] H. M. Stanley; *The Congo and the Founding of its Free State;* Vol. I, pp. 26-7.

CHAPTER XII

LEOPOLD DECEIVES: STANLEY PIONEERS

AMONG THOSE FOUNDERS of the Comité d'Etudes were the Belgian banker Léon Lambert, the Scottish magnate William Mackinnon (who as owner of the British India line with its interests in Zanzibar was an old collaborator of Leopold's, and was already on the track of the concessions which in 1888 took form as the Imperial British East Africa Company), the Dutch 'Afrikaansche Handelsvereeniging', already established at the river mouth, and the Manchester cotton merchant James Hutton. Between them, they raised 742,500 francs out of the 1,000,000 francs in 500-franc shares set as the capital. Lambert, acting for Leopold, bought 265,000 francs worth and paid another 10,000 on his own account. The Dutch subscribed 130,000. Even Greindl put in 5,000 francs of his own.

But Jules Greindl, with his curiously dilettante interest in truth, was on the way out of his master's confidence. A few days before, Colonel Maximilian Strauch had replaced him as Secretary-General of the AIA: now Strauch, instead of Greindl, was made effective chairman of the Comité d'Etudes. Greindl, though permitted to be a board member of the Comité, was despatched suddenly to Mexico as Belgian Minister and passed the rest of his career on the normal diplomatic circuit. His successor, a staff officer at the War Ministry, was too discreet and loyal to leave historians with evidence as suggestive as that of Greindl's several sallies for further information. Strauch 'jauntily wore a moustache and pince-nez. He was a conscientious man who when a Captain in the infantry had enrolled as a student in the Free University of Brussels'[1].

The terms of the Comité's foundation were not published. But in 1918 the German Government, taking perhaps a lead from Trotsky's publication of secret treaties found in the Tsarist files,

[1] H. M. Stanley; *Unpublished Letters;* p. 13.

issued the text of a number of Belgian documents taken from the Foreign Ministry in Brussels whose contents were intended to disconcert those who thought they were fighting a just war for Belgian liberation. Among them was the original agreement of the Comité d'Etudes, and it was discovered, to the considerable embarrassment of Leopold's apologists, that Article VI of the agreement expressly engaged the Comité against taking any sort of political action. And yet not only had the Comité acted as a precursor of the Congo Free State, not only had Leopold in private instructions demanded action which could hardly have any end but a political one, but in the scheme for a 'Confederation of Free Negro Republics', the Comité had actually advertised a political intention to the world. Every subscriber to the Articles, moreover, must have known both that political action was illegal and that his own intervention, appealing to Article VI, would have stopped it. None did so.

The earliest definitions of purpose were careful. At the last meeting of the syndicate, before the Comité was formally created, Stanley had been briefed 'to effect the object for which the committee was constituted. I was to erect stations . . . to establish steam-communication[1] wherever available and safe . . . By lease or purchase, ground enough was to be secured adjoining the stations so as to enable them in time to become self-supporting if the dispositions of the natives should favour such a project. If it were expedient also, land on each side of the route adopted for the traffic was to be purchased or leased, to prevent persons ill-disposed towards us from frustrating the intentions of the Committee through sheer love of mischief or jealousy. Such acquired land, however, might be sublet to any Europeans, at a nominal rent, who would agree to abstain from intrigue'[2]. This sort of land acquisition, it could still be argued, amounted only to the minimal requirements for the maintenance of the commercial enterprise.

In December, Stanley drew up estimates for the first six months of work, and on January 2, 1879, the Comité d'Etudes voted him the money. 'By 23rd of January, all that I could personally effect in Europe was accomplished', and he set sail for Zanzibar to recruit porters from the population which had

---

[1] Stanley referred to river-steamers, not to the subsequent railway.
[2] H. M. Stanley; *The Congo and the Foundation of its Free State*; p. 27.

served him so well on previous expeditions. On the way back, heading for the Congo, Stanley found Strauch waiting for him at Gibraltar. At a secret meeting, on July 7, 1879, in a Gibraltar hotel, Stanley was admitted a little further into the intentions gathering in Leopold's mind.

Baldly, Stanley was to set about the erection of a sovereign state, whose monarch was to be Leopold II. That was the true purpose of the Comité and of the stations to be founded. But to conceal the incredible audacity of this plan, Leopold had devised yet another cloak of good intentions: the State was to bear a superficial resemblance to Liberia, and be presented to the world as a 'Confederation of Free Negro Republics'.

An undated document in the Belgian Foreign Ministry archives[1] appears to be the draft of the instructions which Strauch was to give Stanley. 'It is not a question of Belgian colonies . . . It is a question of creating a new State, as big as possible, and of running it. It is clearly understood that in this project there is no question of granting the slightest political power to negroes. That would be absurd. The white men, heads of the stations, retain all power. They are the absolute commanders of stations populated by free and freed negroes. Every station would regard itself as a little republic. Its leader, the white man in charge, would himself be responsible to the Director-General of Stations, who in turn would be responsible to the President of the Confederation.

' . . . The work will be directed by the King, who attaches particular importance to the setting-up of stations . . . the best course of procedure would no doubt be to secure concessions of land from the natives for the purposes of roads and cultivation, and to found as many stations as possible . . . Should we not try to extend the influence of these stations over the neighbouring chiefs, and then form these posts and their dependencies into a republican confederation of negro freedmen, supported by the participation of the chiefs who had helped to abolish slavery? . . . The President will hold his powers from the King, and this President should be resident in Europe.'

It was a plan difficult for a humanitarian to condemn. Never, of course, put into practice, this promise of an eventual league of negro republics glittered confusingly for many years before

[1] Quoted in H. M. Stanley; *Unpublished Letters;* p. 24.

the eyes of those unenlightened about Leopold's true purposes, as an end which would justify almost any means to achieve it. One of its advantages was that it professed to carry out the anti-slavery campaign for which the AIA had largely been created. Another was the fact that it was not a new idea. There had, of course, been Liberia, and the shortcomings of Liberian demo-cracy had already made a disappointing impression on the world. Thus Leopold was not in conflict with the currents of continental opinion when he noted that 'there is no question of granting the slightest political power to negroes'. On the contrary, he was cleverly synthesizing ideas already in circulation. The German explorer Schweinfurth, whose book *In the Heart of Africa; 1861-1871* appeared in 1875, had suggested that the most hopeful method of suppressing the internal slave-trade in Central Africa would be 'the formation of large Negro states, to unite the terri-tories most exposed to slave raids, which would be placed under the protectorate of the European Powers'. The implication was that the protectorate should be a collective one, and what body was more suited to exercise that protectorate than the Associa-tion which the geographers of the Powers had already set up? A second inspiration clearly came from the discussions of the Paris Geographical Congress in 1875. Here again was the notion of the white *noyau dirigeant,* the total reconstruction of native society into new units forming around posts manned and commanded by Europeans.

Impressive to men of good will, the Confederation plan shocked Stanley by its revelation of what seemed to him an element of ignorant idealism in Leopold's approach to Africa. He wrote to Brussels from Gibraltar, warning the King tactfully that posts should be founded and further groundwork completed before any question of confederating Africans could arise: the local population, in his view, was far too primitive to take part in schemes for political union. With the sixty-eight Zanzibaris and Somalis recruited in Zanzibar, Stanley then sailed on for Banana at the outfall of the Congo.

A secret note from Leopold reached him some time in August, when he was already in Africa, written in a rather more hard-headed tone than the draft instructions for Strauch. There was little talk about freedom or republics. Instead, Leopold repeated his orders that Stanley should acquire territory on a large scale, and spoke for the first time of a 'free state'. The Comité d'Etudes would lay down its laws and appoint its Governor, but Leopold, 'as a private citizen', would be head of state. He explained: 'The King, as a private person, wishes only to possess properties in Africa. Belgium wants neither a colony nor territories. Mr Stanley must therefore buy lands or get them conceded to him, attract natives on to them, and proclaim the independence of his communities, subject to the agreement of the Comité.' Leopold cited Luxemburg, independent and prosperous although its Grand Duke was also King of Holland, and with less assurance, Liberia: 'a little state: it's true that it was formed by American negroes and is not doing very well'[1].

Stanley did not leave the Congo for three years. During that time, with immense labour and at the cost of the life or health of many men, he broke open a route along the banks of the Congo from the shore above the existing port of Boma to the inland sea of Stanley Pool, far above those Yelala cataracts in which he had seen his last European companion die on the transcontinental expedition two years before. Along the river, from Boma upstream, he founded the stations of Vivi, Isangila, Manyanga, Ntamo (Leopoldville), and Mswata above the Pool itself. In those years, Stanley earned for himself his treasured nickname of 'Bula Matadi', the Rock-Breaker.

Nor did he break rocks only. Something of the horrified admiration he won from his subordinates in this climactic period of his life can be found in this letter, written home in 1881 by the dying Engineer Neve: 'Mr Stanley has taken great care of me during these bad days. He brought to bear the sort of care a blacksmith applies to repair an implement that is utterly essential and that has broken down through being used too roughly, an implement he dreads to lose; teeth clenched in anger, he smites it again and again on the anvil, wondering whether he will have to scrap it or whether he will still be able to use it again as before'[2].

But Leopold was not entirely content with Stanley, who seemed to him to lack imagination and above all to move far too slowly. The King had tried and failed to buy the services of

[1] Roeykens; *Débuts de l'Oeuvre;* p. 397. The original of this letter has not been found.
[2] H. M. Stanley; *Unpublished Letters;* p. 44.

Count Savorgnan de Brazza, and now de Brazza was back in Africa, travelling light as usual and coming down towards Stanley Pool from the north. His commission from the French Government, as Leopold soon discovered through enquiries carried out by Sanford, was to hoist the French flag over the Pool if he arrived there before Stanley. But it proved impossible to make Stanley understand the importance of getting to the Pool before de Brazza. In vain, Leopold wrote: 'The interests of the undertaking demand that you should not remain at your first station. Serious rivalry is threatening on the Upper Congo. Brazza will try to follow the Alima down to its junction with the Congo and hopes to get there before you. There is not a moment to lose.' Stanley merely retorted that there could be no rivalry over the Pool, 'for I discovered the place two and a half years ago'.

More agonized letters failed to accelerate Stanley's ponderous advance, and in October 1880, de Brazza arrived on the north shore of Stanley Pool, where he hoisted the tricolour, made a treaty with a local chief named Makoko, and established a post on the future site of Brazzaville, which he left under the command of Sergeant Camara Malamine, a Senegalese NCO in his party.

Leopold was furious. Baron Solvyns wrote: 'Stanley is held to have been stupid to the highest degree. He ought to have begun by securing the most important part of the Congo—Stanley Pool—and one wonders why, as a Californian, he did not think fit to lay his rival low with a rifle shot. He proved as gentle and tractable as those wretched savages that have to be civilized'[1].

The implicit equation of 'civilization' with the morals of Boot Hill is tasty. But there was no time to waste in blaming Stanley: Leopold flung his efforts into a temporarily successful attempt to discourage Ferry and Gambetta from recognizing the Makoko treaty. To Stanley, on the last day of 1881, he wrote patiently: ' . . . it is indispensable that you should purchase for the Comité d'Etudes as much land as you can obtain, and that you should successfully place under the sovereignty of the Comité, as soon as possible and without losing a minute, all the chiefs from the mouth of the Congo to Stanley Falls. Brazza in a very short

[1] H. M. Stanley; *Unpublished Letters;* p. 159.

time has placed under his dependence the chiefs round Stanley Pool. Should we not do as much for the Comité? Others will do it for themselves and against us, and all our work, all our expenditure, will be a total loss'[1]. But Stanley's reply ignored every reference to the acquisition of land.

Meanwhile, the work of opening up communications went forward in the greatest possible secrecy; Stanley had sworn his employees to discretion under pain of a 20,000 franc fine. The inevitable result of this lack of hard news was a recurrence of Press rumours, and in 1881 Leopold had to get the *Etoile Belge* to print a denial of a letter in *The Times* which suggested that Stanley was using chain-gang labour. The *Etoile* was to assert that Stanley employed only Zanzibari volunteers, 'who love him like a father'. On the credit side, the security curtain was effective enough to blind even de Brazza to the eventual aims of the whole project.

Among the secrets of the enterprise was one which even Stanley did not know. On November 17, 1879, the Comité d'Etudes du Haut-Congo had ceased to exist, but Stanley was not aware of this until 1881. Not only was he not informed, but Leopold continued deliberately to refer to the Comité as if it still lived, discussed, and took decisions. The name was useful to him: the substance was not.

It is true that Stanley had been allowed to hear about the first events in this strange process. Returning from Zanzibar in 1879, he had heard at Aden that the Dutch firm, the Afrikaansche Handelsvereeniging, had collapsed, and that a general refunding of subscriptions to the Comité was under study. Leopold's secret letter to him that August had stated: 'The funds of the Comité d'Etudes will soon run out, and it will not find any fresh supporters: the King will therefore offer to take on the responsibility of carrying on the project, reserving for himself an absolute freedom of action'[2].

The failure of the Dutch partners in the Comité was at once turned to advantage by Leopold. On the advice of Sanford, who wrote from New York and returned to Brussels to press his suggestion further, he resolved to evict all the remaining businessmen from control of the Congo operation. Little notice

[1] *Ibid.*, pp. 137-8.
[2] Roeykens; *Débuts de l'Oeuvre;* p. 416.

was taken of worried enquiries from the British subscribers who wanted to instal two British representatives on the board of the Comité. At the annual meeting in November, the shareholders were told that three-quarters of the initial capital had been spent, and that the rest was needed to liquidate contracts already signed. It was a dismal prospect. As the shareholders struggled under the shock, Lambert, acting on Leopold's instructions, came forward with a new proposal: if the subscribers would agree to dissolve the Comité, the King guaranteed to return their original investments to them. He would take personal control of the project, and would offer them preference in any commercial undertaking launched by the stations.

They would have been fools not to accept. The Comité d'Etudes expired, unknown to the rest of the world, and was replaced by the Association Internationale du Congo (AIC): a convenient locution to decribe one man and his money. There were in fact no subscribers to the AIC save Leopold himself, who assumed complete control of the whole Congo operation and provided the capital out of his own fortune. This sum, which is thought not to have formed part of the 15,000,000 francs he inherited from his parents, was probably amassed by clever speculation, possibly in Suez Canal stock. Whatever its origins, it remained attached to Leopold himself: he advanced it to the legal fiction of the 'AIC', where it remained, under the name of the 'Fonds Special', to form the treasury of the Congo Free State itself. Having thus lent his own money to himself, Leopold naturally retained a control over the capital of the Free State whose intimacy bewildered his contemporaries.

The similarity of the name 'Association Internationale du Congo' to the 'Association Internationale Africaine' was a further advantage. Even when the public was allowed to know that the Comité had ceased to exist, confusion between the two Associations was deliberately encouraged, and the impression given that the AIC was just another recasting of the original league of private philanthropists and geographers. On January 8, 1884, Leopold wrote to Strauch: 'Care must be taken not to let it be obvious that the Association du Congo and the Association Africaine are two different things. The public doesn't grasp this. It concludes that there are two phases, the first being disinterested'[1]. Stanley himself, once he had discovered that for two years he had been working for an employer he had never heard of, continued to accept a similar version of what had taken place. ' . . . the Committee at a later period, having satisfied itself that progress and stability were secured, assumed the title of 'Association Internationale du Congo', which, be it remembered, was originally started with the philanthropic motive of opening up the Congo basin . . . '[2]

[1] H. M. Stanley; *Unpublished Letters;* p. 21.
[2] *Ibid.,* pp. 51-2.

CHAPTER XIII

THE PORTUGUESE THREAT

THE FRENCH THREAT to Leopold's plans still remained: for all his friendship with Leopold, de Lesseps, chairman of the French committee of the AIA, could hardly be expected to lobby indefinitely against the interests of his own government. In June 1882, de Brazza returned to Paris triumphant after his victorious race to Stanley Pool, and Leopold resolved to try his loyalty once more. On September 10th, he noted: 'De Brazza seems to think that Stanley is working for Belgium and Britain. We must explain to him that Belgium wants absolutely nothing, that our Comité (sic) is an international one. We shall do well to consult de Brazza on the best way to invite French capital to join our work . . . that will be a way of leading up to an invitation to de Brazza to take an interest in our enterprises and conduct some of them himself'[1].

The meeting, a few days later, was a failure: its only result was to give de Brazza some idea of what Leopold and Stanley were really up to, and to alarm him. Shortly afterwards, he presented the French Government with a high-spirited document arguing that the Makoko treaty should be ratified. 'Mr Stanley acted in the name of the King of the Belgians for Belgium, which at that time wanted to found in Africa a sort of international factory . . . Doubtless the King of the Belgians was quite disinterested. He gave his millions with the sole aim of civilizing the savage tribes. I thought, however, that there was a political ideal at the back of the humanitarian sentiments of the King of the Belgians. I was far from blaming him for this, but that did not prevent me from having a political idea of my own, and mine was very simple. Here it is: if it was a good thing to get hold of the Congo, I preferred that a French flag, rather than the Belgian "international" flag, should float over this magnificent African territory'[2].

[1] H. M. Stanley; *Unpublished Letters;* p. 149.
[2] *Ibid.*, p. 156.

In October, Stanley himself turned up in Brussels. He had been very ill and needed a break, but Leopold was not pleased to see him at a moment when he might have been signing up strategically-placed chiefs in de Brazza's absence. However, he was able to convince Stanley of the importance of making treaties along the whole length of the river, and to excite him with the idea of cutting off de Brazza's claim on the Pool from the sea by a foray into the region north of the Congo mouth: the valley of the Kouilou and its tributary the Niari[1]. Stanley, who once again insisted on the importance of building a railway round the cataracts, agreed to return to the Congo before the end of the year. Rather to Leopold's misgivings, he proposed first to pay a visit to Paris.

The truth was that Stanley had at last been stung by de Brazza's remarks about him. De Brazza had revived for the benefit of the French Government the old stories of Stanley's coarse pioneering methods, and had boasted: 'I never was in the habit of travelling on African soil in martial array like Mr Stanley, always accompanied by a legion of armed men . . . Mr Stanley had adopted the practice of making himself respected by dint of gunfire: I myself travelled as a friend and not as a belligerent.' Stanley decided to hit back. On October 20th, he attended the Stanley Club dinner in Paris (organized by Mr Ryan of the *New York Herald*), and launched off into an ornate and boastful speech in which he accused de Brazza of fooling Makoko over the contents of the treaty, perverting the ideals of the AIA, and introducing 'an immoral diplomacy into a virgin continent'.

But Stanley had underestimated the sleek assurance of de Brazza's character, a man derived not from a Welsh workhouse but (so he let it be known) from Doges and Emperors. As poor Stanley foamed up towards his peroration, de Brazza hurried smiling into the room, seized Stanley's hand in his, and addressed the diners in his own charmingly accented English. 'I see in Mr Stanley not an antagonist,' he said, 'but simply a labourer in the same field . . . Gentlemen,' he ended, lifting a glass, 'I am a Frenchman and a naval officer, and I drink to the

---

[1] These rivers, now in the 'Brazzaville' Congo Republic, are sometimes spelt 'Kwilu' and 'Njari'.

civilization of Africa by the simultaneous efforts of all nations, each under its own flag'[1].

His adversary's guns spiked, de Brazza returned to the attack on his own government. On November 30, 1882, France officially ratified his treaty with Makoko, and the following month, the Assembly voted credits to him for another expedition. In the interval, Makoko had become a favourite target for Parisian music-hall satire, but his actual identity and status remained the subject of intense dispute. Not for the last time, a European had sought to establish authority over a region of Africa by picking out a 'paramount' chief and buying up his powers; not for the last time, a European had managed to identify a 'paramount' chief in a society where supreme political authority was in fact not vested in any individual. De Brazza convinced himself that Makoko was the 'big chief' of the Bateke, claiming allegiance from lesser chiefs and having full authority over their land. Makoko seems to have hastened to accept this theory of de Brazza's, as one might expect, but in fact he had no more than a certain priestly seniority. When Stanley arrived—and this bears the ring of truth—another chief explained to him: 'There is no great king anywhere. We are all kings—each a king over his village and land. Makoko is chief in Mbe; I am chief of Malima . . . But no chief has authority over another chief. Each of us owns his own lands. Makoko is an old chief: he is richer than any of us'[2]. None of these arguments, however, dislodged Sergeant Malamine or prevented de Brazza in 1884 from extracting another treaty out of Makoko which professed to grant him rights on the south, 'Belgian' shore of the Pool.

Back in the Congo, Stanley retrieved his reputation by narrowly beating the French to the occupation of the Kouilou country, after a series of brilliant marches by his lieutenants Grant-Elliott and Vandervelde. They were charged with treaty-making, now a major objective of AIC policy. Just before Stanley returned to the Congo, Leopold had noted to Strauch (October 16, 1882): 'The terms of the treaties Stanley has made with native chiefs do not satisfy me. There must at least be added an article to the effect that they delegate to us their sovereign rights over the territories . . . the treaties must be as brief as possible, and in a

[1] H. M. Stanley; *Unpublished Letters*; p. 155.
[2] *Ibid.*, p. 69.

couple of Articles must grant us everything'[1]. His model at this time was a cutting from *The Times* giving details of the treaties signed a few years before by Mr Dent and Baron Overbeck with the Sultans of North Borneo[2], and when complaints about the validity of his treaties arose, he was able to recruit British lawyers, among others, to argue that he was acting within his rights. In 1883, he despatched to the Congo the elderly and ailing Sir Frederick Goldsmid, a retired Indian civil servant, whose instructions were to push ahead with the 'confederation' scheme by getting the assent of chiefs to a treaty form which bound them to be governed and policed by the AIC, under its flag of blue with a gold star. By December, Goldsmid had to be invalided home, but assistants in Leopold's service extracted more than 300 signatures from the Congolese chiefs. These treaties were in effect a purchase of sovereignty by an organization whose flag was not recognized by the outside world as anything more than the ensign of a commercial company, but Leopold, on Sanford's advice, defended them not only on the precedent of the North Borneo treaties but on that of the agreements made by the early settlers in North America with the Indian nations. Sir Travers Twiss, of Oxford, and Professor Arntz of Brussels were engaged to provide legal opinions confirming the right of a trading company to make such treaties, and they contributed learned references to the practice of the Teutonic Knights and the Maltese Knights of St John.

In the year 1883, Stanley established a dominance over the Congo which de Brazza was not able to challenge again with any real hope of success. In exchange for gin, bits of cloth and discarded uniforms[3], the riverain chiefs signed away their independence, discouraged from any subsequent change of allegiance by the military strength of Stanley's following. By about the end of the year, he had built up a strength of a hundred white men and six hundred Africans, armed with four early machine-guns, twelve Krupp guns, and disposing of a stock of a thousand quick-firing rifles with two million rounds of ammunition: eight steamers provided rapid transport to the scene of trouble. As

[1] H. M. Stanley; *Unpublished Letters;* p. 161.
[2] The Dent-Overbeck treaty's legality is currently disputed by the Philippines Republic, which claims British North Borneo on historical grounds.
[3] Leopold planned at one time to dress loyal chiefs in the uniform of 'Beefeaters'. See Ruth Slade, *King Leopold's Congo;* London 1962; p. 25.

early as the summer of 1881, there had been a punitive raid which left some fourteen dead, and at least one campaign of reprisal by the burning of villages. In August 1883, Stanley was able to move his whole armada steadily upstream from the Pool, founding stations as he went, until on December 1st he reached Stanley Falls and established the post which was to become Stanleyville, more than a thousand miles from the Atlantic.

But Leopold, in spite of these successes, remained dissatisfied with the dogged and unimaginative quality of Stanley's leadership, and continued to look for other commanders to supervize or replace him. When Stanley was in Brussels in 1882, the question of a successor had been discussed, and Leopold had suggested that Lovett Cameron might be sounded, as long as Stanley could make sure that he wasn't drinking too much. Leopold's main hopes, however, lay for several years in General Gordon.

As early as October 1879, Strauch had been urged by the King to make approaches to Gordon, through the intermediary of William Mackinnon. In July Gordon had resigned his post as Governor-General of the Sudan for the new Khedive Tewfik, and Leopold hoped by appealing to his generous hatred of the slave-trade to persuade him to lead an East African expedition to found a chain of posts linking the Indian Ocean with the head-waters of the Congo. Gordon had already shown interest in the AIA in 1877: in February 1880, Mackinnon arranged that he should visit Brussels, and his meetings with Leopold took place in March. Enthusiastic over the version of the AIC's purposes which Leopold produced for him, he agreed in principle to become Governor of the Congo once the AIC flag had been recognized by the Powers as that of a sovereign state. That condition, however, was a long way from being fulfilled in 1880, and Gordon was in any case passing through a period of agitated indecision; shortly afterwards, he left to take up a post as secretary to the Viceroy of India which he did not occupy for as long as one week.

In 1883, Leopold acknowledged that the Congo was too small for Stanley and Gordon together; 'it will only increase the disorder and disunity from which our affairs are suffering. I do not think Gordon need be told how the Confederation plan stands. He is most indiscreet. The British do not understand the meaning of the word "confidential" '. He offered Gordon employment in the Congo again, and once more Gordon came to Brussels and accepted, with reservations. But by now Leopold's own reservations about Gordon were multiplying. At the time of their meeting, on January 3, 1884, he noted to Strauch: 'If Gordon says to you "In England I shall be a general in three years", tell him: "With us, you can be a field-marshal in the new state". You know as well as I do that when such eccentrics are stiff-necked, one should run over the arguments again briefly and forcefully and then leave them to think it over. If they hesitate, one should insist, but not at too great a length—to avoid making them lose patience. Stanley, you will remember, before going back also led us to believe more than once that he would refuse'[1]. He added another inducement: he disclosed that he hoped to extend the dominion of the AIC over the arid horizons of the Bahr-el-Ghazal, that huge and empty tract of the Sudan to the west of the upper Nile. This was the first time that Leopold acknowledged an ambition which was to plague and exhaust his officers for the next fifteen years, but even this offer was forgotten by Gordon when, back in England, he agreed to undertake the pacification of the Sudan against the Mahdi. He never came back to the Belgians and almost his last transaction with the pioneers on the Congo confirmed Leopold's black views on his lack of discretion: he wrote to a thunderstruck Stanley at Vivi and let him know about the Bahr-el-Ghazal plan.

Leopold's growing interest in the north-east limits of the Congo basin did not blind him to the dangers which still threatened his precarious hold on the mouth of the Congo, the project's only outlet. He had an uncertain grip on the outfall of the Kouilou, to the north of the great estuary, but there was a steady revival of Portuguese claims in the area, spreading northwards from Angola to reclaim districts which had not been under effective Portuguese control for several centuries. Further, Leopold realized that he stood fair to be the victim of a Franco-Portuguese deal which would return the north bank of the Congo estuary and his acquisitions in the Kouilou-Niari region to France in exchange for a recognition of Portuguese claims to the south bank of the river. Meanwhile, the dealings of the AIC with territorial chiefs round Boma brought down a Portuguese warship, and for some months a war of nerves was prosecuted

[1] H. M. Stanley; *Unpublished Letters*; p. 166.

between Leopold and Lisbon, fought by the King with a flurry of diplomatic notes across Europe and by the Portuguese with flag-bearing landing parties.

The seaward danger came to a head suddenly and from an unexpected quarter, when in late 1882 it became apparent that Portugal was arranging a deal with Britain. Effectively, the initiative was a British one, generated by the news of de Brazza's treaty with Makoko at Stanley Pool; France had to be blocked off from winning a position astride the Congo mouth and Portugal—the AIC being from the Foreign Office's point of view a diplomatic non-entity—was the obvious piece to move. In return for assurances of free trade on the river and certain other concessions, Portuguese sovereignty over *both* banks of the estuary was to be recognized by Britain. Against this project, Leopold's associates William Mackinnon and James Hutton appealed to the commercial and humanitarian interests of a British public which identified Portugal with protectionism and slavery. Leopold himself wrote a letter of entreaty to his cousin the Prince of Wales—he was by now aware that the Queen was not prepared to treat him with the favour she had shown to his father—imploring his intervention to save the high causes of negro emancipation and free trade as embodied in the Association. The development of the protest campaign, rather than this letter, produced results. In March 1883, Granville, the Foreign Secretary, submitted to the Prince of Wales that he might reassure Leopold by letting him understand that Britain would not allow the Portuguese claim to extend as far as the port of Boma, and would sedulously defend the freedoms of trade and navigation on the river.

In effusive gratitude, Leopold answered his cousin: 'My dear Bertie; Many thanks for the excellent news which you sent me . . . I will allow myself to ask you to continue to keep an eye on this affair until it is concluded . . . '[1] As he knew, it was far from concluded. A public and parliamentary campaign against the treaty, carried out by Leopold's British friends and elaborately orchestrated from Brussels, forced Gladstone's government to drop the project in April 1883. But negotiations between Portugal and Britain were soon renewed, the British government insisting more strongly than before upon various guarantees of

[1] Zuylen; *Echiquier Congolais;* p. 63.

free trade on the Lower Congo and (for the benefit of Mackinnon's powerful lobby) upon keeping the port of Vivi out of
Portuguese hands, and in spite of hectic agitation against the
terms by the Association and its friends, an Anglo-Portuguese
Treaty was signed on February 26, 1884[1].

It was a moment of apparent disaster for the King. It is true
that the treaty was aimed not so much at his own pretensions as
at the possibility of a French foothold at the Congo mouth; the
fact remained that a cork was about to be thrust into the wind-
pipe of his infant State. But the publication of the Treaty, which
might have been accepted in Europe if it had been duly signed
in the spring of 1883, now met a violently hostile international
reaction. In Britain, anti-slavery groups and Chambers of Commerce renewed their attack through Parliament, and there were
references to the 'betrayal' of the AIC to the 'callous and servile'
Portuguese. The French, naturally, reacted fiercely, and the
Americans, already under skilful and sustained pressure to
recognize the AIC diplomatically, expressed their own disapproval.
Ratification of the Treaty became finally impracticable in June
1884 upon Bismarck's flat refusal to accept it.

Suddenly and ubiquitously, statesmen were alert to the coming
of a major crisis over European ambitions in West-Central
Africa. The demarcation of spheres of influence, which free
competition and indirect methods of control had failed to bring
about, could not safely be postponed any longer. Talk of a
general settlement was already in the air when in Munich the
International Law Institute, at its ninth congress, quoted the
analogy of the Danube disputes and called for a conference of
the Powers to settle the dangerous rivalries developing in the
Congo basin. From Brussels, Leopold heard them. The success
of such a conference could only be founded on a compromise
between the colonialist Powers, nations at once intensely suspicious of each other's expansion and reluctant to undertake the
peril and material outlay of expanding further themselves. What
could attract them more than the suggestion of neutralizing the
whole region in dispute under some benign, innocuous, uncommitted regime which would allow them all the privileges of
trade without the responsibilities of government? If there had

[1] For the Treaty and the organized agitation against it, see R. T. Anstey;
Britain and the Congo in the Nineteenth Century; Oxford 1962; Chapters 5-7.

been no other motive to set up a League of Nations than the need for an authority of Mandate, it would probably have come into being when it did. But in 1884, there was no League: only an 'International Association of the Congo'. The Powers were thankful to raise Leopold's amorphous authority to the official rank of a 'Free State'.

CHAPTER XIV

THE CONGO AND THE BERLIN ACT OF 1885

FROM BRUSSELS, Leopold spoke of confederations and states. On the Congo, his men looked around them and smiled. The famous 'stations' which the King advertized as free ports were a few thatched sheds of clay, dominated by an ambitious flagstaff. The 'fleet of fast steamers', supposedly turning the Congo into one of the great industrial waterways of the world, was no more than a flotilla of pretty little launches with stove-pipe funnels and canopies, bobbing at its moorings down at the river bank[1]

Around these fragile phenomena, the African peoples of the upper river pursued their own way of life with robust indifference. In contradiction to the tales of Neanderthal barbarism purveyed about them in Europe, they were highly organized and possessed a degree of technological culture often in advance of the East African Bantu of the interior. The German explorer von Wissmann, who travelled up the Kasai river for the AIC, found a heavy population living along the banks, organized in elaborately-planned villages and equipped with canoes which could hold as many as eighty men each. Food was carefully grown and abundant: for relaxation, there was palm-wine to drink and hemp to smoke. In spite of the spreading chaos on the upper Congo and the Lualaba, following the activities of Arab slavers and their allies, an extensive riverain trade in brass and ivory and fish still survived over long distances, and among the Baluba, von Wissmann found glazed pottery and furnaces for iron-ore with adjustable draughts[2]. Such prosperity was not to last. Far to the north, on the Aruwimi tributary of the Congo, Stanley watched corpses floating downstream from villages raided by slavers, and saw whole populations spending the day

[1] For a description of the Congo at this time, see Charles Liebrechts; *Léopold II, Fondateur d'Empire;* Brussels 1932.

[2] H. W. Von Wissman; *My Second Journey Through Equatorial Africa from the Congo to the Zambesi in the Years 1886-7;* London 1891.

afloat on their canoes and only venturing ashore to visit their fields àt night[1]. And in Europe, the Powers prepared to transfer the whole world of the Congo and its tributaries to the care of a man who regarded it no more than 'a slice of a cake'.

The challenge of the Anglo-Portuguese Treaty had stimulated Leopold into a passion of activity. A ceaseless landslip of letters, orders and memoranda descended from his study upon the staff of secretaries and equerries who dealt with the business of the Congo, and was passed on to destinations throughout the world. Leopold's immediate aim was to marshal European opinion favourable enough to his professed ambitions and suspicious enough of Britain and Portugal to make the Treaty impossible to ratify. Joined to this task was another: to get for the AIC the full and final rank of statehood, through diplomatic recognition of the blue and gold flag, recognition which would make the enforcement of the Treaty almost a *casus belli* to those Powers which had accepted the AIC as a friendly state. To win this recognition, Leopold appealed cleverly to a mixture of high principles and concealed fears. On the positive side, he made noisy invocation to the principles of negro emancipation and of free trade.

Leopold, as his earlier views on forced labour show, was not a free-trader by conviction. But the tactical value of promising free trade over the vast Congo basin was too precious to be ignored. His secretary Jules Devaux, in 1883, had written to William Mackinnon: ' . . . if England, alone or with other Powers, were disposed to proclaim the neutrality of the Congo mouth and to recognize the neutrality of our stations, he (Leopold) would engage himself not to establish either customs duty or tariffs on our routes of communication. If you could find a suitable chance to press for this, His Majesty gives you full powers in the matter'[2]. The same suggestion went to the German banker Bleichröder a month later, and Stanley was instructed to include clauses allowing free entry to traders of all nations in the treaties he made with the Congo chiefs.

The King concentrated his campaign for recognition on the United States. In November 1883, Sanford arrived in New York bound for Washington with a letter from the King to President Arthur, which Sanford had helped Leopold to draft and which

---

[1] Liebrechts; *Léopold II, Fondateur d'Empire;* p. 75.
[2] Dated April 6, 1883. Quoted in Zuylen; *Echiquier Congolais;* p. 70.

E

placed heavy emphasis on trading opportunities. In his baggage he brought not only particulars of treaties signed on the Congo but historical extracts referring to treaties made by Roger Williams in the seventeenth century with the Indians of Rhode Island. (Congress, he later told that body, would not now exist 'if our forefathers had boggled at such trifles'.) Moving to more recent history, Sanford made much public play with the foundation of Liberia by private individuals, and returned to the present with interesting descriptions of the free negro republics now in formation across the Atlantic.

Secretary of State Freylinghausen, conscious of his own ignorance, treated talk of the 'republics' with caution. But the President's annual message to Congress, read on December 4th, was, though muzzy, distinctly friendly: the AIC was referred to as the AIA, and credit given to it for establishing 'embryo states' around the stations, especially in view of the fact that 'it does not aim at permanent political control'. Sanford's grandiose lies were showing dividends already: all through the New Year he went on entertaining and lobbying, directing most of his attention to Senator John T. Morgan, of the Senate Foreign Relations Committee, who had been detailed off by Freylinghausen to look into the claim for recognition.

If he had bothered to study papers already in his possession, Morgan would have seen that the various organizations named in them were not coterminous. If he had troubled to make serious enquiries in Europe, he would have discovered that the AIA now existed only in memory and in imagination. But he preferred to accept it flat from Sanford that 'a branch of the Association was formed . . . under the name of the Comité d'Etudes du Haut-Congo . . . ' On February 25, 1884, a joint resolution by both houses of Congress recommended recognition of the AIC flag as that of the 'Congo Free States'. The plural is significant.

Freylinghausen did not accept, as Morgan did, that the 'states' already existed. But he believed that they would shortly exist, and that meanwhile the flag of the 'Association', their creator, should be recognized in order to assist the process of their birth. The final declarations, exchanged on April 22nd, expressed warm American admiration for the humane purposes of the AIC, and while managing at least to name it correctly, betrayed a quite erroneous belief that its purpose was to 'wither away' beneath the emergence of the Free States of Africa[1].

Victory in America was followed, within twenty-four hours, by a victory in Europe. On April 23rd, Colonel Strauch for the AIC and Jules Ferry, the French Prime Minister, issued a joint statement which read as follows:

'The International Congo Association, in the name of the free stations and territories it has established in the Congo and in the Niari-Kwilu valley, formally declares that it will not cede them to any power, reserving the special conventions which might be drawn up between France and the Association to fix limits and conditions to their respective activities. At the same time, the Association desires to give fresh proof of its friendly sentiments towards France, and engages to offer her the right of first option if unforeseen circumstances should drive the Association one day to realize its estates.'

These two sentences, amiable and precise in wording, conveyed France into the deadliest and most elegant of all Leopold's diplomatic snares. Ferry was nervous and perhaps distracted: the conquest of Tonkin was involving France in war with China. Leopold knew that he was worried about the Congo, desiring it and fearing the consequences for the French territories in West Africa if it fell into the hands of another major European Power: thus the first sentence of the declaration, with its bold guarantee against alienation to any of France's rivals, was a handsome reassurance to Ferry. It has even been suggested[2] that he only asked for the first sentence, and accepted the second as an unsolicited favour. The effect of this second sentence, however, was less to favour than to fetter.

In the first place, it was fairly evidently in contradiction to the spirit of what had been said before. If the territories of the AIC were not to be ceded to any power, then the offer of an option on them was meaningless: both declarations could not be valid. In the second place, and crucially, the rest of Europe, in particular Germany and Britain, was committed to maintain the State in being in order to stave off those 'unforeseen circumstances' which would allow France to annex it. France had in

[1] For these negotiations, see R. S. Thomson; *Fondation de l'Etat Indépendant du Congo;* Brussels 1933.
[2] Thomson; *Fondation de l'Etat;* pp. 163-9.

effect been granted a right which she could never safely use.
Lastly, Ferry's implicit agreement that the AIC could dispose of
territory as it chose was seen afterwards to amount to recognition
of the AIC as a sovereign state: full diplomatic recognition inevitably followed. Leopold, in short, gained everything from this
transaction. France gained nothing and came to resent the fact
bitterly. As late as 1960, during the Brussels Round Table conference which prepared for Congolese independence, General
de Gaulle's government informed the Belgian Ambassador in
Paris that it considered the *droit de préférence* still to be in force.

Leopold lost no time in passing the papers of this agreement
to Bismarck, with the bland observation that he had entered it
from fear of Portugal rather than out of love for France. He
sent an emissary to Berlin to press the suggestion for a conference, and to bring the Chancellor more documents on the
ostensible purposes of the AIC. These papers included a map of
suggested AIC boundaries which included the Congo mouth, a
band of territory extending to the Indian Ocean, and the regions
of the Sudan abandoned by Egypt—this last 'to cut off the slave
trade at its roots'. The State would be ruled by the King of the
Belgians, as 'owner' and treasurer, aided by a council composed
of members of the Royal Family and a few nominees.

Bismarck was impressed with the need to arrive at some
settlement, but Leopold's insinuating approach disgusted him.
'Schwindel!' he noted beside the pious remarks about slavery,
and 'Fantasies' beside the project for a council. Later, he relieved
his feelings more thoroughly: 'His Majesty displays the naïve,
pretentious egoism of an Italian who assumes as a law of nature
that everything will be done for him for the sake of his *beaux
yeux* and nothing of equal value asked of him in return'[1]. He
told Granville, however, that the Anglo-Portuguese treaty was
not viable, and after prolonged bargaining and in return for
well-defined commercial privileges, Germany ultimately recognized the AIC as a friendly state on November 8th.

On November 15, 1884, called at the initiative of France and
Germany, the Berlin Conference opened. It was well packed with
Leopold's friends, since the AIC, recognized so far only by Germany and the United States, could not send an official delegation. The Belgian party included Lambermont and Banning;

[1] Quoted in Thomson; *Fondation de l'Etat;* p. 182.

Strauch was present; Stanley acted as technical adviser to the Conference; and Sanford, though still in Leopold's service, ran the affairs of the American delegation. But the agenda set before the fourteen nations who attended went beyond Leopold's own purposes. Suspicion of the British occupation of Egypt was a major motive in bringing Bismarck and Ferry together, and the conference was designed to define the formalities of effective occupation in West Africa, to secure free trade on the Congo, and also to secure freedom of navigation not only on the Congo but on the Niger.

Within this larger struggle but outside the official sessions of the conference, Leopold fought tenaciously against the French and the Portuguese. Early in December, he heard that British recognition was imminent, in return for Belgian support against the internationalization of the Niger, and he became for a moment over-confident, writing on December 10th: 'If I had all the left bank of the Congo, the right bank of the Upper Congo, an indemnity for the Kouilou-Niari and enclaves on the coast, I should not complain.' A few days later, when the French had shown their teeth over the Kouilou-Niari, he was screaming with pain and fear. 'For the last six years, I have been putting my whole fortune at the service of the Association du Congo. I can go no further, and if the French refuse to refund my expenses on the Niari, I will not accept their terms, for I cannot. I shall wait till they invade the Kouilou, and I shall then withdraw from Africa. You must keep the Germans and the British up to date about this situation . . . '[1]

He was threatening, in other words, to sabotage the whole Congo settlement by creating a dangerous vacuum there if he did not get his way, and another note to Strauch the following day suggested how the threat might be phrased: 'To the Germans and British, you must show yourself distressed by France's ruin of our work. Say that you are at least glad that the Association has been able to survive long enough to win the sympathy of Europe . . . our defeat is an honourable one, and it is better to admit and accept it at once than to drag out a painful existence . . . '[2]

[1] Leopold to Strauch, December 20, 1884. Quoted in H.M. Stanley; *Unpublished Letters;* p. 169.
[2] *Ibid.*, p. 169-70.

From Brussels, working day and night, Leopold was able to keep his agents under almost telephonic control, never leaving them uncertain of the line they should take or often of the very language they should use. Gradually, using his own weakness as a wedge and the mutual fear of the Powers as a lever, he prised Portugal away from those who pretended to be her allies and made his own concessions to France. Britain was obliged to repudiate the treaty with Portugal. On February 5, 1885, France recognized the AIC, and Leopold abandoned the Kouilou-Niari. Most of it went, without indemnity, to France: a smaller area to the north of the Congo mouth went to Portugal. He retained twenty-two miles of coastline on the Atlantic, co-sovereignty over the mouth of the Congo, and a corridor along the south shore of the estuary to the highest navigable point, to allow for a railway between an ocean wharf and Leopoldville. The main Conference was now about to end. Only the Portuguese representatives, caught between what they knew could not be avoided and the pressure of public opinion at home, still raised objections, until the Powers obliged them by sending Lisbon an ultimatum which could decently allow them to agree.

The Berlin Act, finally signed on February 26, 1885, declared a free trade zone covering 'the Congo basin and its affluents', and covering also the Indian Ocean coast of Africa between the mouth of the Zambezi and the Somali coast[1]. No power exercizing sovereignty in the area could concede a monopoly or special commercial privilege: all powers in the area were bound to improve native conditions, to protect missions, to allow liberty of conscience, and to put down the slave trade. The whole area was proclaimed to be neutral. There was also a dangerous provision worrying to Leopold, which provided for the setting-up of an International Commission, to oversee Congo navigation and if necessary to raise loans for its own expenses: a possible rival to his own administration.

There was no mention of the Association. But the question of political form of the Congo basin had been at the back of the delegates' minds, and at the last session of the Conference, they formally welcomed the new State into existence. Kind words

[1] Only the Berlin signatories were committed to this second zone: other and subsequent sovereign states in that area would observe it only at their express consent.

were spoken about Leopold and his ideals, and Bismarck, as chairman, read the Congo State's declaration accepting the terms of the Berlin Act. Around the convenient armature of Leopold's political structure, Europe had modelled an economic charter to control the scramble for central Africa within certain decencies. But Leopold, from within, was now to make this model come alive and work for him alone.

CHAPTER XV

BELGIUM: THE 'GREAT LIBERALS' AND THE SCHOOL WAR

A S POLITE APPLAUSE descended on Leopold and his newly sovereign Association, two nations remained conspicuously surly. One of them was Turkey, irritated at the easy abuse heaped upon Islam in the person of the Arab slavers and, after the loss of Egypt two years before, unenthusiastic about European penetration into Africa. The other was Belgium.

During the hectic search for diplomatic recognition, Banning had suggested that as a last resort, Belgium might be persuaded to take over the Congo at once and to occupy Boma. With Leopold's approval, Frère-Orban was approached. But the old Liberal, now leading his last government, was no more impressed than he had been when the young Leopold, so many years before, had dumped on his desk that marble slab with its crude *Il faut à la Belgique une Colonie*.

Now he repeated his original answer: 'Belgium does not need a colony. Belgians are not drawn towards overseas enterprises: they prefer to spend their energies and their capital in countries which have already been explored and on less risky schemes. They don't like emigrating, but if they were forced to do so to seek a living, they have at their doorstep a perfectly adequate colony. I mean France, where thousands of our compatriots go and settle. Still,' he assured the royal equerry who had been detailed to sound him out, 'you can assure His Majesty of my whole-hearted sympathy for the generous plan he has conceived, as long as the Congo does not make any international difficulties for us'[1].

Jules Malou, the moderate Catholic leader, was equally sceptical. With an effort to end his comments on a less impolite note, he told the equerry that he supposed it was 'not a bad thing that

[1] Daye; *Léopold II*; p. 203.

a King as busy as ours should have a favourite hobby to drain
off his surplus energy'[1]. It was not Liberal or anti-colonial
principles which created this indifference; it was the self-obsession
of contemporary Belgium, absorbed in social and ideological
conflicts which seemed to their partisans to hold universal consequences. To the Liberal, the very concept of a civil Belgian
state was in danger; to the Catholic, Masonic conspiracies
threatened the souls of his children by blocking the channel of
grace through Christian education; to the Socialist, victory
would bring a new world to birth, while defeat would prolong
the era of famine and beggary, and of the tremendous mine
disasters which punctuate the decades of Belgian working-class
history. When such issues were at stake, the diversion of energy
to some costly exhibition of philanthropy in cannibal Africa
seemed to absurd to be contemplated.

In 1878, the June general elections had dislodged Malou and
brought back, by a narrow majority, Frère-Orban and the
Liberals. This was the last and stormiest ministry of the old
aristocratico-métallique, who took the portfolio of Foreign
Affairs as if to leave to younger men the hard fighting over
internal politics which he knew was about to break over Belgium.
But he was still an imposing and formidable figure.

Frère was near to the essence of the nineteenth-century local
politician. His province was small, but his gestures and his
references were gigantic: his voice rose and fell in speeches
ardently heard but now profoundly soporific. He acted out-
rageously, because he believed that only theatricality could
convey conviction. 'He would start up slowly, dropping his first
sentences into the silence. And at first his familiar gesture was
to grasp the lapel of his frock-coat and stroke its fold in a down-
wards direction. Then he would warm up, the debate would get
into its stride, and he would throw out his arm from his chest
in a wide and always measured way. Even when carried away,
he remained in entire control of himself, of his gestures and of
his words. Rage would empurple his face, blood would congest
his cheeks, his forehead would go red, his eye would flash fire;
yet, by a phenomenon familiar to orators, from the back of his
mind he kept a precise control over every word and gesture . . .
His voice—full, rich with sap and warmth, a fleshy voice spout-

[1] *Ibid.,* p. 203.

ing up from the depths of his chest—echoed, gleamed and glittered like flashes of lightning; the vastness of his gestures, his majestic accents, his sublime brow, all gave to this man the splendour of a demi-god'[1].

Supported by his 'Great Liberal' cabinet, Frère-Orban planned a massive counter-offensive against the encroachments of the Church on the functions of the State. Belgian Catholicism was still dangerously Ultramontane, in the year of Pius IX's death, and the Liberal right and left wings had found temporary unity in their fear of an advance towards theocracy. Inevitably, the field of battle was to be the schools, as it was in every country where the Napoleonic lay state came into conflict with Ultramontanism, and the new cabinet's first move was to set up a Ministry of Public Education.

In the period of Belgian 'unionism', the question of education had been skirted by common consent between the parties: there had been hostility over estimates for school expenditure, but the general attitude was that of Lebeau, who in 1833 refused to enter a discussion on the subject while 'the ultimate sanction of our national existence depends on our unity'[2]. During the forties and fifties, laws on primary and middle schooling had given the Church an increased share in educational management, until only the two state universities of Ghent and Liège were left as 'neutral': it remained for the doctrine that 'error has no rights' to make the share of each side seem to the other an intolerable usurpation. In January 1879, the government introduced an education bill designed to establish lay and neutral primary education which would be under centralized state control and, not, as hitherto, under the control of the local commune authorities and of the parish. Each commune was to set up an official school of the new kind, and the communes were forbidden to subsidize or assist the 'free' (Catholic) school. Teachers were all to have qualifications from state teacher-training colleges. For the problem which was central to the whole dispute, the teaching of religion, the bill laid down that any kind of religious instruction could be given by any kind of priest or minister, provided that it was given out of school hours and that attendance was not compulsory.

[1] Paul Hymans; *Frère-Orban*. (Article in *Le Soir*, August 1923.)
[2] Quoted in Henri Pirenne; *Histoire de Belgique*; Vol. VII, p. 96.

This bill has gone down to history as the *Loi de Malheur*. Even admitting the irrationality of the volcanic reaction against it, and the sanity of many of its provisions, it still remains unforgivably pugnacious and provocative. Instead of extending civil liberty, it diminished it, both by stamping on the tender toes of the commune *bourgmestres* and by dealing a powerful blow against the originally Liberal principle of freedom of education. For a Flemish village, solidly Catholic and possessing perhaps only one building suitable for use as a school, in which most of the teachers were trained by the Church, the bill was tyranny.

The Belgian hierarchy's first reaction was to promise excommunication to those who sent their children to one of the new primary schools, and to those who taught in them, unless they were forced to do so under threat of prosecution. Their second was to throw their weight behind the political campaign launched against the bill by the Catholic party. But the bill had become law on June 18th, after a vote in the Senate so desperate that a man literally a few hours from death was carried into the lobbies, and Leopold, concealing the fury he felt at the Liberals who had put him in such a position, was obliged to give his assent. For carrying out this constitutional duty, the Catholics hastened to insult him, and it was in vain that he appealed, as he did at Tournai in August, for a return to 'that wise and manly frame of mind which built up Belgian nationality on the foundations of co-operation between the parties'.

In revenge, priests added to their Litany the prayer: 'From Godless schools and faithless teachers, good Lord deliver us!' It was said that the new act would release 'a Socialist torrent which threatens to overwhelm order and property'. But this was the reverse of the truth: it was the Catholic campaign against the *Loi de Malheur* which released a torrent of popular emotion and almost for the first time associated the masses with the conflicts of the two major political parties. Pirenne points out that the ultimate consequence of the measure was to raise the masses against the *Pays-Légal*. Another consequence, achieved partly by the brusquely centralizing aspects of the law, was to strengthen the bond between the Catholic party and the growing Flemish movement, already breaking away from the cultural domination of Brussels.

The immediate aim of the campaign was to construct in every parish in the Kingdom a free Catholic school, and to have these schools open for the beginning of the school year in October. It was a spectacular success. By October, 40,000,000 francs had been raised, and at the start of the new term a third of all the pupils and a fifth of the staff went over to the new schools. Two years later, more than half the pupils and staff had migrated. Many communes refused to build lay schools which would remain empty, and disorder spread. The splendid celebrations of the *Cinquantenaire*, to mark the fiftieth year of Belgian independence, were overcast by the knowledge that the Church had decided to take no part in them. On June 5, 1880, Frère-Orban broke off diplomatic relations with the Vatican.

But the tide was turning against him fast. In 1879, the new Pope Leo XIII had done Belgian Catholics the service of destroying the basis of the Ultramontanism which alienated them from the electorate. The Belgian Constitution, he told journalists, 'contains some principles of which as Pope I cannot approve, but the position of Catholicism in Belgium after fifty years' experience shows that in the conditions of modern society, the system of liberty established in that country is best for the Church. Belgian Catholics therefore ought not only to refrain from attacking the Constitution, but to defend it'[1]. The following year, Leo went so far as to advise the Belgian bishops to use moderation in their campaign: this counsel was seized upon by Frère-Orban to back up an assertion that the Pope considered the bishops deplorably intransigent, and it was the subsequent remonstrations which ended in diplomatic rupture. Meanwhile, however, the Catholics were able to lean heavily upon the argument that the law was in breach of the article of the Constitution which guaranteed liberty of conscience.

On the Left, after a year or so of calm, the Radicals led by Paul Janson began to demand from Frère the price of their brief loyalty. Eleven years after the Paris Commune, they returned to their campaign for universal suffrage, and in 1883, to the apprehension of the older Liberals, a new law widened the franchise at provincial and local elections. To the *Censitaires* were added the *Capacitaires*: a category defined not by wealth but by their educational standard and by the nature of their work. En-

[1] H. Pirenne; *Histoire de Belgique;* Vol. VII, p. 238.

couraged, the Radicals tried to follow up their success by proposing the Constitutional revision necessary to widen the
parliamentary franchise, but the right wing of their party considered that enough had already been conceded. In the summer
of 1883, Janson's bill for revision received only eleven votes
against 116, a defeat which decided the Radicals to make a
formal breach with the Liberal party association.

The elections of 1884 were a Catholic landslide, from which
the Liberals did not recover for the rest of the century. They
were replaced by a Government thirsty for revenge. Led by the
ageing Malou, the tone of the cabinet was set by the presence
of the extremists Jacobs and Woeste, architects of the electoral
victory and the free schools campaign, and its first acts were to
restore relations with the Vatican, to abolish the Ministry of
Public Education, and to return the control of primary schools
to the communes, which were in many cases forced to adopt and
subsidize the free schools erected during the *Guerre Scolaire*.

Leopold realized that there would be trouble from the Liberals,
especially from the anticlerical mob of Brussels, and he suggested that the bill should be at least modified. 'After 1878,' he
wrote to Malou, 'the Liberals behaved as if there were no Catholics in Belgium. The Catholics now have an interest to remember
that there is a very large number of Liberals in this country'[1].
On the day he wrote this, the police only just prevented a major
riot as two political processions collided in Brussels, but the
elderly Malou, nervous and over-excited, told Leopold that the
Liberals numbered only a fifth or so of the population and that
the parliamentary majority had every right to pass clerical legislation if it wished to. At a cabinet meeting, Charles Woeste, who
knew well that Leopold hoped for his fall, attacked the King for
failing to support his ministry in public. Boiling with rage, Leopold was forced to promise his assent. But before he did so, on
September 7th, wild rioting broke out in Brussels as Liberal
groups attacked a Catholic victory rally, and the Queen was
jeered at on her way to the Opera.

Leopold signed Woeste's law, but as soon as the commune
elections in October gave him an excuse by showing a Liberal
swing, he dismissed both Woeste and Jacobs. Malou had to go
with them, as Leopold knew he would, and was replaced by a

[1] Daye; *Léopold II;* p. 246.

younger man, Auguste Beernaert. Leopold had a perfect right to
dismiss ministers: that was admitted: but the episode cost him
as much popularity with his Catholic subjects as he had already
lost from the Liberals by signing the education bill. On the
credit side, he was finally rid of Woeste, whose anti-militarism
he feared much more than his views on schooling, and he had
at least restored the monarchy to an even keel, if only by ensuring that it was liked no better by one faction than the other.
Men had shouted *Vive la République!* in some of the Brussels
riots: it was time to end the war of parties and move away from
the fanatical commitments of the recent past.

It is said that Leopold liked Beernaert because his nose was
nearly as big as his own. Unlike Leopold, he was given to scratch-
ing it when perplexed, a habit which relieved contemporaries who
found the rest of his exterior too smooth and cold to be comfortable. He was a successful lawyer, well shaved and rather rich;
a moderate Catholic in politics who fancied his own taste in
painting, and who served Leopold with almost excessive loyalty
and discretion for ten years. His special virtue, in Leopold's eyes,
was that he could be relied upon for support in the affairs of the
Congo; he had become a member of the Belgian Committee of
the AIA in 1876, and in 1878 had acted as its vice-chairman. Yet
beneath his sleek manner, Beernaert, like many lawyers concealed
a sarcastic sense of humour, springing out of deep contempt for
the men and policies he had to deal with. He occasionally used
this derision on the King himself, who appreciated it: introduced at a reception by Leopold as 'the greatest cynic in the
Kingdom', he retorted that he would not dare to take precedence
over His Majesty. Pierre Daye observed that from 1885 the affairs
of the Congo and of Belgium were run by Leopold as a single
policy, no longer in two compartments. This was only made
possible by the skill and compliance of Beernaert, at Leopold's
service until, strangely reversing the usual sequence of a politician's ideas, he became an idealist in his old age.

CHAPTER XVI

THE CONGOLESE CROWN AND THE
SEARCH FOR MONEY

ONLY SIX MONTHS after he had torpedoed the Malou cabinet, the last explosion in the six-year war over religious education, Leopold had to persuade his subjects to confer on him the Crown of the Congo. As he was well aware, Article 62 of the Constitution forbade a Belgian King to accept the throne of another state without the assent of both Chambers of Parliament given in a two-thirds majority, a precaution originally inserted as a defence against absorption by France. Leopold had already discussed this process with Malou, who was gloomy and evasive about the chances of raising the necessary support in Parliament, and who warned Beernaert, as he handed over the control of the Government, that 'you are going to be lured on to an extremely slippery slope'[1].

Before venturing into the business of Article 62, there were other preliminaries which allowed Beernaert to test the feeling of the nation on the Congo project. The end of the Berlin Conference and the appearance of the AIC as a political state with boundaries visible on a map took Belgium by surprise. It was felt, immediately and correctly, that for all the fake internationalism of the AIC, Belgium had been involved in Africa without having been consulted, and that the Belgian taxpayer would sooner or later be asked to pay for what had been done. An Antwerp paper wrote: 'We must protect ourselves against appeals to Quixotry in such a grave and important business'[2]. An address of congratulation to Leopold was voted unwillingly by both Chambers: on March 10th, Beernaert put down a bill to ratify the Berlin agreements in a noticeably frosty atmosphere. Malou, not without malice, sent Beernaert the draft of his congratulatory address to the King with the request: 'See if you can work a few sparks of enthusiasm into my glacial prose'[3].

[1] Quoted in Thomson; *Fondation de l'Etat;* p. 284.
[2] *L'Escaut*: quoted in Pierre Daye; *Léopold II;* p. 286
[3] Lichtervelde; *Léopold II;* p. 216.

Leopold, warned by these portents that he faced the supreme humiliation of being denied by his own Parliament the powers which had been conferred on him by the combined empires of Europe, set Banning to work persuading the deputies that the Congo offered Belgium a prospect of commercial privileges without liabilities. In particular, bearing in mind that a simple governmental majority would not be enough, Banning was told to concentrate on the Liberal opposition. Leopold wrote to Beernaert on March 29th that 'I think I ought to confirm to you that the best way to talk round the leaders of the Left to the idea of allowing me to become the Sovereign of the Congo is to tell them that the Government is satisfied that the new State has adequate sources of revenue'[1].

But there was another source of anxiety beside the notoriously tender Belgian pocket. The point of Article 62, conceived in an age of monarchs bound to their Parliaments by constitutions and charters, was that a King with two Kingdoms would be bound to obey the dictates of two different assemblies, which might be expected at times to conflict. Would there be a Congolese Parliament, forcing upon Leopold measures damaging to Belgium and contrary to the policy of the Government in Brussels? Leopold lost no time in letting his critics know that he would be an absolute King in the Congo, and that such a problem could not arise. The letter, drawn up under his supervision and read by Beernaert, which asked the Chambers for their approval of his new sovereignty, insisted that the union between Belgium and the Congo would be purely a personal one, committing Belgium to no kind of responsibility for Leopold's 'international colony'.

Without much enthusiasm, the Opposition under Frère-Orban at length gave the necessary support to the bill granting Leopold a second crown. Whatever they thought of the matter, they could not make a fool of their King before the eyes of all Europe and the United States. Only one deputy, M. Neujean, attacked the bill and voted against it. In a speech often quoted in the years to come, Neujean warned 'that the union may to a certain extent embroil us in the fortunes of a State which is remote, embryonic, and which exists more in theory than in fact'[2]. He

[1] Quoted in Thomson; *Fondation de l'Etat;* p. 290.
[2] Lichtervelde; *Léopold II;* p. 218.

added: 'Events may force on Belgium a duty to support her King out of her own pocket in an enterprise which she has encouraged . . . '[1]

Even Beernaert, seeking perhaps to protect his Government against retrospective blame for whatever might happen to Belgium in future on the Congo's account, pleaded: 'This is a project which has nothing whatever to do with this government; it is neither Catholic nor Liberal; it is exclusively the King's affair.' It is not surprising that after such a speech from the chief minister, the Opposition refused to regard itself as committed to supporting the Congo adventure by the vote it had just given: later, Frère-Orban was to say: 'I have never had anything to do with this business (the Congo); I had no hand in it . . . '[2]

Leopold, in granting all these assurances of the Congo's financial and political independence of Belgium, had paid a very high price for permission to acquire his second Kingdom. Did he mean those assurances seriously? It is hard to believe that he still imagined that the Congo could pay for itself without massive financial assistance for the investments necessary to open it up, especially for the railway. The Berlin Act forbade him to levy import duties, and he had made the additional gesture of banning the sale of alcohol to the African population. Well before the Berlin Conference, he had been aware of the problem of finding capital, and had examined numerous schemes for raising money. In 1882, he had suggested to Stanley through Strauch that a toll might be levied upon European travellers using the stations along the river and upon their caravans, but Stanley told him plainly that the idea was impossible. 'The mere rumour of such a course in Europe would bring general condemnation on our heads'[3].

Leopold has been called 'the master of the limited-company', and the following year he produced a sketch for a much more characteristic scheme involving foreign capital. It should be remembered that Belgium, although rich almost to the point of unbalance in finance and investment banks like the Société Générale, was still a very small country, and it remained true throughout the history of the Congo Free State that the Belgian

[1] Thomson; *Fondation de l'Etat;* p. 293.
[2] *Ibid.,* p. 295.
[3] H. M. Stanley; *Unpublished Letters;* p. 136.

money market was never adequate for Leopold's capital needs. He was obliged to cadge and to bargain his way into the stock markets of his great neighbours, especially those of Paris, Berlin and Vienna, and this constant dependence on the goodwill of foreign governments made it all the more necessary for him to form the elaborate Press and propaganda bureau which for decades lauded the material wealth of the Congo and attempted by every means to suppress the growing volume of criticism.

The new scheme envisaged the formation of a French company to build the vital railway, the capital of 400,000,000 francs to be provided and raised by the financier Jaubert and guaranteed by the French Government. As a financial inducement, the company would be allowed to keep one of the two tracks at the expiry of the concession; as a political inducement, France would get a frontier 'rectification' in the Kouilou-Niari. But this typical plan came to nothing, and by the end of the Berlin Conference, as the new State was proclaimed at Boma, Leopold was becoming thoroughly alarmed. The stations above the Pool were temporarily abandoned so that the main effort could be concentrated on Leopoldville and the construction of a shipyard there. He told Beernaert that the State would receive 1,000,000 francs a year in 'royal subsidy', and another 500,000 in taxation, but even in 1886 the product of taxation and dues was no higher than 74,200 francs[1]. The real state of Congo finances was suggested in a note to Strauch written by Albert Thys, a young army officer who had just been added to Leopold's Congo staff. Leopold, Thys complained, 'repeats ten times a day that we are going bankrupt, that he doesn't know how he can pay up, that the bankers won't lend him any more money, etc., etc. Our gracious Sovereign is like this all the time: your days with him must be tougher than I supposed . . . '[2]

The King next turned to the British for his railway. In 1885, the 'Royal Congo Railway Co.' was founded in Manchester by James Hutton, William Mackinnon, Stanley and others, and on July 24th a provisional concession to build and exploit the line was signed. But there were Belgian protests; the British tried to drive a better bargain; and Leopold finally offered Thys six

[1] About £2,900 at exchange rates of the day (twenty-five Belgian francs equalled £1).
[2] R. P. Ceulemans; La Question Arabe et le Congo; A.R.S.C. 1959; p. 194.

months to form a company of his own: the result was the
'Compagnie du Congo pour le Commerce et l'Industrie', god-
father to the 1889 'Compagnie du Chemin de Fer' which got the
first locomotive to the Pool in 1898.

The broader financial problem remained. The year of 1886
was excruciating for Leopold: the gate-keepers of the European
exchanges dawdled with their keys as Congo operations slowed
down towards a condition of paralysis. At the time of the Berlin
Conference, Ferry agreed by private letter to let Leopold run a
20,000,000-franc lottery in France in return for the Kouilou-
Niari, but though the region was occupied, Ferry fell from office
before the loan could be further discussed. Successive French
governments stalled and havered, and it was only in 1887 that
Leopold at last arranged a bond issue, after two other *com-
binaisons* had fallen through.

This issue formed the basic public debt of the Congo State.
Leopold had at last persuaded Beernaert to authorize an issue
of 150,000,000 francs' worth of premium bonds, and after a
rather hostile debate in 1887, the Chamber concurred. Permission
to offer up to 80,000,000 worth of this issue on the Paris Bourse
was won as part of a complex deal with France, struck on
April 29th, by which France was allowed another 'rectification'
on the Ubangi in return for allowing the Congo shares to be
quoted and for a highly guarded hint that the right of French
pre-emption would not be held to stand in the way of an ultimate
cession of the Free State to Belgium.

Even when the issue had been cleared with the governments
concerned, there remained the problem of finding a guarantee
for prospective shareholders. The Société Générale, Rothschilds
and the French banks all refused to help: Leopold was reduced
to a plan by which the Congo would rely on the *moral* support
of a *Regie* including the Banque Nationale, the state issuing
bank of Belgium. It may have been the sheer desperation of this
scheme which persuaded Beernaert to arrange a compromise
with the banks, and the bonds came on the market at last in
February 1888, three years after the foundation of the Congo
Free State.

At first they sold well. Then terrifying fluctuations of price
began to occur, especially on the nervous Belgian exchange, and
Leopold was driven to massive purchasing of his own shares in a

vain effort to hold the price steady. When General Boulanger, the aspiring dictator of France, retreated to Belgium in April 1889, Leopold rushed at the chance that he might be used as a bargaining counter to buy access to the Paris Bourse for more Congo shares. He wrote to Beernaert: 'I would not be at all alarmed if the French Government asks us to keep an eye on Boulanger, and thus offers us an excellent chance to remind France of her obligations towards the Congo . . . '[1] But Beernaert's nerves were not strong enough, and he expelled Boulanger to Dover in the same month.

The second instalment of the premium bond issue was already due to be floated, but the market price of the first half of the issue had now fallen below the proposed starting price of the second half. Leopold was growing thin and grey: he shook and appeared half-distracted to his ministers. Marie-Henriette, watching him pacing up and down, wailed, 'Mais Leopold, tu vas nous ruiner avec ton Congo!' and it was true that the King, about this time, was mortgaging the livery of his servants and the orders presented to him by foreign monarchs. This may have been done more to attract sympathy than to raise important sums of money, like a famous decision to cut a course out of his lunches, but the first half of 1889 was certainly a moment at which no normal financier would have persisted with a venture so obviously crumbling. Leopold, however, was a King. Beernaert offered to lend him 50,000 francs to bring the first half of the issue up to par, and Leopold was still able to refuse the loan as an 'act of patriotic madness'[2].

Only a third of the second issue was taken up in the event, even though the Belgian government agreed to buy, and the whole loan only raised 30,000,000. Leopold had apparently hoped that it would raise the secret 'Fonds Special' of the Congo (which, it will be recalled, actually remained his own property) to about 50,000,000. It was now almost impossible for him to see any event, personal or political, except in terms of its possibilities in credit. He had tried to involve the Belgian hierarchy, by a letter to the Pope, in supporting the premium bond loan as a work of evangelization. He had almost certainly drawn upon his mad sister Charlotte's inheritance, by foul means rather than fair;

[1] Alain Stenmans; *La Reprise du Congo par la Belgique;* Brussels 1949; p. 71.
[2] *Ibid.,* p. 74.

and his mild, deaf brother the Count of Flanders was set to entertaining important financiers who visited Belgium.

Of all this period of obsession, perhaps the most repulsive manifestation was Leopold's attitude towards the Mayerling tragedy. In what was almost certainly a suicide pact, his son-in-law Rudolf, the Austrian heir, and his mistress Marie Vetsera had been found dead in a hunting-lodge in January 1889. It is said that Leopold's first action, on getting out of the coach in Vienna, was to make an appointment with the chairman of an Austrian bank: only then did he turn to his waiting daughter Stephanie. It is certain that in reply to a message of sympathy from the Belgian Government he wrote: 'We thank you for your kind expressions regarding the disaster that has fallen on us. We know the feelings of Ministers, and count on their sympathy in the terrible trials which God has laid upon us. Do whatever you can to help M. Van Neuss to place some more shares on the market: this would be most agreeable to me. Once more, I thank you'[1].

It was clear by 1888 that the normal methods of raising money on the stock market would not be adequate to pay even for the effective occupation of the Congo, while the amount produced by export duties remained insignificant[2]. Instead, three totally new possibilities presented themselves to Leopold, in his search for funds. The first was a revision of the Berlin Decrees to permit an import duty. The second was political action to extract a direct loan from the Belgian Treasury. The third, and the decisive cause of the immense disaster which was to overtake the African population of the Congo, was to devise a new economic system for the production of wealth by the state apparatus itself. In 1885, a proclamation had assigned all 'vacant lands' to the Free State, and this was to be the foundation on which Leopold constructed his new system—inevitably, a system of state monopoly to the exclusion of private enterprise[3].

[1] Quoted in Ludwig Bauer; *Leopold the Unloved;* London 1935; p. 216.
[2] According to the Belgian lawyer Félicien Cattier, the Congo exported goods worth about 886,000 francs in the second half of 1886, rising to 4,250,000 for 1889.
[3] Leopold could already have seen the Berlin Act violated with impunity, as in the case of the practical monopoly granted in 1886 to the Royal Niger Company. (See *Africa and the Victorians* by R. Robinson, T. Gallagher, and A. Denny; 1961; pp. 182-3.)

CHAPTER XVII

REFORM AND REFERENDUM

WITHIN A FEW YEARS of the schools crisis, another and far more significant upheaval began in Belgium, which ended in the destruction of the old *censitaire* system and in the arrival of organized Socialism as the governing factor in Belgian politics. The schools war had been for Leopold little more than a nuisance, offering him no opportunities and diverting the national attention at a moment when he wanted it to fasten upon the Congo. But the advent of universal suffrage, in itself highly unwelcome to the view of monarchy he had inherited from his father, involved a major revision of the Constitution. In return for his assent, Leopold tried unsuccessfully to include in the revision certain ideas and principles which were central to his ideas of a new monarchy.

Leopold's new enemy, the Belgian labour movement, was now growing rapidly from foundations which had taken a long time to lay. The first significant co-operative, the 'Vooruit' of Ghent, had been founded in 1881. Other co-operatives and unofficial trades unions followed, but politically growth was still delayed by the movement's division into Walloon and Flemish parties. Two things helped them towards unity. One was the firedamp explosion in a colliery at Frameries, in April 1879, which killed 123 men and brought the whole region out on strike. Another was the middle-class Radical campaign for universal suffrage which revived in the early eighties. In the spring of 1885, after a hard winter of strikes and hunger, the various 'Socialist' groups finally united into the 'Parti Ouvrier Belge', whose 'Antwerp Programme', drawn up in August, contained a list of aims to be achieved by the conquest of parliamentary power through the franchise rather than by revolution. These aims included 'liberal' points like free and universal lay education and the separation of Church and State, as well as the legalization of trades unions and modern labour regulations: the party's immediate objective was the introduction of universal suffrage.

Revolution overtook the POB from behind. On March 18, 1886, an Anarchist group in Liège organized a meeting to commemorate the fifteenth anniversary of the Paris Commune. On the previous day, the miners of Jemeppe had begun a strike, and the meeting on the 18th turned into a major riot. In the next two days, the whole Liège area stopped work. Troops were sent in, but the strike spread quickly southwards into the Bassin du Centre and the Borinage.

The first of the great Walloon general strikes, of which the 1961 strike was the most recent, had begun. There was destruction of plant, on a massive scale; there were processions calling for a Republic and following the Red Flag; finally, there were deaths as troops began to open fire. When the strike finally subsided, the Government hunted down Socialist leaders, but 30,000 workers marched through the streets of Brussels in August, demonstrating for universal suffrage and threatening another general strike if nothing was done to satisfy them.

This unrest coincided with a lasting and important new movement within the Catholic party which called for state intervention to protect the worker against the consequences of free competition. The European wave of Christian Democracy was reaching Belgium. As the 1886 strike exploded, the 'social' Catholics Verhaegen and Helleputte were preparing the first of the Liège congresses[1] at which the party's left wing strove to persuade their colleagues that paternalism was outdated and that a militant Christian trades union was not necessarily a contradiction in terms.

Less idealistic Catholics saw that social reforms also offered a tactic which would embarrass the Liberals and disarm the Socialists. Beernaert, with Leopold's approval, resolved to remedy some of the grievances which both men considered a major cause of the undesirable tumult over the franchise. In a speech from the throne, Leopold said: 'We may have put too much confidence in the effectiveness of the fruitful principles of liberty, and it would be just if the law gave a special degree of protection to the weak and the unlucky.' A Commission of Inquiry set up by Beernaert revealed, among other things, a proportion of child

[1] 1886, 1887, 1890.

labour as high as a third of the work force in some factories: legislation was now introduced to regulate working conditions and to licence the activities of trades unions.

After two years of relative calm, broken by a public scandal over the use of police agents to provoke another strike, the universal suffrage movement returned to the attack in 1890 with a demonstration 80,000 strong in Brussels. Its organizers, the Socialists Anseele and Volders, sent an intoxicated telegram to the King: 'For your information: you asked for instructions from the nation. These instructions are: Universal Suffrage.' With the threat of another strike looming over Belgium, these demands could no longer be ignored, and Beernaert permitted the Radical leader Janson to move a revision of the Constitution.

The parliamentary committee examining Janson's motion was preparing to reject it, when once again a mining strike escaped the control of the POB and spread over the industrial area of Belgium. Lamely adopted by the Socialists, the strike changed the minds of the committee, who on May 20, 1891, accepted the principle of revision. But by now Leopold had entered the lists himself.

He wished to include in any revised Constitution three points of his own: the right to extend Belgian territory; the right of the King to control royal marriages; and the right of the King to call referenda. The inclusion of these demands and the agreement of all parties upon them, he told Beernaert, formed the *sine qua non* of his assent to a revision, and he hinted at possible abdication if they were not accepted. The first point was intended to help him when he came to hand the Congo over to Belgium, and to ease the ordeal of passing colonial legislation through an unwilling Parliament. The second harked back to Leopold's obsession with the patrimony as the backbone of a successful dynasty. He was claiming the right to use his sons and daughters, in the traditional Coburg fashion, as pawns in the game of alliance by marriage. Further, he hoped to escape the obligation imposed on him by Belgian law to divide his property among his children, which doomed him to waste his fortune on the husbands of his detested daughters at the expense of the male heir to the throne, his nephew Albert[1].

[1] Second son of the Count of Flanders. Baudouin, the elder son, heir to the throne after the death of the child Count of Hainaut, had died earlier in 1891, on January 23rd.

The demand for the right to call a popular referendum was entirely new. Then as now, the device evoked memories of Louis-Napoleon, and charges of 'Caesarism' were raised by Woeste on the Right as well as by the democrats of the Left. Leopold retorted with energy, calling in examples and useful quotations from history-books and newspapers collected from all over the world (where such approving articles had not be written, his agents tried to ensure that they were written at once). From London, he wrote to Beernaert: 'Dear Minister; Lord Salisbury attaches the utmost importance to the 'Royal Referendum'. He considers that no measure could be so useful and effective. He has been thinking for a long time about having one for England, and hopes one day to take a leaf out of Belgian legislation and introduce it over here'[1].

But hostility to his plan grew rather than diminished, and he was forced to explain his motives to Beernaert in greater detail. 'A referendum is a prudently democratic and patriotic measure. It is more of a widening of the powers of the electorate than an addition to the powers of the Crown. It allows the electorate the right to *reply*. It is in no way a step towards allowing the people to make laws directly. To try and ensure the smooth running of the parliamentary system can only strengthen it and thus discourage and prevent the substitution of any other system'[2].

In the long term, the institution of a 'Royal Referendum' would obviously have granted Leopold and his successors a control over the Cabinet which would have been intolerable in a constitutional monarchy. It would not only have acted as an immensely strengthened royal veto on a measure already approved by both Chambers (referendum *post legem*); it seems likely[3] that Leopold intended to use it as a lever to force the government of the day to introduce legislation he thought necessary. Leopold probably hoped to present Beernaert and his party with a massive popular majority in favour of personal military service and the abolition of *remplacement*. In such a case, could the Government have safely refused to carry out the popular will? It was against this referendum *ante legem* that the fiercest opposition was raised, led by the unforgiving Charles Woeste

[1] Daye; *Léopold II;* p. 382.
[2] Quoted in Daye; *Léopold II;* p. 385.
[3] See Count Louis de Lichtervelde; *Léopold II;* Brussels 1926; p. 332.

who called it 'the end of the political liberty which we have been enjoying for sixty years', and the King was ultimately driven to ask for the *post legem* variety by itself.

Even this failed to win the support of the Constituent Assembly, formed in 1892 to revise the Constitution. Leopold won both the control over royal marriages and the right to extend Belgian territory, but all forms of referendum were firmly rejected. Paradoxically, the King's proposals might have received more support if there had been Socialist deputies in the 'Constituante', for the Parti Ouvrier Belge, in drawing up its recommendations for revision, included both proportional representation and the right of popular referendum, and the idea of a plebiscite was a plank in the Socialist platform at the 1894 elections. Nor did Leopold entirely abandon the point. Before giving his assent to the new Constitution, he deposited a memorandum in a sealed envelope, to be opened after his death. This was done, in December 1909, and from beyond the grave Leopold's own obstinate, hectoring style was recognized for the last time.

'As I sanction the revised articles of the constitution, I wish posterity to understand that if I did not insist on the inclusion of a referendum in Article 26, it was because I was convinced that there is nothing in the Constitution to prevent the Government consulting the electorate directly. The passing of a bill is all that is necessary to permit such direct consultation'[1]. If he had really thought so, he left no indication why he had not bothered to say it at the time of the revision. But this phoney legal opinion—Leopold knew little about law and disregarded what he did know—helped to ensure that the referendum issue would become a recurrent nuisance in Belgian twentieth-century politics.

In March 1893, the Radicals in the Constituent Assembly agreed to accept universal suffrage (for men only) at the age of twenty-five, tempered by the grant of a double vote to heads of families. The right wing of the Liberal party and most of the Catholics refused to accept this compromise, and the Assembly was finally moved to reject the principle of universal suffrage altogether. The same night, that of April 11th, the Parti Ouvrier Belge launched its first deliberate General Strike, which brought

[1] Lichtervelde; *Léopold II;* p. 336.

out labour not only in the Walloon regions but in the cities of Flanders. Perhaps twenty people were killed in fights with security forces before, fearing a full revolution, Parliament for the second time surrendered to strike action. Only a week later, on the evening of the 18th, the Chamber passed a revision granting the vote to males of twenty-five, reserving plural votes for various categories, and the strike ended next day.

The Socialists proclaimed 'a first victory for the working class', but they were right to treat it as no more than a preliminary. It became apparent, as tempers cooled, that the plural votes allowed for were so numerous that only the poorest category of worker would have a single vote, and this discovery brought a number of disillusioned Radicals across into the POB[1]. This was tactically astute on their part, to say nothing of their deeper convictions, for the Parti Ouvrier Belge had become a formidable and efficient political organization during the years of agitation as the revision was being deliberated. And some of them remembered Frère-Orban's old warning that a wide breach in the franchise qualifications would let in a Catholic flood. Belgium was no different to the rest of Europe: with the introduction of universal suffrage, the progressive Liberals were about to achieve their mission of sawing off the branch on which they sat.

Meanwhile, the Catholic party worked hard to put harness on the newly-enfranchised Catholic masses. They had to be headed off from Socialism, and the new Encyclical *de Rerum Novarum* (1891) had come in time to provide useful instructions for the formation of Christian social and economic organizations. In the Flemish countryside, the new Catholic left had founded the 'Boerenbond' (Peasants' League) in 1890, and Helleputte founded his 'Ligue Democratique Belge' for the Catholic worker in the year of the Encyclical. In a massive and enduring shift of aim, the Catholics were turning their guns away from the highly-educated lawyers, teachers and aldermen of the towns, and sighting them on a new enemy. From 1894 onwards, the deepest preoccupation of politics was the determination of Catholic and Liberal to keep the Socialists out of power.

Leopold could see perfectly well that the soundest tactics for

---

[1] The total number of voters was multiplied almost by ten: to 1,370,000. But only 850,000 voters had a single vote, the remaining 520,000 disposing of 1,240,000 votes between them.

the Catholic party in future would be to outbid the Left by a programme of social legislation. As usual, he thought that he could get something out of this situation for himself. In 1886, he suggested to Beernaert that his party could profitably abolish the purchasing of exemption from military service—*remplacement*—as 'the only possible sop to Democracy which would also strengthen the fabric of society'. Like many elder Catholics, Leopold would have preferred a paternalistic Welfare State to universal suffrage.

Beernaert, however, would not play. The suggestion of abolishing *remplacement* always roused hysteria from those Catholics who regarded barracks at Satanic academies for the introduction of Catholic youth to swearing and brothels. Instead, he chose to help Leopold on another military matter which did not touch on the 'educational' neurosis. For years, the King and his propagandists had been calling for the fortification of the Meuse. Brialmont had only succeeded in antagonizing Frère-Orban when he suggested this plan in his *Situation Militaire de la Belgique*, published in 1882, but Emile Banning's memorandum 'Considérations politiques sur la défense de la Meuse', fell on the more sympathic ears of Beernaert and that in the more promising year of 1886. A noisy but largely false crisis was advancing on Europe. Another Bulgarian upheaval was opposing Russia and Austria-Hungary, and Bismarck, for his own purposes, was affecting to fear imminent attack by France. In France itself, General Boulanger was enjoying his brief but menacing day of influence, and the word *revanche* was popular. Neither side perhaps had any intention of attacking the other, but a game of ostentatious preparation was played, involving the usual jockeying for position around Belgium.

Subsequent history and a look at the atlas suggest that if you defend the line of the Meuse by fortifying Liège and Namur, you are trying to stop the Germans coming north-west towards the Channel. In the nineteenth century, people did not think that this was necessarily so. Not only the French but the Germans asked Belgium to put up forts along the river. When Count Brandenburg came to put this request to Beernaert in January 1887, it was the third time in less than thirty years that a German envoy had done so. It was too good an opportunity to miss, especially as Banning's secret memorandum had suggested that the forts would in the end be more useful against Germany herself, and after a struggle, Beernaert with the support of the King managed to get his Cabinet to agree to the preparation of a Meuse forts bill.

Leopold, however, wanted to go on still further and launch an attack against *remplacement* itself. He was in a state of high nervous excitement. Over the Meuse forts, he had written to Beernaert: 'I implore you with clasped hands, dear Minister, to demand and if necessary to insist that this be so!' He had seen Bismarck use the crisis to push a highly advantageous army bill at the Reichstag in November 1886, and then get his political enemies smashed at the polls for rejecting it. Perhaps something like this could be done in Belgium (the referendum quarrel was later to demonstrate Leopold's conviction that the masses were with him over the introduction of 'personal' military service). Imitating Bismarck again, the King offered Pope Leo XIII various privileges for the hierarchy in return for a little pressure exerted on the Belgian bishops in favour of conscription reform. But the cases were not really similar. There were no serious disabilities to be lifted from the Church in Belgium as there had been in Germany, and Leo finally refused to intervene.

Beernaert, though personally in favour of the measure, knew that in getting their support for the Meuse forts he had pushed his followers as far as he dared. Leopold invited and harangued deputies of both parties without much result, writing wildly to his Prime Minister: 'A majority in favour of personal military service does exist. If that majority cannot combine to vote in its favour, you will excuse my candour if I say that it will obviously be your fault.' But the measure—Leopold could rely only on a relation of one of his courtiers to introduce it—failed to pass.

In a famous speech at Bruges on August 15, 1887, a month after his bill's defeat, Leopold blew off steam and made his own appeal to those who soon would hold the vote. 'The Flemish Lion must not doze off . . . All liberty is born and dies with independence.' But popular interest in the topic of *remplacement* was already deflating, and stayed flat for a decade. The Catholic party retreated into cloudy schemes for a territorial *volontariat*, which would remove the need for any kind of conscription.

A few weeks later, Beernaert's appropriations for the Meuse forts were grudgingly voted by the Chamber. France had been echoing all year to rumours that the British were planning to allow German troops right of passage across Belgium, and Lord Salisbury evaded Beernaert's requests for a clear restatement of the British guarantee of Belgian neutrality. When the Meuse bill passed, part of the French Press affected to see the forts as a German rampart against France, especially after a Belgian official in the Ministry of the Interior named Nieter had sold France secret documents on the purpose of the new defences. Nastily edited, these documents were thrown back at Leopold by Paris newspapers in the course of 1888.

The years of crisis now gave way to a period of consolidation.

From the decade of conflict which opened in 1886, Belgium had emerged as a modern nation. The principles of universal suffrage and of state intervention to protect the weak against the strong had both been forced upon the two middle-class parties. Those who had made the 1831 Constitution to suit their own idea of the balance between liberty and order were now surrendering the controls of their machine to a class which might well decide to scrap it altogether. The Monarchy had been set up to defend liberty: Leopold tried in this period to transform it into the guardian of order. He wanted to use the 'Royal Referendum' to win a Belgian King powers proper to a chief of the executive, an initiator of laws. Secondly, he wanted to settle once and for all the form of the Army which the King constitutionally commanded, an essential protection against parliamentary interference. In both cases, he failed.

The fall of Beernaert in 1894 upset Leopold to the point of tears. Yet the two men were done with each other, and had disagreed about the Constitution, about the Army, about the Congo, and now about Beernaert's attempt to introduce proportional representation, which led to his defeat. More widely, Leopold could see now that all his plans to extend the influence of the Crown had done no more than keep pace with the growing power of Parliament. In the elections that autumn, thirty-four Socialist members entered the Chamber for the first time, facing fourteen dazed Liberal survivors and no less than 104 Catholics. To deal with this threatening future, Leopold was left with whatever use he could make of his existing powers, his money and his Congo. And in 1896, the Congo for the first time balanced its budget.

CHAPTER XVIII

EXPLORATION AND IVORY

THE BASIN OF A RIVER is not always easy to define, least of all in a continent still unsurveyed. A succession of maps suggesting progressively broader frontiers for the Free State had left Leopold's rivals with differing ideas about the shape of the political entity they had recognized at Berlin. Effective occupation was therefore a first task for him: a second was to take advantage of the general uncertainty by pushing the frontiers as far outwards as they would go.

The late eighties in the Congo formed a period of expeditions: its consequence in the early nineties was a period of Arab wars and Bantu mutiny. In 1888, in spite of the enduring lack of money, Leopold organized expeditions up the Uele and the Aruwimi, tributaries of the Congo which led towards the interesting and unoccupied regions of the Bahr-el-Ghazal and the upper Nile. Other parties prepared to take the Congo flag southwards into the Lunda country, towards the fringe of Portuguese influence in Angola, and into the remote Garangaze, the land which came to be called Katanga.

At Bunkeya, now a small town on the road running north from Jadotville, a highly organized and autocratic African state had set its capital. Dr Slade has described it as 'the latest of a long series of conquest states going back at least to the sixteenth century'[1]. Ruled by Msiri, the son of a Nyamwezi trader, the state followed the tradition of earlier Luba-Lunda states by trading with the Portuguese at the ocean coasts to east and west. For guns and gunpowder, Msiri returned copper from the Katanga mines, ivory and slaves; the traders who came to his court, through the fence knobbed with human skulls which surrounded it, were followed in 1886 by British missionaries who failed to change Msiri's way of life but who felt it necessary, through one of their number sent back to London in 1888, to

[1] Ruth Slade; *King Leopold's Congo;* London 1962; p. 119.

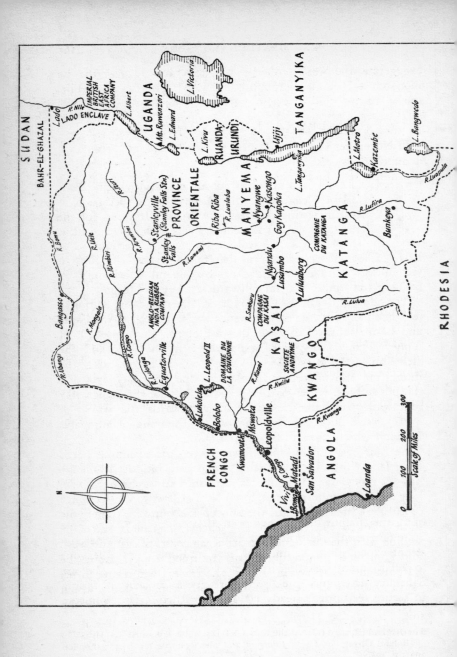

exaggerate the wealth of the kingdom and to describe its monarch as ' . . . a thorough gentleman'[1]. The British public, inured to this kind of preliminary to an appeal for funds, was not greatly impressed. But from the south, Cecil Rhodes believed he saw an opening for his British South Africa Company.

In November 1890, Vice-Consul Sharpe turned up at Bunkeya, despatched by Rhodes' friend Harry Johnston, consul at Mozambique. The missionary Swan spoiled his chances of getting Msiri to accept a cession treaty by translating it in full to the King, but this failure was not known for some time in Europe, where Leopold was fighting persistently to get Rhodes off the Katanga. In July 1890, he protested to Lord Salisbury that Harry Johnston was circulating maps showing the Free State falling short of Katanga and was touting political treaties in Free State territory to the south-west of Lake Tanganyika. 'I fear that there will be complications,' he ended, 'and I am forced to take protective measures'[2]. Belgian expeditions were preparing, but it was a long journey to the Katanga.

If Leopold thought that the Foreign Office was giving orders to Rhodes, he was wrong: Rhodes was leading and the Office reluctantly followed. But he was right about Johnston. On August 25th, in London, Johnston wrote a foolishly aggressive letter to Salisbury in which he attacked Leopold's claims to 'the richest country in minerals (gold and copper) in all Central Africa'. He argued, prematurely, that Msiri was now ready to place his territories under Her Majesty's protection, and that 'the King of the Belgians has no right to it (the Katanga). On the official maps of the Congo Free State territory issued by him after the Berlin Congress, he does not even include it in his dominions. Of late, though, through the indulgent carelessness of British mapmakers, it has been allotted to the Congo Free State on the map, and now the King . . . is about to despatch a strong expedition there under M. Delcommune . . . to endeavour to collar Garangaze either by cajolery or force.' Five days before, Salisbury had signed the Anglo-Portuguese Convention, failing to secure territories already claimed by Rhodes, and Johnston

[1] *Ibid.*, p. 127. The black-spectacled Godefroid Munongo, 'Minister of the Interior' and effective ruler of the Katanga secession, is a grandson of Msiri's.
[2] Roland Oliver; *Sir Harry Johnston and the Scramble for Africa;* London 1961; p. 194.

F

hoped to prevent a similar disavowal in Katanga. Leopold, he jeered, 'has by many a hook and crook, by many a wile and intrigue, by much expenditure of his own and not a little subscribed by the rich English people whom he bamboozled, created a fine African empire for little Belgium. But why his enterprise should be viewed by *us* . . . with indulgence . . . I cannot conceive'[1].

Effective occupation of the Katanga was the only satisfactory answer to these British experiments: as he waited for his expeditions to arrive, Leopold fought back by personal diplomacy. In London, when he came over in March 1891, he raised another fuss with Salisbury and tried to block Johnston's posting as Consul-General north of the Zambezi. When in April the South Africa Company asserted that Msiri had granted a concession, he protested to Queen Victoria and the Prince of Wales, as well as to Salisbury who was obliged to admit on May 29th that the rumour was false. In the Congo, Lieutenant Paul le Marinel arrived at Bunkeya and founded a Free State post nearby in April. Alexandre Delcommune joined him in October, and at the end of the year a strong expedition led by the British mercenary Captain Stairs for the new 'Compagnie du Katanga' came in from the East coast. Stairs was a brusque man who soon tired of Msiri's evasions and hoisted the Congo flag over Bunkeya. Taking fright, Msiri retreated a few miles to a village where he was overtaken by Stairs' colleague Captain Bodson: in the course of a violent and mysterious quarrel, Bodson killed the King of Garangaze with his revolver and was fatally shot in the stomach by the bodyguard.

Bodson had certainly behaved like a *condottierre*, but the whole region rejoiced to be free of Msiri's tyranny. Stairs installed a pliant successor, who set his mark to all the necessary treaties, and despatched the engineer Jules Cornet to make the first scientific survey of the Katanga's mineral wealth. The frontier between the Katanga and what was later to become the British protectorate of Northern Rhodesia was settled in a section of the Anglo-Congolese Agreement of May 12, 1894.

Several hundred miles to the west, the territory of another old Luba-Lunda empire was being quietly slipped out of the hands of the Portuguese. Another vagueness of mapping had left un-

[1] *Ibid.*, p. 194, note 2.

defined the Angola-Congo border to the east of the Kwango, a large river which flows roughly northwards from the centre of Angola and empties into the Congo above Leopoldville, and the Portuguese had suggested in 1888 that the position ought to be cleared up. To the east of the Kwango lay the confederation of Lunda peoples whose traditional ruler held the title of 'Mwata Yamvo'. The Portuguese now claimed that the Mwata Yamvo was bound to them by treaty, and that the frontier eastwards from the river might therefore be drawn as a continuation of the agreed frontier on the west bank. This lay along the parallel of six degrees south, and its extension threatened Leopold's projects up the Kasai with uncomfortable constriction.

Without telling anybody, Leopold sent out an expedition to the Kwango commanded by Lieutenant Dhanis, later to become the most famous of all Free State soldiers. Obeying secret orders, Dhanis plunged southwards up the course of the Kwango as far as Capenda-Camulemba, a point almost at nine degrees south which even now is far into Angola. On June 10, 1890, Leopold proclaimed a new district of 'East Kwango' to incorporate the ground which Dhanis had won, and a furious quarrel opened beween Brussels and Lisbon. Leopold looked around for suitable weapons to use against the Portuguese but found none. However, his opinion of Portugal remained a poor one, and he appears to have decided that Lisbon might secretly thank him for some sort of ultimatum which would allow honourable withdrawal, comparable to the ultimatum which the Powers had been obliging enough to issue at the end of the Berlin Conference. How could the infant Congo show teeth it did not possess? Leopold decided to hire a gunboat.

Later in 1890, the incredulous Lieutenant Liebrechts found himself in a London hotel, charged by his King to purchase a second-hand gunboat with ammunition and crew which would sail up the Tagus and hold the city of Lisbon up to ransom. Liebrechts mooned about shipping agencies, arousing bewilderment and then suspicion. He left one hotel because the staff were being asked awkward questions and moved to another; finally he found a gunboat in dock at Poplar, armed and more or less ready to sail. It was at this point, according to Liebrechts[1], that the wildness of what he was doing broke on his conscious-

[1] Liebrechts; *Léopold II, Fondateur d'Empire;* p. 182.

ness, and ignoring further orders to buy the vessel at Poplar, he came home to Brussels and was severely reprimanded. It is a good story, but in some particulars a fishy one. Something definite might emerge if records of British police surveillance were available, but in the meantime it seems not unlikely that the whole episode was rigged to impress the Foreign Office at a moment when the Anglo-Portuguese boundaries in Central Africa were under discussion.

Whether the British intervened for Leopold or not, a cabinet crisis in Portugal led to a change of Foreign Minister, and to a new readiness to negotiate. At the talks which began in February 1891, the Portuguese brandished their treaties with the Mwata Yamvo, and there ensued another sanctimonious European wrangle over the nature of Bantu political authority. However, Leopold's representatives were able to demonstrate that the Lunda kingdom was in disintegration—in 1887 the Bachokwe tribe, a well-armed nation of slave-raiders, had invaded the Kwango region and chased the Mwata Yamvo into western Katanga[1]—and the final agreement with Portugal left the Congo with most of Dhanis' claims up the right bank of the Kwango.

But the Kwango and even the Katanga were not the most important targets of Leopold's expansion. The copper of the Katanga, promising as it was, would take time and great capital expenditure to exploit. The Kwango brought him little but a tactical advantage over Portugal. Economically, Leopold wanted the quick profits of a commodity which required no processing before sale and with very high value by weight. Ivory, and later wild rubber and copal, suited this piratical and primitive view of exploitation. Strategically, Leopold wanted to occupy an inland region which would allow him to command Central Africa, and here there was never any choice between possible alternatives: he wanted a foothold on the Nile. It was a decisive coincidence of interests that these drier north-eastern lands of the upper Nile plateau and the south Sudan were the home of great herds of elephants.

A few years later, Leopold asked one of his ministers if he found nothing exciting in the idea of becoming a Pharaoh[2]. His

[1] Biebuyck and Douglas; *Congo Tribes and Parties;* London 1961; p. 21. M. Moise Tshombe, 'President' of Katanga, is the present Mwata Yamvo's son-in-law.

[2] Daye; *Léopold II;* p. 413.

first involvement with Africa had been his visits to Egypt and the sight of the great trenches of the Canal works, and he had retained a weakness for tinselly historical comparisons, whether to Rameses of Godfrey de Bouillon. Such romanticisms, however, did not for a moment relax his vulpine attention to the chances presented by the political misfortunes of greater countries.

The Sudan remained under the control of the Mahdists. Khartoum had fallen in 1885, and the last outpost of Egyptian rule was the crowded camp at Lado where Gordon's eccentric German subordinate Emin Pasha sat tranquilly beleaguered with 10,000 men and women in his garrison and a stock of ivory worth £60,000. In 1886, a mild letter from Emin reached Europe, suggesting that he would like to be rescued by England. The British Government, to the disgust of public opinion in its own country, hastily passed the responsibility to Germany: British negligence might have allowed the Mahdi to conquer the Sudan, but Emin (a Moslem convert) was a German subject. This did not distress Leopold, who had been fishing for an invitation to help Gordon and his officers ever since the revolt began. Mackinnon and Hutton set about organizing a private expedition, and cabled Stanley in America with an offer of the leadership. Leopold and Strauch fiddled about with a scheme to use Stanley themselves to extricate Emin and to send London a bill for £60,000, the price of Emin's tusks. This coming to nothing, Leopold put pressure on Mackinnon and Stanley to send their expedition up the Congo instead of by the obvious and easier route from the East Coast and Zanzibar, and at a meeting with Stanley in January 1887, persuaded him to offer Emin 300,000 francs down and an annual salary of 37,000 francs to become Governor of an Equatorial province of the Free State on the upper Nile.

Stanley went to Zanzibar to recruit porters. There he met Tippo Tib, the princely and intelligent Arab who ruled a slaving empire on the upper Congo and the Lualaba, and whose presence as chief of a state within the Congo State was causing Leopold increasing difficulty. After conversations conducted in the British Consulate, Tippo Tib accepted the ruthlessly logical short-term solution which Leopold, through Stanley, proposed to him, and became 'Governor of Stanleyville' for the Free State at a salary of £30 a month. Leopold intended to use the Emin Pasha expedition for his own ends: those ends demanded that the expedition should arrive from the Congo direction, and that could not be achieved unless the Arabs were prepared to let Stanley pass. For such a result, accusations of hypocrisy raised by humanitarians in Europe were a small price to pay. The Congo State, founded with the purpose of abolishing the slave-trade had just installed the most powerful slaver in Africa as Governor of part of its territory. Questions were inevitable: in reply, Leopold was able to produce an undertaking signed by Tippo Tib to prevent slave-trading by Arabs or Africans within his province. Leopold cannot have taken this document seriously. Curiously enough, Tippo Tib did, and his attempts to interfere in the trade of his vassals raised resentment against his authority which later exploded into disastrous rebellion.

With 800 of Tippo Tib's men and a huge retinue of local Africans, some of whom were cannibals, Stanley fought his way up the Congo and north-west into the Ituri forest. The country lay devastated in his wake, but the terrain through which he now marched was the most appalling he ever had to encounter in a life of travelling. He swore, bullied and flogged: his men died by the hundred. Emin, once reached, refused Leopold's offer on the grounds that the Congo Free State was too fragile a structure to last long, and inflamed Stanley by hinting that perhaps he would rather not be rescued after all. Lugged down to the east coast by Stanley, which they reached only in December 1889, Emin fell shortsightedly off a balcony during their first evening of civilization at Bagamoyo and fractured his skull. Stanley left him in hospital and went off home to Europe, where, on his last return from Africa, he received the welcome of a hero. In Brussels, in a Bourse decorated with Congolese spears and with 400 elephant tusks sprouting from a monstrous centre-piece of foliage, Leopold himself spoke in Stanley's honour. He had already picked his brains elaborately in a series of private interviews, but the truth was that Stanley had failed in the last job entrusted to him by the King of the Belgians. The upper Nile was still unclaimed.

In letters to Greindl, now Belgian Ambassador in Berlin, Leopold was not ashamed to suggest to Bismarck that the presence of the Free State as far east as the Bahr-el-Ghazal and Lake

Tanganyika would help the German operations against slavers on the coast, and he won some support in Berlin[1]. From the British, he gained an illusory triumph by a convention signed on May 24, 1890, with Mackinnon's Imperial British East Arica Company, allowing the Congo's 'sphere of influence' to come up to the left bank of the upper Nile to face the British sphere on the right bank. Unfortunately, this agreement conflicted with Salisbury's decision in late 1889 that the Nile and its affluents should remain 'inviolable'[2], and a month after its signature, it was pushed contemptuously aside by Salisbury's Anglo-German Agreement, the major treaty defining British and German frontiers in East Africa, which the Prime Minister personally emended to give Britain 'the western watershed of the Nile'. This seemed to include the Bahr-el-Ghazal through which a Congolese expedition would have to approach the river[3].

The interval of power in the south Sudan would not last long. Bands of Emin's troops still survived along the course of the upper Nile, although the departure of their commander had cancelled their claim to form an outpost of Anglo-Egyptian occupation. Leopold had to act fast, before the British advanced north from Uganda or the French made the long leap across the plains from the Atlantic. Jerome Becker, a secret emissary, was sent to Tippo Tib to make him an offer for his ivory and to promise him 200,000 francs if he would establish three posts up in the Bahr-el-Ghazal and another on the Nile itself, but Tippo Tib, already in difficulty with his own subordinates, found a reason to refuse.

Every attempt to get to the Nile on the cheap having failed, Leopold was forced to finance an expedition of his own. In 1890, Van Kerckhoven and Ponthier set off up the Congo. Leopold hoped that their small army would pay its way by collecting ivory as it marched, but the troops were too busy killing and burning to look for tusks; Ponthier involved himself in a savage war with the Babuja tribe, north of the Congo. On the Uele, the river which forms the northern border of the Congo, treaties were signed with the chiefs and reinforcements bought in

[1] R. P. P. Ceulemans; *La Question Arabe et le Congo;* Académie Royale des Sciences Coloniales; Mémoires (nouvelle série) Vol. 22, pp. 145-6.
[2] Quoted in Robinson, Gallagher and Denny; *Africa and the Victorians;* p. 285.
[3] *Ibid.*, p. 295, note 5.

exchange for rifles, but in August 1892, Van Kerckhoven himself was accidently killed in a battle, and command was taken over by Lieutenant Milz. Emerging into the Bahr-el-Ghazal, Milz managed to make contact with survivors of Emin's forces, and on October 9th, indifferent to the British claim of 1890 to the western watershed of the river, he arrived on the bank of the Nile.

CHAPTER XIX

NILE INTRIGUE AND ARAB WAR

L EOPOLD WAS ON THE NILE at last, but his position seemed a highly precarious one. Physically, it was so far stretched from its Atlantic base as to be almost untenable, and a revolt among Emin's ex-officers in 1893 (they had tried to do the same thing to Stanley) actually drove Milz's successor off the river. Diplomatically, the position defied the Anglo-German Agreement of 1890, and the fort built by Milz at Ganda in the Bahr-el-Ghazal defied the Franco-Congolese arrangements after Berlin which had set the Congolese boundary of influence at four degrees north.

Once again, Leopold used the very weakness of the Congo State as a source of strength. In 1892, the British pressed him to renounce the Mackinnon Agreement, and for a time, Leopold allowed France to suppose that he might be prepared to share the Upper Nile basin with them. Did the British want a direct clash with France at this point? Salisbury argued nervously that he had never approved the Mackinnon Treaty, but Leopold had personally shown the unsigned draft to him in London, and a letter from Salisbury to Leopold exists, dated May 21, 1890, in which the Prime Minister tells the King that 'I have assured myself that no objection will be raised by the Foreign Office concerning the engagements contracted by Your Majesty as Head of the Congo State and by Sir William Mackinnon's Company'[1]. A month later, in the middle of the Anglo-German negotiations, Salisbury regretted his generosity and told Leopold that rights granted to the Congo by a private company could not be sovereign rights. Leopold's rough-and-ready view of constitutional law had always been that a company could indeed dispose of sovereign rights, but he sent Salisbury a modified definition of the rights ceded him by Mackinnon. Neither he

[1] Quoted in Baron P. van Zuylen; *l'Echiquier Congolais;* Brussels 1959; p. 238. Letter in Palace Archives; Brussels.

nor Mackinnon actually signed this 'codicil', as Salisbury noticed, so neither the Treaty nor the British objection to its validity were changed.

If he had been Britain's only rival on the upper Nile, Leopold could not have resisted for a month. But he was not. On May 3, 1893, Carnot, President of the Republic, made the decision that French forces must prepare to march east across the continent and occupy Fashoda on the White Nile[1], and by early 1894 the Foreign Office was aware of these plans. From being very weak, Leopold's position now stood revealed as rather strong: he was already at the Nile, which British forces were not, and some temporary recognition of his position there would at least provide the British with a useful buffer against the French advance from the west.

As soon as certain news came from Paris about French intentions, the British opened secret talks with Leopold. In return for the abandonment of the Mackinnon Treaty and recognition of the British sphere of influence as defined in the Anglo-German Agreement, he was offered a lease of the Bahr-el-Ghazal and of the left bank of the Nile as far north as Fashoda. Leopold haggled over the duration of this lease, which he originally wanted to be terminable 'only if Belgium became a republic or if the Congo passed to other hands': an interesting reminder of Leopold's underlying intention to use the Congo as the treasury of the Belgian Coburgs. The Foreign Office rejected this transparent invitation to guarantee the Belgian system of monarchy, and the final terms of the agreement gave Leopold the left bank up to Fashoda for his lifetime, the Bahr-el-Ghazal being let to him and his successors in an arrangement 'terminable by notice'[2].

The Agreement was signed on April 12th, so privately that even the Congo's deluded foreign affairs secretary observed on April 20th that the French 'seemed to imagine that the Congolese government is somehow in league with the English . . . '[3] A French delegation led by Hanotaux had in fact arrived in Brussels to buy Leopold off the path to the Nile, only a few days too late, and Leopold managed to persuade the British to post-date the treaty to May 12th.

[1] A. J. P. Taylor; 'Prelude to Fashoda: The Question of the Upper Nile, 1894-5'; *English Historical Review;* January 1950; p. 54.

[2] *Ibid.*, p. 56.

[3] *Ibid.*, p. 55, Note 3.

He felt already that he might have gone too far, and he was right. To the dismay of Belgian ministers, as ignorant of the existence of the Anglo-Congolese Treaty as anybody else, the publication of the Treaty brought furious reactions from France and Germany. The French objected to the Congolese barrier raised across their line of advance; the Germans protested against Article 3 of the agreement, which leased Britain a strip of Congo territory (next to German East Africa) for the passage of the mythical Cape-Cairo railway, and added threats to the British position in Egypt. Gradually, the British sector of the Anglo-Belgian front began to crumble, leaving Leopold fatally exposed. In June, Britain abandoned Article 3 and the 'corridor'. A few weeks later, the Liberal cabinet (in power since 1892) refused to allow Rosebery, the Foreign Secretary, to support Leopold against French pressure, and in August, Leopold had to sign a new convention with France, which left him only the west bank of the Nile as far north as 5 degrees 30 minutes, a remnant which came to be known as the 'Lado Enclave'. Leopold had been officially registered on the Nile at last, but only at the price of recognizing the far stronger British and French claims in the region. Wary though he was, Leopold had let himself be used by the British as Portugal had been used on the lower Congo in 1883-4, and in the face of international protest, he was discarded with the same alacrity.

In these years, when he needed all his available resources for the north-eastern thrust into the watershed of the upper Nile, Leopold's effort in the Congo had been largely diverted between 1891 and 1894 by war with the Arabs of the Manyema. These wars, which began as Tippo Tib's authority on the upper Congo disintegrated, were fierce and difficult: the courage of Belgian officers in action against the slavers gave rise to a cycle of generous legends which are still precious to their countrymen and which play an important part in the patriotic education of Belgian children. Inevitably, the necessity of the myth has done strange things to the personalities involved in it. The Arabs, even Tippo Tib, appear as pagan fiends with carmine lips, bottomlessly deceitful and cruel. The Belgian officers, Dhanis and Lothaire, Chaltin and de Bruyne, charge with the sainted fearlessness of those Belgian Papal Zouaves who fell for Charlotte in Mexico, while at home their snow-bearded King rides across the park at Laeken and dreams of more enslaved millions to emancipate.

The Arab presence in Central Africa, however, did not bring the Bantu peoples unmitigated evil, any more than Leopold's motives in destroying it rose exclusively from concern for the slaves. It was true that slavery had been inseparable from the Arab trade in ivory which brought them steadily further into the interior in the course of the nineteenth century, for only slave-labour could produce the porters necessary to carry the heavy tusks down to the coast. In the coastal regions, and even on the shores of Lake Tanganyika, the Arabs had bought slaves for iron goods or cloth from local chiefs. Further inland, in the forest regions of the Manyema to the west of the Lakes, African society was fragmented into isolated villages often at war with each other, and it was easier to collect slaves by raiding or by inciting raids than by buying them. The result was anarchy and depopulation which spread steadily down the Upper Congo from the Lualaba and the Lomami, where in the 1870's Tippo Tib was establishing his empire[1]. Villages blazed to ashes and recalcitrant populations were massacred, as often by their neighbours greedy for the slave-price of guns and powder as by the Arabs themselves. Slave-raiding had been a practice in Central Africa long before the Arabs arrived, but with their encouragement it became a devastating plague. Yet there was something to be allowed to the credit of the Arab presence as well. Where the tribes were sufficiently centralized to be able to learn, the Arabs had much to teach about administration, and through the use of scribes working in Arabic, offered local rulers the elements of a modern bureaucracy, as they had once offered the Normans in Sicily the services of a treasury department. Except in a few places, their influence in Africa did not last long enough to be effective, but they brought about the spread of Swahili as a common language throughout East and Central Africa, and economically they were responsible for a revolution in African diet, introducing mango, orange and avocado trees, beans, onions, garlic and tomatoes to the continent.

Some British administrators in East Africa have regretted that the Arabs did not establish a fully-fledged political empire over the whole area, providing the incoming European overlords with a sophisticated class with whom to collaborate. But to Leopold,

[1] Ceulemans; *Question Arabe;* p. 33.

allowing for his attempt at co-existence while Tippo Tib was Governor of Stanley Falls, the Arabs seemed a force not of collaboration but of competition. It would be facile to explain the Arab wars as a fight for the wealth of the Congo: it was as much an inevitable clash over political sovereignty, and moral indignation against slavery certainly came into play on the Belgian side. But commercial rivalry was an important determining cause both of tension and of the outbreak itself.

When Stanley first founded the Falls station in 1883, he had urged the Arabs to export their ivory down the Congo rather than across the difficult land route to the Indian Ocean and Zanzibar. On the East Coast as well, there was a general move by European companies to channel the ivory trade and to collect the high profit margin between the Arab price and the price obtainable in Europe. But it was clear from the start that this profit would be still higher if the Arabs could be eliminated and the ivory bought directly from African hunters. Coquilhat, a senior Congo official, found that he could buy ivory from Africans for 82 centimes a pound and could sell it in Liverpool for 12 francs 50 centimes—a profit of over 1500 per cent, before deduction of transport costs[1].

He had, in fact, no business to do so. The charter of the Congo Free State, in the opinion of the rest of the world, allowed it to construct and police the great market-hall of Central Africa, so that the private companies of the West could safely do business there. It was not at all the rôle of the State to buy and sell in the Congo on its own behalf. But almost from the beginning of its legal existence, the desperate lack of money had forced the State into commerce, principally in ivory. State agents, already playing the parts of administrator and explorer, were encouraged to add the duties of trader, although this activity was as far as possible concealed from the public in Europe and America. In 1888, however, the steamers of commercial companies appeared on the Upper Congo and headed for the piles of tusks stored at the Arab landings. It was no longer possible to disguise the fact that the State was in direct competition with private traders, and a Dutch company soon began to lodge protests at Brussels. Both sides were prepared to sell the Arabs arms and ammunition in exchange for ivory, in spite of the State's own regulation for-

[1] Ceulemans; *Question Arabe;* p. 195, Note 2.

bidding the use of firearms as exchange, and in the same year
Liebrechts, commanding at Leopoldville, managed to impound
the Dutch company's stock of guns in its warehouse at Stanley
Pool. This was a great help to Leopold's emissaries Becker and
Tobback, who arrived at Stanley Falls in February 1889 to buy
ivory from Tippo Tib, as well as to propose that he should found
stations for the State in the Bahr-el-Ghazal (the State at this
period was paying one bolt rifle for 275 kilograms of ivory[1]).

In the same year, the Brussels Anti-Slavery Conference had
been manipulated by Leopold to allow him to impose a ten per
cent import duty on goods entering the Congo, and to renew
his mandate to suppress the slave-trade on behalf of the Powers.
The import duty infuriated the Dutch and exacerbated the
struggle for Arab ivory on the Upper Congo. A damaging piece
of evidence on State methods rose to light in 1891, in the form
of a letter from Lieutenant Tobback at Stanley Falls which was
forwarded to Tippo Tib at Zanzibar; addressed to his subordinate Arab rulers in the Manyema, it suggested that they should
sell ivory only to State agents and should entirely exclude the
offers of the private traders. Tippo Tib, who knew as well as
Leopold how to play off the strong to the benefit of his own
interests, showed this letter to the British Consul in Zanzibar,
and the British Government complained to Brussels of a flagrant
and radical violation of the Berlin Act[2]. Van Eetvelde, who was
Leopold's 'administrator-general' for the foreign affairs of the
Congo, announced that the letter was a forgery, but he was not
generally believed, and German and to a lesser extent British
traders continued to offer arms and ammunition for ivory in
breach both of the Brussels Act of 1889 and of the Congolese
regulations. If the State was acting illegally for commercial
advantage, why should not they? Even in Belgium, where private interests in the Congo were principally represented by the
'Société Anonyme Belge pour le commerce du Haut-Congo'[3],
founded by Albert Thys, there were outcries against the unfair
competition of State trading in ivory, to which Beernaert tranquilly retorted: 'In spite of pressure, the Belgian State has not
abolished productive work in prisons . . .'

[1] Ceulemans; *Question Arabe;* p. 205.
[2] *Ibid.*, pp. 218-9.
[3] Usually abbreviated to 'Société Anonyme Belge'

A head-on collision between monopoly and free-trade was now becoming inevitable : its consequences were to govern the future existence and ultimate destruction of the Congo State. But meanwhile, a rapid worsening of political relations between Europeans and Arabs inflamed the basic antagonism of the rival intruders. Stanley, emerging at last on the East Coast with Emin Pasha, had sued Tippo Tib for failing to support his expedition as he had promised : the Governor of Stanley Falls had been deeply offended, and leaving his province to his nephew Rashid, set out in May 1890 for Zanzibar to argue his case. The tail of the Van Kerckhoven expedition had already devastated the countryside it traversed and plundered ivory from the Arab caravans it encountered. In May 1892, Africans apparently instigated by Arabs attacked a private trading expedition led by M. Hodister, and its members were tortured, killed and in some cases eaten.

Tippo Tib, who might have controlled the situation, was now down at the coast, more than a thousand miles away, and the unity of his own satraps began to break up. Van Kerckhoven's men had taken more than 2,000 tusks off their caravans, ruining their credit with the private trading companies; now a Belgian anti-slavery post on Lake Tanganyika began to interfere with east-bound caravans, not only to liberate the slaves but to levy export duty on the ivory they were carrying. The final provocation came in late 1892. Tippo Tib's favourite slave, Ngongo Lutete, who had been in charge of his master's interests on the upper Lomami, was defeated in a clash with Dhanis and surrendered his allegiance to the Free State. An ultimatum from Sefu, Tippo Tib's son, was rejected, and in November the Arabs attacked Ngongo Lutete and were in turn attacked by the Congo 'Force Publique'.

The war had begun, and it is arguable that Dhanis himself did much deliberately to provoke it[1]; launching an immediate offensive, he won victory after victory against the Arabs, delayed in his advance only by a lack of trained reinforcements, for Ngongo Lutete's men, though brave enough, preferred to follow victory by a banquet off the dead than by a proper pursuit[2].

[1] See Slade; *King Leopold's Congo;* p. 110.
[2] O. Michaux; *Carnet de Campagne;* Namur 1913; quoted in Slade; *King Leopold's Congo;* p. 111.

Ngongo Lutete himself was executed for treachery in September
1893 by a junior officer who did not bother to consult Dhanis or
to verify the charges, and the resentment which this ungrateful
act ignited among Ngongo Lutete's Batetela followers came
home to roost a few years later in the first of a series of cata-
strophic 'Force Publique' mutinies led by Batetela soldiers.

By early 1894, Dhanis had won his war. Islam's latest and perhaps most astonishing empire collapsed under the fire of Belgian
machine-guns and Krupp artillery, before its walls had time to
harden. Its two elaborately-planned capitals, Kasongo and
Nyangwe, the great plantations of rice and potatoes, the orchards
of citrus fruits and the fields of sugar-cane fell into the hands of
the Congo State, which took care to maintain them and to keep
locally in being something of the 'indirect rule' relationship
between Bantu chiefs and central authority which the Arabs
had established.

In Belgium, the destruction of the slave-trade and the honours
won for Belgian arms earned Leopold's Congo a huge, if
transient, popularity, and abroad gained him a certain respite
from international criticism of his commercial and administrative methods in Africa. It encouraged the German campaign
against the Arabs, and, among other effects, presented the British
with a useful argument for the retention of Nyasaland: Sir Percy
Anderson, in charge of the 'Foreign Office Empire' in Africa,
minuted in February 1894: 'Nyasaland cannot be abandoned.
The Arabs, hard pressed by the German and Congo State forces,
would make it their stronghold'[1].

Leopold could now assert effective authority throughout his
monstrous African estates. No third party diverted his attention
from the private companies gnawing at wealth he regarded as
his own. The Berlin Act was a scrap of paper to the King of the
Belgians: the foreign traders no more than squatters in the
Palace grounds. Once these traders had helped him. Now they
obstructed the great design of exploitation which was already
raising its walls around the Congo[1].

[1] Quoted in Oliver; *Sir Harry Johnston*; p. 245.
[2] The British Government, at least, had been aware of the Congo's move
towards State monopoly as early as 1884, before the Berlin Act created the
Free State. See R. Oliver; *Sir Harry Johnston*; p. 49.

CHAPTER XX

LEOPOLD AND THE
ANTI-SLAVERY CONFERENCE OF 1889

LEOPOLD WAS NOW FIFTY-FIVE. The deviously slow maturing of a Coburg was complete: his attitudes towards his family and his governments had taken permanent form behind almost impassible barriers of formality. His way of life, with compartments for unbridled enjoyment hidden behind a hard cladding of routine, was established.

To his parents, he had been an alarmingly feeble child. As a young man, a 'weak chest' and a noticeable sciatic limp suggested that he might not live long, and added to the helpful legend of his 'spiritual' nature. The truth was that Leopold enjoyed a constitution of iron, and his daily routine exhausted not only the minds but the bodies of his equerries. He would get up at half-past five, take a shower followed by a massage (like many robust men of high nervous energy, he was a terrible hypochondriac), dress, and attack the morning papers and his first post, which he would open and read as he walked about the garden at Laeken. Some of these letters would already have been answered by breakfast-time, when Leopold would sit down to a massive English meal of poached eggs, fruit, weak tea, toast and an astonishing quantity of marmalade. His care for his own health did not prevent him from eating whatever was put in front of him, and in a Paris hotel he once called for and ate a dish of buttered potatoes which had just been refused by a jockey at the next table. This greed was offset by a habit of drinking glasses of hot water as an emetic, which were brought to him at intervals through the day, and by the fact that a large proportion of his business was conducted on the march. With rapid, limping strides, he kept moving along the alleys and drives of the Laeken gardens, sometimes in bleak silence, sometimes dictating letters to a male secretary who had trouble in keeping up with him. When forced to sit in his office to receive officials, he remained an intimidating and difficult master, elusive and yet mercilessly sarcastic, glaring through his pince-nez when too closely pressed and constantly fiddling with the end of his fan-shaped white beard or the plaque of an Order on his tunic. Lunch was a silent, gobbling break between more walks in the garden and the slitting open of more posts.

His favourite moment of the day was probably the arrival of *The Times* from London, the paper which remained his oracle all through his life. Leopold was a skilled corrupter of journalists and could usually get important papers to use the stories he provided for them, but the fact that he could not get round *The Times* did not lessen his affection for it. Every afternoon, the guard of the Ostend-Basle express would slip it into a special sheath and throw it out of the train as it ran through Parc-Royal station, to be picked up by a Palace attendant, ironed by a footman to kill the germs and make it easier to read, and finally handed to the King to be studied and annotated in bed at night.

In February 1909, however, *The Times* at last conceded its approval to the anti-Congolese campaign which was publishing such deadly evidence about Leopold's methods in Africa. The old King made a great show of stopping his subscription. 'This paper is systematically malicious,' he told a courtier, 'and there is no point in Our reading it. Many statesmen consider that it's better to read no newspapers at all: Lord Salisbury, Mr Balfour and M. Clemenceau share this view'[1]. His gesture made, Leopold secretly arranged that his valet should travel daily to the Gare du Nord in Brussels and buy *The Times* off the station bookstall.

Leopold was becoming obstinate, in small matters and in his political tactics. The episode of the Brussels Anti-Slavery Conference, which opened in 1889, revealed that while Leopold was as alert as ever to the broader possibilities offered by a situation, he was becoming dangerously inflexible in the detailed business of political bargaining. He was finding it increasingly difficult to make any sort of concession, even a tactical retreat which would bring a greater advance in some other field, and several

[1] Leopold, like any skilled public-relations man, enjoyed massing big names to back his views, but there is no evidence that these men did not read the papers. The story comes from J. Stinglhamber.

of the advisers who were trying to get the best possible terms for him at the Anti-Slavery Conference found themselves fighting on two fronts and were in the end permanently estranged from the King.

The Anti-Slavery Conference was made possible by the powerfully emotional campaign against the slave-trade in Africa which was launched in 1888 by Cardinal Lavigerie. It is enough to say about the much-described character of Lavigerie that nobody since the Spanish missionaries in southern America had so completely identified the spread of Christendom with the spread of the territorial influence of their own country. Like Leopold, he made clever use of spurious historical comparisons to create nationalist enthusiasm for his projects, invoking not only the Crusaders but Charlemagne's wars as precedents for the French *mission civilisatrice* towards the lands of the heathen, and his influence, whether in the form of the *Alliance Française* or of the attitudes towards Algeria found recently in the better type of Army officer, is still active in contemporary France. But he stood in need of allies, and the fervent Catholicism of Belgium was always a reassurance to him. In the late seventies, when he was Archbishop of Algeria, it was largely out of Belgian veterans of the Papal Zouaves that he had formed his escorting corps for his new order of White Fathers: at a service in the basilica of Notre-Dame d'Afrique, on the hill above Bab-el-Oued in Algiers, they had each received his blessing and a sacred sword for their operations among the pagans of Africa.

Created Archbishop of Carthage and 'Primate of Africa' in 1884, Lavigerie's work brought him into close contact with the Association Internationale and its sovereign. A plan for the foundation of a hospital station staffed by Belgian monks was warily discussed between them in 1879, but it was Lavigerie's foundation of the 'Société anti-esclavagiste' in 1888 and his subsequent tour of Europe to preach a new African Crusade which brought him and Leopold closely together. In Paris, and London, he called for money and for military volunteers. Leopold, a little uneasy about this last point, made sure that Lavigerie had been properly briefed before he spoke in Brussels. The sermon was to be delivered on August 15th; on August 10th, Lavigerie and Leopold had a private meeting at Ostend. 'I am going to try to get him to say that the Congo State should and can take part in this crusade', the King warned Lambermont[1], and to Albert Thys, he wrote even more candidly: 'If the Cardinal raises some money, I intend to sponge it up by proposing to him that we should get a steamer launched on Lake Tanganyika . . . I wouldn't like to offer the Cardinal any temptation to spend his money some other way'[2]. Briefing Van Neuss, the official who dealt with Congolese finances, to be ready with propaganda in case the Cardinal made the error of criticizing the Congo State, Leopold left in a mood of some confidence for a West Highland yachting holiday with Sir William Mackinnon.

Lavigerie behaved splendidly. In his sermon, he compared Leopold to the Sower of the parable, and shook his head over the Belgians for failing to support his Congo enterprise with the funds it needed. A Belgian branch of the 'Société anti-esclava-giste' was founded and announced that it would indeed launch steamers on Lake Tanganyika to attack the Arab slavers, an embarrassment to Leopold who was still employing Tippo Tib as Governor of Stanley Falls and who wanted to control any steamers himself.

Elsewhere, the Cardinal's appeal had profoundly upset the public conscience, and nowhere more than in Britain; it was Lord Salisbury who proposed that an international conference on the suppression of the slave-trade should be called, and he suggested that it should be convened by Leopold in Brussels. He might not have done so if he had known that Lavigerie was suggesting to Leopold in early 1889 that he should take advantage of the Moslem *coup d'état* in Buganda, cross the Nile, and establish himself on the north shore of Lake Victoria; a plot which Leopold was sorry to abandon before Lambermont's alarmed warnings. But Salisbury's motives, apart from their element of genuine concern about the slave trade, included an uneasy suspicion that the growing Arab resistance to the European presence in East Africa was somehow a southward extension of Mahdism in the Sudan, and that a danger of concerted Moslem upheaval existed[3].

The Conference opened in the autumn of 1889, in the offices of the Belgian Foreign Ministry, attended by the Powers signa-

[1] Ceulemans; *Question Arabe;* p. 290.
[2] Daye; *Léopold II;* p. 309.
[3] Oliver; *Sir Harry Johnston;* p. 139.

tory to the Berlin Act and by delegates from the Congo State. Emile Banning was a member of the Belgian delegation; the Congolese party was led by Van Eetvelde, the foreign affairs administrator, and by the pliable Van Maldeghem, the State's attorney-general, with the assistance of a team of advisors which included Charles Liebrechts and Coquilhat. A further strategic position in the Conference was secured for Leopold by the appointment of Lambermont as chairman.

In its main task, the formulation of an agreement upon methods to be used for the suppression of the slave-trade, the Brussels Conference was successful and served humanity well. A programme was drawn up for the construction of fortified stations along the slave-trails, for the limitation of sales of alcohol and firearms, and for the eventual building of telegraph lines, roads and railways. For Britain, the most important outcome was a useful recommendation for the building of a railway line inland from Mombasa to Lake Victoria, later to be realized in the Uganda Railway. But the Conference, one delegate recalled, also had its moments of vulgar comedy. Vain arguments from certain quarters suggested that 'trade spirit' was actually good for the health of the African body, and that breech-loading rifles were not offensive weapons, while constant embarrassment was caused by the presence of a Turkish delegate, Caratheodori Effendi. Delegates carried away by their ideals would begin to evoke the lusts of the Islamic harem as a market for the slave trade: Lambermont or their colleagues would send them desperate signals, but Caratheodori Effendi, roaring with laughter, would assure the hall: 'Please go on, gentlemen; say anything you like!'[1]

Like a great trustful dove, the Conference had settled on Leopold's doorstep. Its success would bring greater glory to his name, but he wanted to get more than glory out of it. For one thing, he feared that the Conference would bring international brigades of liberators into the very debatable lands where expansion of frontiers was still possible for the Congo State. He warned the Congo delegation in private that the Powers 'have unlimited resources which in spite of the Congo State's advance would allow them to arrive first on the Lakes, in the Bahr-el-

[1] Liebrechts; *Léopold II, Fondateur d'Empire;* p. 147.

Ghazal, and on the Zambezi. We must not push the Powers into thrusting and advancing into the interior'[1].

Secondly, Leopold thought that he could get money out of the Conference by rushing it into a revision of the fourth Article of the Berlin Act which forbade him to levy import duty, an alteration which would actually violate the second point in the Article allowing for revision only after twenty years. The suggestion that a five per cent import duty would help Leopold's anti-slavery expenses had already been tried out on British delegates, and Leopold was evidently encouraged to raise his sights. In May 1890, as the Conference approached its end, Lambermont read out a draft motion asking for a ten per cent entry duty on goods entering the Congo. Britain and Italy backed the motion; others were less keen; the American delegate Henry Sanford, once Leopold's most useful henchman, was appalled, and both the United States and Holland appealed to the sacred principles of free trade enshrined in the Berlin Act—an Act which the United States had never in fact ratified. So persistent was the opposition that Banning suggested that Leopold ought to give up hope of getting the entry dues inscribed in the formal Act of the Conference, and settle for a separate Declaration with the signature of the Powers.

Leopold would not hear of this, and continued to resist the chorus of warnings delivered by his advisers on the Belgian and Congo delegations. He wanted his entry dues, and he wanted them in the Act, or there would be no Act worth speaking of at all. On May 30th, in a council of war at the Palace, Leopold told his team: 'I have certain scruples, now that the moment of signing has come . . . ', and ordered the Congolese party to declare that unless he was granted the entry dues, he would be unable to fulfil his duties under the Act. Without the co-operation of the Congo State, in which the surviving bases of the slave-trade were located, the resolutions of the Conference would be futile; Leopold was holding the noble project up to ransom for his ten per cent.

His staff had not realized how far Leopold would go to get his way. Emile Banning, Lambermont and Van Neuss were deeply shaken, and implored the King not to abort his own conference

[1] Ceulemans; *Question Arabe;* p. 260.

for 'a secondary question of purely pecuniary significance'[1]. Van
Eetvelde and Van Maldaghem, whose loyalty was tougher and
less conditional, kept quiet, and at the next meeting of the Conference, Van Maldeghem read out a message from Leopold
warning that his resources were now exhausted, and that 'if
through lack of funds I later find myself unable to honour my
engagements, I want it to be understood that no blame can be
attached to me . . . ' Once again, Leopold was threatening to
create a European crisis by letting the Congo State collapse.
Lambermont, in the chair, dropped his head into his hands and
feigned a stupor while Van Maldeghem spoke. Banning, at the
end of the session, grabbed Liebrechts and burst into a violent
tirade against the Congo for trying to break both the Berlin Act
and the old Geographical Conference. Liebrechts, one of the
younger 'realists' who owed his career to Leopold, retorted with
anger.

'I tried to calm him,' Liebrechts wrote later; ' . . . the truth
was that the Berlin Act had been imposed on us and in many
of its provisions, formed a strong barrier to the economic
development of the Congo. I ended by telling him, for we could
reach no agreement, that we were living on earth and not in
some sphere of dreams and illusions'[2]. But he failed to bring
Banning to heel; the shock had been too great for a man whose
enthusiasm for Africa since the age of twenty had always centred
on the abolition of the slave trade. For Emile Banning, at this
moment, began realization that the man in whose cause he had
spent most of his energies was out for his own ends.

Leopold ultimately had to accept the principle of a Declaration on import duties separate from the Act of the Conference
itself. Holland, with a large commercial interest on the Upper
Congo, held out against the grant of the duties long after the
Act had been signed, and it was only British pressure, perhaps
encouraged by a begging letter from Leopold to Queen Victoria,
which at last obliged the Dutch to sign the Declaration in
December 1890. They knew perfectly well that Leopold was out
to wreck the trade of the Dutch companies competing with the
State for ivory on the edges of the Arab zone, but everybody
seemed to be against them. Even the Americans, after an inter-

[1] Emile Banning; *Mémoires politiques et diplomatiques;* Brussels 1927; p. 141.
[2] Liebrechts; *Léopold II, Fondateur d'Empire;* p. 150.

minable exchange of telegrams with President Blaine about raising liquor duties and getting an international guarantee for Liberia, had given in.

The Conference, most of its signing done, continued to sit and talk at intervals until 1892. Meanwhile, Leopold was well aware that his diplomatic triumph over import duties, though essential and brilliantly carried off, was not going to produce anything like the money which the Congo needed if it were to carry out the programme of internal consolidation and external conquest which had been drawn up. In the summer of 1890, Camille Janssen, the Governor-General, drafted plans to raise 1,250,000 francs through direct taxation, the raising of export duties, and an increase in the price of licences to sell alcohol, in case the Conference did not grant Leopold his import duties. In spite of his success in Brussels, Leopold was unwilling to let this scheme be scrapped, and the end of 1890 saw him engaged in a series of frantic quarrels with his advisers, who fought to keep these additional duties in their pigeonhole. He threatened again to abandon the whole enterprise: Banning and Lambermont, now recklessly outspoken, dared him to do so for the sake of a few thousand francs of revenue. In the end, the King retreated. Stagily telling Lambermont to take his papers and get out of the office, Leopold called him back from the doorway and magnanimously agreed to discuss fresh cuts in the duties.

In the following year, Leopold showed the extent of his confidence in his staff by presenting them with a fudged version of the Congo annual report. To a meeting, Lambermont declared coldly that he could take no responsibility for the report, because the King had removed the trade figures from it and abbreviated the general statement of accounts.

'The end,' he said, 'entirely from the King's hand, expresses a policy of adventure and conquest entailing excessive spending and liable to destroy private enterprise under intolerable burdens. There is only one possible view to take: the report must not include these final pages, which would make Belgian annexation quite impossible and thus, by opening the way to French pre-emption, create the possibility of a serious conflict between France and England'[1].

Again, Leopold made minor emendations. But Emile Banning

[1] Quoted in Banning; *Mémoires;* p. 316.

considered that 'financial exaggerations and hostility to the Belgian trading companies remain the keynote (of the report) . . . experience has taught nothing on this score'[1]. Though he continued to serve Leopold a little longer, Banning was finished with the King. Leopold found it hard to believe this of the man who had lent the priceless asset of genuine moral passion to the propaganda he had written for the great African operation, and came repeatedly to see Banning when he retired dejectedly to Middelkerke for a rest by the North Sea. Both limping, the two men would set out together along the beach on one of those immense Leopoldian walks, while the King tried to persuade Banning that the Congo would have to be run as a private Royal estate if it was to pay its way. Gradually he realized that it was moral disgust which prevented Banning from accepting the disagreeable logic of what he was saying, and he took an offence so deep that it lasted for the rest of Banning's life. For Banning's part, he used the eight years left to him in writing bitter memoirs and railing at the King's new policies for the Congo. At a New Year's Day reception, Leopold deliberately turned his back when Banning was announced, and asked his courtiers: 'Do you think old Hobbler takes the hint? I shall do the same thing next year.'

There were still others ready to obey him, and to assure him that the world would in time understand the nobility of his motives. Perhaps the most biting, because unconscious, sarcasm expressed on Leopold's activities at the Anti-Slavery Conference is Baron Zuylen's shocked comment on the attitude of the Dutch. 'The opinion of other nations, who had greeted the Brussels Act as a great moral and political event, was disgusted to see such sordid particular interests endangering a high humanitarian enterprise'[2].

[1] *Ibid.*, p. 317.
[2] Zuylen; *l'Echiquier Congolais;* p. 197.

CHAPTER XXI

THE TESTAMENT AND THE
BROWNE DE TIEGE SWINDLE

LEOPOLD'S PURPOSE FOR THE CONGO was a double one. He certainly intended that part of its revenues should remain in his own possession: transformed into great trusts safely based in Europe, this money would form an endowment for him and for his male heirs, a privy purse out of reach of Parliament which he and his successors would use on major public works. At the same time, he still intended that the Congo should ultimately become a Belgian colony. Obviously, the timing of the second intention was governed to some extent by the progress of the first: if there was any danger that a Belgian Colonial Ministry might cut off his personal siphoning of the Congo's wealth, then he must extract the capital he wanted from the State before he handed it over to Belgium. But there would certainly be a hand-over one day, and therefore it seemed reasonable to Leopold that Belgium should be asked to put down a deposit in advance.

He proposed to the Government that in return for a loan he should publish a Will leaving the Congo to Belgium. This bargain was discussed with political leaders during the Brussels negotiations over the revision of the Berlin Act. Beernaert was frightened of Left-wing reactions, knowing that the younger and more socially-conscious politicians regarded the Congo as an expensive nuisance, whose acquisition would either ruin the Treasury or flood the country with the products of cheap labour. Frère-Orban, for the Opposition, disliked the Will idea but admitted to the King that it would probably get through Parliament. The plan was worth trying. Leopold wrote to Thys: 'I shall sign the Will and its covering letter when the loan is signed: the Will and the letter will both be ante-dated. That won't affect the basic situation. Before the Will is signed and witnessed, I must have in my hands a formal promise to hand the proceeds of the new loan over to the Congo State'[1].

It might be necessary to stiffen Beernaert's backbone, while the project was still secret, and in London in March, Leopold drafted for him a fervent sales brochure. 'The Congo State, having completed its period of formation, is now entering its period of development . . . To develop the Congo is to work for the wealth and the development of Belgium.' Getting into detail, Leopold went on, 'We know that we have marvellous soil where excellent coffee grows wild (see the Antwerp Chamber of Commerce letter). Since Stanley's journey, we have known that we are the owners of the largest and richest slice of the world, with its valuable woods and countless rubber vines; we know that we shall harvest excellent tobacco and superb ground-nuts and that the soil can refuse us nothing—not cocoa, cotton, tea, rice or anything else. Cattle are numerous and fine, and could be bred in limitless numbers. In the ground there is copper, iron, gold, granite, and lime, and we have not begun to go looking for them. To search for them will require more money than we possess. To make a profit out of the millions hidden in the great forests, we will have to spend money . . . In the recent scramble,' he boasted, 'we have drawn the winning ticket . . .'[2]

All finally went smoothly. On July 3rd, the day after the signing of the Brussels Act, Beernaert and Van Eetvelde signed an agreement for a Government loan of 25,000,000 francs to the Congo. Five millions would be paid at once, the rest in 2,000,000 instalments over ten years. At the end of the ten years, it was for Parliament to choose whether to annex the Congo or to demand repayment of the loan.

Beernaert introduced the loan bill into the Chamber in July 1890, and Leopold's Will was read to the deputies. It had only just been drafted, but to prevent any undignified suggestion that the document was just half of a sharp deal, he back-dated it 'August 2, 1889'. An accompanying letter, back-dated to August 5th the previous year, explained to the Belgians the priceless nature of the heirlooms for which they had just paid 25,000,000 francs.

It was a peculiar transaction. Count Louis de Lichtervelde,

[1] Leopold to Thys, April 15, 1890. Quoted in Daye; *Léopold II*; p. 323.
[2] Daye; *Léopold II*; pp. 320-21.

one of Leopold's most indulgent biographers, felt driven to comment: 'The King of the Belgians, so closely fettered by constitutional rules and by the traditions of parliamentary monarchy, had found a way to display the absolute power which he exercized in Africa to a degree which would have been denied to Louis XIV or to a Tsar of All the Russias. This transmission of sovereignty by testament—as if sovereignty were part of a patrimony—recalled the high Middle Ages and is still without parallel in the modern world'[1]. Hostility on the Left had been placated by the emphasis on the commercial opportunities offered to Belgium by the Congo, and by avoiding references to the word 'colony'[2], but Frère-Orban still felt that the arrangement was a rickety one.

'It would have been worthier of a free people,' he remarked, 'not to be tied to the Congo by a trick, but to have founded the link on thoughful agreement, after mature discussion and inspired by the high intention of taking part in a civilizing undertaking'[3]

A condition of the new loan was that Leopold should keep the Belgian Government informed of the state of Congo finances, and that he should not undertake further borrowings without Belgian permission. The years following the Will of 1890 saw the establishment of the 'Domain' system in the Congo, and the triumph of State monopoly over free trade, which will be described later; as early as 1891, as Lambermont had complained, the King was concealing financial data even from the Congo's own staff, and he continued to carpenter a variety of schemes to raise further credit. Beernaert found it difficult to defend his master against the powerful lobby formed by the Belgium private companies trading in the Congo when he had constant grounds for suspicion that Leopold was not only withholding information from him but secretly acting in breach of the 1890 Agreement. In 1894, six months after Beernaert had fallen and been replaced at the head of the Catholic Government by Jules de Burlet, the uneasiness of Parliament over the way in which Leopold was fulfilling his part of the bargain came to a head.

The crisis of the 'Browne de Tiège Loan' is one of the most

[1] Lichtervelde; *Léopold II;* pp. 246-7.
[2] Daye; *Léopold II;* p. 328.
[3] Quoted in Daye; *Léopold II;* p. 328.

important and mysterious affairs of Leopold's reign. It is important because Leopold nearly lost the Congo to Belgium before he was ready to part with it. It is mysterious because the latest studies made into the episode by Professor Stengers reveal an entirely new level of deceit below the superficial floor of dishonesty; a bewildering discovery whose implications will take time to follow out. In the circumstances, it may make things a little clearer if the original hypothesis is narrated first, and the new facts examined afterwards.

Towards the end of 1894, de Burlet's Government became aware of a vast new money-raising apparatus which was being erected by Leopold apparently in breach of the 1890 Agreement. In 1892, part of the Congo had been given over to concession companies to exploit and administer under licence. Now, ministers understood, Leopold was negotiating with Colonel North[1], the chairman of the concession company known as the 'Anglo-Belgian India-Rubber Corporation' (ABIR), for the lease of enormous territories in the State. The 'Société du Manyéma', or 'Société Générale des Cultures', would have received a lease of over 42,000,000 acres in return for a payment of 6,500,000 francs. With a capital of 8,000,000, the company would have remained under the control of the Congo State to the extent that the State would appoint the members of its Board, and approve replacements for them. Most of this capital, the Government was led to believe, would be British, and it may have been this which encouraged them to intervene.

The Prime Minister objected that the proposed concession was too large, and that his Government would be running political risks in taking over a colony which contained a foreign-owned company of such size and power. His Cabinet felt that the only solution to these dangers and to the King's reckless search for money was immediate annexation of the Congo by Belgium, and both Lambermont and Banning advised that this should be done. On November 4th, the Cabinet unanimously demanded that Leopold should drop the 'Société du Manyéma' project and provide them with full accounts of Congolese finances, and at the end of the year, de Burlet's Foreign Minister, Count de Mérode, sponsored a bill for immediate annexation of the Congo.

[1] If these negotiations ever took place, they must have been interesting. North was a puppet, and his money was principally Leopold's.

For a moment, Leopold seems to have believed that he was going to lose the Congo. Before Mérode's bill had even been drafted, he announced that in direct breach of his obligations to the Government, he had borrowed 5,000,000 francs from the Antwerp banker Alexandre Browne de Tiège in 1892, and that the loan was due to be repaid, with six per cent interest, on July 1, 1895. He would now be unable to repay Browne, the 'Société du Manyéma' having failed to materialize and provide him with the money he needed, and as security for the loan he had mortgaged 16,000,000 hectares of the Congo to the banker and his associates.

This revelation appalled the Belgian Government. Annexation seemed all the more urgent, but another 5,000,000 francs had been added to the costs of the operation, since Leopold's debt would have to be paid by the Treasury, and the expenditure of public money on the Congo was the surest way to bring anti-colonial passions in Belgium to the boil. With ominous docility, Leopold, through Van Eetvelde, accepted Mérode's draft for the annexation bill on January 9, 1895. The Government and the private trading companies guided by Albert Thys stuck to their plan for an immediate takeover, while Mérode with great difficulty bought off an energetic French attempt to use the right of pre-emption to set up something like a French protectorate over the Congo. But public indignation was already mounting.

On the other flank, Socialists, progressive Liberals and even a number of Catholics attacked the draft bill of cession. Anti-colonialism, in the Belgian Socialist sense, owed less to humanitarian feelings for oppressed populations overseas than to concern for the effect on Belgian welfare of massive overseas public spending. One Socialist commented: 'If we contrive one day to fling off the yoke of capitalism which oppresses us and win genuine civilization for our European population, then will be the time to consider sharing this prosperous situation with the coloured races'[1]. Nor did public opinion like the prospect, played up by the opponents of annexation, of maintaining a Belgian Army in the Congo to fight interminable wars against slavers and native mutineers. In February, de Burlet confessed to Leopold that the transfer was going to be even more difficult than he had expected.

[1] J. Stengers; *la Première Tentative de Reprise par la Belgique;* ARCS; p. 37

Leopold's optimism began to revive. He saw that de Burlet was frightened by the reactions of the enormous new electorate, ten times the size of the old *Pays Légal*, which had voted for the first time five months before and had put thirty-four Socialists into the Chamber. Mérode was sticking to his guns, but de Burlet's courage was leaking away visibly. The *Patriote*, a newspaper which supported the Catholics, wrote cunningly: 'We have defended the Congo enterprise against its habitual enemies. Now we are defending it again against those who are using shock tactics to rush the Right into a vote which would spell its doom at the next elections, and which in the eyes of the working class of the towns and the countryside would discredit all plans for a colonial policy, if not the monarchy itself.'

The Times wrote a judicious long leader which came down with surprising firmness against annexation. ' "When in doubt, do nothing" is a prudent and wise maxim for the Belgian nation to adopt, in the present case at least.' Dodging the missiles of Albert Thys and the King's creditors from one side and the mud flung by a furious public from the other, Jules de Burlet may have laughed rather wildly at this advice to be a good boy and sit still. Some 900 words later, the leader summed up: 'It does seem to us doubtful whether the moment has arrived for Belgium as a nation to saddle herself with a responsibility the actual extent and ultimate outcome of which cannot at present be gauged. Nor can it be forgotten that, after all, she might not be working for herself but for France, to whom in an unfortunate moment of irritation against England, the sovereign of the Free State gave a pledge which has hampered the enterprise in the past and will continue to hamper it in the future'[1]. Many supporters of the Government assumed that Leopold must have suggested this article himself.

In March, Charles Woeste admitted to Van Eetvelde that annexation was becoming impractical, and that the only alternative was a rapid financial settlement of the King's debts. Mérode, meanwhile, was growing more obstinately attached to his bill as his colleagues grew less willing to take it any further. It was clear enough to them that Belgium did not want the Congo, and if they had to, they would throw Mérode overboard

[1] *The Times;* March 18, 1895.

before he sank the whole Government with his annexation project.

Ministers dithered, but Leopold's hopes continued to rise, as two events gave him new grounds for confidence in the Congo's future. One was the arrival at Antwerp of impressive shipments of rubber and ivory, proof to him that the monopolistic methods of his State were taking effect, and, to the public, proof that the Congo really was rich enough to pay its own way without Government intervention. Another, less easy to explain to his critics, was the installation in January of his old friend Felix Faure as President of the French Republic. Faure had stayed with him three years before, in the enormous old chalet which the King used for his Ostend holidays, and he shared Leopold's admiration for State monopoly as an economic system for colonies: his rise to power told Leopold that there was now a chance to make an arrangement with France over the Bahr-el-Ghazal. He would play on French fears of a British return to the Upper Nile, as in the previous year he had played upon British fears of the French, coming close to success in establishing himself as a 'neutral' buffer between the two advancing rivals. He had arranged a visit to Paris in May (in the event, Leopold's health forced him to go and 'water' at Aix-les-Bains, and the trip did not take place until September), and the annexation bill must therefore be killed at once.

He reminded the Cabinet that July 1st, the day when Browne de Tiège had to be paid or acquire permanent rights over a gigantic estate in the Congo, was drawing closer. Why not abandon the hopelessly unpopular annexation bill, and advance the King the money he required? After three consecutive days of argument ending on May 15th, de Burlet's Cabinet agreed to pay Leopold his 5,000,000 francs. In the limpness of surrender, they accepted his demand for an extra 1,500,000 for good measure. Mérode refused to give up his bill: he had already warned the Government that if they merely paid Leopold's debts and were content with a few vague controls over how the money was spent in future, they would be perpetuating 'an era of difficulties and conflicts, which can bring Belgium into grave danger'. Abandoned finally by his colleague Smet de Naeyer, the Finance Minister, Mérode realized that he was beaten, and resigned late in May as his bill, to which he was formally com-

mitted before Parliament, was thankfully buried by the rest of
the Government.

Leopold had been extremely lucky. His impatience and his
obsession with short-term results had very nearly lost him the
Congo, and only the sudden storm of opposition to the Treaty of
Cession had surprised him with a demonstration that everything
was not yet lost. The feature of Belgium politics which had
always disgusted him, its small-minded ability to raise shrill and
rapid factional tumult over an issue which affected the deepest
destinies of the Belgian state, had done him a service at last.

He had been lucky, too, in the credulity of his Cabinet, for
the truth is that Leopold never borrowed 5,000,000 francs from
Browne de Tiège at all. At the end of 1894, he had been certain
that he was about to lose the Congo. Was he to get nothing for
all the millions he had put into it? This thought was unbearable,
and to ensure that he would at least not be out of pocket when
he gave the Congo up, he invented the Browne de Tiège loan.
Browne de Tiège did exist; he and his brother Constant were
leading bankers in Antwerp, and both of them were deeply
involved in the concession companies formed in 1892. Alexandre
being chairman of the 'Société Anversoise de Commerce au
Congo', better remembered as the 'Anversoise'. He did many
things for his King; he did not, however, lend him 5,000,000
francs in 1892.

Professor Stengers has discovered that Leopold extracted the
5,000,000 from the Government by telling them a flat lie about
a debt which was pure fiction. His pretended confession certainly
helped to quicken the public reaction against adopting a debt-
burdened Congo, but that does not seem to have been its original
purpose. Leopold did not intend to relinquish the Congo without
the most majestic of 'golden handshakes'; as things turned out,
he was able to keep the Congo and the golden handshake as well.
It will be remembered that the Treasury of the Congo State and
Leopold's private fortune, though outwardly separate institutions, were in fact a single entity, through their relationship to
the *fonds special*. The product of some of the share issues floated
by the Congo State had thus been used to pay off some of Leopold's real debtors, especially the Rothschilds. The 5,000,000 of
the fictional loan were solemnly paid over by Smet de Naeyer
and the Belgian Treasury to the Congo State; instead of being

G

transmitted to the account of Alexandre Browne de Tiège, most
of the money was in turn 'paid' by the State Treasury to Leopold
himself, to cover 'advances' made by the King to the State. Leopold had thus repaid himself for an advance made by himself
to himself, and done so with somebody else's money. Perhaps
the angels wept, but Midas looked down in envy.

CHAPTER XXII

MONOPOLY AND THE RUBBER SYSTEM

O N THE UPPER CONGO, the unequal war between the
State and the private traders continued to rage. Ivory,
still the most important source of short-term profits,
would not last for ever, and there was a growing
interest in balls of wild rubber tapped from the Landolphia and
Clitandra creepers, which was traditionally used by Africans for
odd jobs like covering drums or fixing arrowheads to shafts. But
although rubber would fetch about eight francs a kilo in Europe,
the main commercial struggle took place while ivory still ruled
the export market.

In 1888, the private traders had launched their steamers on
the upper river. But the State retained the enormous advantage
that it paid no duty either on its own illegal exporting or on its
imports, and paid its own agents, supposedly administrators, a
bonus on their ivory collection. Early in 1890[1], the State violently
tightened the screws on the competitors it was supposed to be
serving by raising export duty from 50 to 200 francs per hundred
kilograms of ivory. In June, during the negotiations over the
Government loan and the Will, Leopold tried to explain away
this apparent move towards monopoly in a letter to Beernaert
which argued that the Congo State was not really engaged in
trade, but only 'harvesting' the produce of its own estate, and
that the behaviour of the private companies getting rich on the
sacrifices made by the State was 'immoral and scandalous'[2]. This
outburst was no substitute for serious reasoning, and on July 9th,
the day Beernaert introduced the loan and the Will into the
Chamber, a Congolese decree defined the area open to private
ivory buying as that lying between the Pool and Stanley Falls,
and below the first falls of the Congo tributaries. Such a concession did not deter the State's competitors from pointing out

[1] Decree of March 25th.
[2] Letter of June 27th. Quoted in Ceulemans; *Question Arabe;* p. 206.

that it was still acting *ultra vires* in excluding any territory in the Berlin 'conventional basin' from the operations of free trade.

Goaded by the Prime Minister and his own staff to reduce discriminatory taxation, Leopold made the revealing retort that 'you know that I would prefer to harvest my ivory myself . . . '[1] Beernaert begged him by return of post to think of the consequences of offending Holland, France and Portugal by hindering their commerce. In the Congo, however, Captain Coquilhat was posted to Boma a few months later as Deputy Governor of the State, with secret orders to prepare a plan for the imposition of a new monopolistic system on the whole State.

One of the first acts of the Congo State, in 1885, had been to claim possession of *terres vacantes* or unclaimed land. This measure, which did not define what sort of African occupancy might constitute a claim to land, formed a useful basis for what was now to follow. A secret decree of September 29, 1891, accompanied by detailed instructions, asserted the State's right to its *fruits domaniaux*, the produce of the supposedly empty lands which belonged to the State. Special orders to commanders on the Aruwimi, the Uele and the Ubangi warned them to take steps to protect the State's rights to ivory and rubber there.

The 1891 Decrees, as has been pointed out[2], only provided an official justification for what had already been going on. Money was needed for the Nile expeditions and, it could be argued, to mount operations against the slave-trade. Nor was the 1885 claim to vacant lands without precedent. Most colonial powers in a new territory, including the British, declared that forest and unoccupied land was the property of the colonial government; a policy of 'nationalization' which was to have interesting results on African attitudes to Socialism in the middle twentieth century. In German East Africa, in the Cameroons under the German South-Cameroon Company, in the French Congo, in Ceylon, similar measures had been passed. From the point of view of the local population, the essential difference between these systems was in the degree of their application and the extent to which the colonial government recognized the fact that to survive, a village needed far more land than the area under cultivation at a given moment, to say nothing of its depen-

[1] Letter Leopold-Beernaert, September 25, 1890.
[2] Ceulemans; *passim.*

dence on fish, game and fruit taken from the surrounding country. In Ceylon, these facts of tropical life eventually received official recognition. In the Congo State, Leopold's rights were pushed to their most extreme interpretation, until the essential practice of shifting cultivation to maintain fertility was made impossible and it became a crime to trap a bird or hunt in the forests outside the villages.

The lawyer Félicien Cattier, later to become one of Leopold's most formidable enemies, opined in 1892 that the State's claim to the produce of vacant lands was not in breach of the Berlin Act, and that the State was fully entitled to be judge of its own actions in the application of this undoubted right. But the storm was already breaking, as news of the Decrees leaked out, and there followed particulars of the detailed circulars issued to the traders working on the Congo which warned them that it was a criminal offence to buy ivory and rubber from Africans in the restricted areas, just as it was an offence for Africans to hunt elephants and keep the ivory or to tap rubber without handing it over to the State authorities.

Leopold's adversary, in the slanderous duel which now opened in Belgium, was Albert Thys, the organizer of the 'Société du Haut-Congo', the 'Compagnie du Katanga', and a group of lesser companies known generically as the 'companies of the Rue de Brederode', after the street in which they had established their offices. Thys was a dangerous enemy. The Socialist Emile Vandervelde recalled:

'With his Emperor's face, his powerful jaw prematurely tooth-less, his brick-coloured complexion, his reddish hair, his yellow wild-beast eyes, Albert Thys could at once be seen for what he was: another Cecil Rhodes, a sort of capitalist Pizarro or Cortez, a conquistador whose inflexible will knew no obstacles . . . '[1]

Thys, builder of the railway from Matadi to the Pool and Secretary-General of the Congo State, gave in his resignation and placed his case in the hands of A. J. Wauters, the editor of the *Mouvement Geographique* magazine. Camille Janssen, the Governor of the Congo, resigned as well. The discreet Strauch and the Congo's financial secretary Van Neuss had already deserted Leopold. Banning wrote a pamphlet about free trade and the Berlin Act to show that the new measures were illegal.

[1] Emile Vandervelde; *Souvenirs de'un Militant Socialiste;* Paris 1939; p. 77.

When Thys took the matter directly to the Government, both Lambermont and Beernaert told the King that he should withdraw his instructions before there were serious international complications.

Leopold made a show of alleged malpractice in the running of the 'Société du Haut-Congo', but there had already been questions in the Chamber about ivory-buying by the State, and Beernaert himself was now threatening to resign. The King was obliged to come to terms. In October 1892, a new set of decrees cleared away the tangle of rights and illegalities, and attempted to make a fresh start.

The Decree of October 30, 1892 divided the Congo into three Zones. The first Zone, in which private trading was forbidden, was defined later as the *Domaine Privé* of the State. A second Zone was 'provisionally reserved' for the State. The third Zone, down the Kasai, was reserved for private trading companies. It was provided that the Decree would become void when Belgium was ready to take over the Congo as a colony.

In the Free Trade Zone, a number of small Belgian and Dutch companies were already operating, taking rubber from the Bantu population and paying at least a nominal cash price for it, which was more than the State would have done. The Congo State in practice continued to harry and to obstruct their work even in the zone reserved for them, refusing whenever possible to permit them to acquire land or even to lease it. In self-defence, Thys and others planned to consolidate the companies into one major combine, to be known as the 'Compagnie des Caoutchoucs du Kasai', an offshoot of the old 'Compagnie du Congo'. The capital was raised, but the State, warned by the Belgian motto that unity made strength, managed to keep the combine in suspended animation for years. When at last it appeared in public, it had become another Leopoldian robot. The episode anticipates the narrative, but it arose directly out of the terms of the 1892 Decree.

Granting rights to free commerce along the Kasai, the Decree had included the proviso that it would cease to have force when Belgium was in a position to take over the sovereignty of the Congo. The precise wording of this stipulation, overlooked at the time, proved fatal to the freedom of the 'Compagnie du Kasai'. In 1901, at the end of the ten-year term of the 1890 loan, Belgium

did indeed stand in a position to take over the Congo. But
unluckily for the Congo's inhabitants, Belgium decided not to
do so. The Decree of 1892 became null and void, but Leopold
was still in possession. He had won an opportunity to stamp out
the flickering embers of free trade in the Kasai, and he took it.
The fourteen companies which had survived in the zone were
invited to subscribe half the capital for a new 'Compagnie du
Kasai', the State providing the rest, and in return for a share of
the profits, to renounce their trading rights in the zone for thirty
years and to hand over their installations to the new trust. They
were relieved to accept the offer. The 'Compagnie du Kasai', now
just another of the huge concession trusts which were exploiting
the Congo by forced labour and a tax in rubber, took over the
region. Leopold appointed to its Board the Belgian deputy who
had moved in the Chamber that annexation was no longer
necessary.

The other zone—the provisionally-reserved zone soon merged
with the *Domaine Privé*—was divided into several categories.
Part of it was sold to owner-companies. The Rue de Brederode
companies, as a consolation, were sold areas on the Busira River,
south-east of what is now Coquilhatville. An arrangement had
already been made in March 1891 over the Katanga: Albert
Thys, the banker Léon Lambert and others had co-operated
with the Congo State to found the 'Compagnie du Katanga',
which became another owner-company under the new arrangements. Leopold was never deeply concerned with Katanga
minerals, which offended his preference for commodities offering a quick return on investment. The Katanga was a long way
from the sea and, worst of all, inaccessible by any major river
which was deep enough to get ore down to the Atlantic. Anyway,
the deposits were only then being surveyed for the first time by
Cornet, and even in 1895 *The Times* could comment that 'our
information about them is at present too vague to justify our
regarding them as a valuable asset'[1]. It was left for the 'Compagnie du Katanga' to initiate the mining combinations which
became so significant in the history of the Katanga after Congolese independence in 1960.

In 1900, the Congo State and the 'Compagnie du Katanga' set
up the 'Comité Spécial du Katanga', charged to develop the

[1] Leader of March 18, 1895.

region, on whose Board Congo State representatives predomi-
nated. A little later the same year, by an agreement signed on
December 8th, the 'Comité (CSK) conceded to the British-owned
Tanganyika Concessions Ltd. ('Tanks') a monopoly of mineral
prospecting over the Katanga. For the exploitation of the metals
found, the CSK and 'Tanks' would each provide half the capital,
and half the companies formed to exploit the deposits were to
have their headquarters in London, but the profits would be
divided in the proportion of sixty per cent for the CSK and only
forty per cent for 'Tanks'. The instrument of exploitation which
was set up to embody this deal was the 'Union Minière du Haut-
Katanga'. A few years later, the 'Tanks' holding in Union
Minière was substantially reduced in an arrangement to pay for
the building of the Benguela Railway to the Atlantic coast in
Angola.

Up to Congolese independence in 1960, the CSK remained the
authority granting all mining concessions in the Katanga. It
was then wound up, and a complex distribution of shares was
planned, although the secession of the Katanga has prevented
a final settlement so far. The effect on the Union Minière was
to be that 22·5 per cent of its shares were to pass to the Congo
Government—whether to Leopoldville or to the rebel Tshombe
administration in Elisabethville is a question at issue—20·5 per
cent to the British interests, and over 19 per cent to the Yggdrasil
which to a greater or lesser extent had financed all these bodies
from the 'Compagnie du Katanga' to 'Tanks' itself: the 'Société
Générale'.

A second category of the State Zone was that reserved for the
concession companies. The practice of exploiting an undeveloped
region by wholesale concession to private trusts was well-known,
though disliked by progressive colonial officials, and operated in
the neighbouring French Congo with enough success to
encourage Leopold to take shares in the companies, but in the
Congo State, the concessionaires operated almost as private
governments, subject to no effective restraint of any kind by the
State and not even obliged to publish the terms of their agreement. The largest was the 'Anversoise', assigned a fifty-year
concession of the Mongala basin to the north of the upper Congo.
Both the Browne de Tiège brothers were Board members; so was
Baron Constant Goffinet, one of the cross-eyed twins who were

Leopold's most trusted equerries, and in 1898, at a recasting of the company's structure, the Congo State acquired half its shares. The atrocities committed by 'Anversoise' agents in the Mongala in their extortion of rubber became so notorious that in July 1904 the Congo State was forced to intervene and suspend the concession.

Another large concession was granted to the Anglo-Belgian India-Rubber Company (ABIR), whose first chairman was the Englishman Colonel North. ABIR's concession lay to the south of the Congo, roughly opposite the 'Anversoise' territory, and its reputation was little better. Here again, there was a recasting, which led to the withdrawal of British capital and the formation of a new Board which included the usual Leopoldian friends and equerries; Leopold himself owned half the nominal capital[1]. In both cases, the recasting transformed the concession companies into 'Congolese law' concerns, and rescued them from Belgian tax and property regulations. Other concession companies existed, some on paper and others in reality, most of them controlled by Leopold's direct shareholding, by 'men of straw' investing on his behalf, or by his placemen on their Boards.

But the most significant division of the *Domaine Privé* was the secret allocation of an area which eventually became ten times the size of Belgium to Leopold himself. In 1892 or 1893, a paper was furtively lodged in the archives at Boma to register the lands round Lake Leopold II and Lake Tumba in the name of 'the Duke of Saxe-Coburg-Gotha'. This was the nucleus of the institution later to be known as the *Domaine de la Couronne*— the Crown Estate—exploited directly and with ruthless haste to provide the King with funds of his own. The *Domaine de la Couronne* was designed to be at once the instrument of personal power, providing Leopold with the money needed for his programme of public works in Belgium, and the main source of the great endowment which he intended to leave to his successors. Even the Belgian Government had for many years no idea that the *Domaine* existed, and its history has been reconstructed provisionally by Belgian historians[2] working only with fragmen-

[1] E. D. Morel; *Red Rubber;* London 1906; p. 141. It now appears that North himself, who was supposed to own most of the original ABIR capital, was a man of straw using Leopold's money. See R. T. Anstey; *Britain and the Congo in the Nineteenth Century;* p. 209, Note 4.

[2] See Stengers; *Combien le Congo a-t-il coûté à la Belgique ?;* ARSC 1957.

tary data. The first that was officially heard of it was the publication in 1901 of a Decree dating ostensibly to March 9, 1896, reserving the region as Crown property. This document however, was a forgery; no Decree had existed until it became convenient to confection one, and Leopold had to warn Van Eetvelde in 1901 to remember not to sign himself as 'Baron', a title he had not received in 1896.

Except for the titular 'Free Trade Zone', the Congo State was now a set of closely-interrelated monopolies. The main object of their operations was to win wild rubber. The absence of competition, and of imported goods which the African population could buy meant that no money economy existed in these regions; the lust to save overheads and the degree of political control which the exploiters held over the helpless population discouraged them from introducing one. In such conditions, as outside observers could guess for themselves, forced labour and extortion were inevitable.

To most European colonial governments, taxation in money was one accepted way of forcing a native peasantry to earn wages by productive labour on plantations or public works. The Congo State and the concession companies took the shorter and cheaper cut of imposing a tax in labour itself. In most cases, this was commuted into a tax on produce, a system of forced deliveries of wild rubber, copal[1] or food grains. Villagers whose economy had already been ruined by the 1891 Decree reserving 'vacant land' and its produce to the State, now found themselves obliged to spend days in the forest searching for a steadily-declining number of rubber vines, doing unpaid labour as porters, or working as woodcutters for the river steamers. The amount of the rubber levy varied greatly from station to station, but failure to deliver was punished by corporal punishment, collective fines in kind, imprisonment, or by punitive expeditions which burned villages and on occasions massacred their inhabitants. Nor could Leopold's subjects escape: the corollary to a tax in produce or labour was a prohibition on movement and migration, just as the serf in a developed feudal system had been forbidden to leave his village without permission.

The enormous machine of exploitation by force had been erected. Now it was put in motion. But its efficient lifetime, as

[1] Copal: a form of resin used for varnishes

Leopold never admitted, was necessarily very limited. Producing great wealth at first, for little cost beyond a high bill for rifle ammunition, the system rapidly wore out its component parts. The rubber vines grew rarer and rarer, mortally slashed for their latex by desperate hands who feared death if they did not deliver as much as the trunk contained. Only at the end were a few rubber estates of Landolphia and the Fantumia Elastica tree planted: conservation was thought unnecessary in the Congo. And as the search for wild rubber grew more difficult, the African population itself began to dwindle, through clandestine migration, massacre, epidemic and starvation, until there was a shortage of labour to seek it. The Congolese system was too viciously wasteful, too recklessly short-term in its conception, to deserve even the term of exploitation. It was no more than a prolonged raid for plunder.

CHAPTER XXIII

THE DAUGHTERS: LOUISE

THE 'DOMAINE DE LA COURONNE' had been founded to enrich Leopold's dynasty and his successors. To do so, it had to remain intact as it passed from one generation to another; there must be no question of a sharing-out of the capital at his own death between the various members of his family. Leopold intrigued continuously to find a way round the Belgian civil code, to which as a Belgian citizen he was subjected by the Constitution, and to avoid its provisions against the disinheritance of children. He envied the British system, under which a man could leave his entire fortune to one of his sons or, if he pleased, to a cat's home: under Belgian law, he would have to divide the great endowment among his daughters and see it carried away to pay the bills of worthless husbands in remote European courts. By the time that he had won from the constitutional revision a right to control the marriages of his children, Louise and Stephanie had already married and only the timid Clémentine remained at his mercy. Attempts to persuade successive Ministers of Justice to change the law of inheritance for the Royal Family had already failed. In the middle nineties, the King and the close friend of his old age, the rich lawyer Sam Wiener, examined possible methods of evading the law without actually breaking it. These, too, came to nothing, and in the end Leopold resorted to massive and clandestine illegalities in a vain effort to make sure that his wretched daughters got no share of his main fortune.

He had never made any secret of his contempt for his two elder daughters. He resented them on dynastic grounds, and he hated them personally because they reminded him of Marie-Henriette, because they were weak, and because they were alive and his son was not. Louise his eldest child received the full impact of this dislike and grew up to return it with interest. She used to tell a curious story to explain Leopold's attitude towards her, recalling that her father once caught her as a small child carrying a sealed note to her mother from a secret admirer; she had refused to give it up to him, and he had never forgiven her. Though the incident may never have taken place—Louise was certainly a compulsive liar—the story does suggest two mental needs which distorted her adult life: the need to assert herself through defying and wounding her father, and her need to explain away her mother's withdrawal of affection. Louise had been eleven when her brother Leopold died, and Marie-Henriette's interest in her other children had abruptly ended. Possibly Louise could not face this simple explanation, and found it necessary to invent some excuse for her mother's treachery. Against all the evidence, and although she remained surprisingly fond of Marie-Henriette, she always insisted that she had been involved with a succession of mysterious lovers.

Like her mother, Louise was nearly destroyed by the shock of sexual initiation to a marriage with a stranger. When she was seventeen, she was married to Prince Philip of Saxe-Coburg, her cousin, who at thirty-one was already a dingy, bumbling figure with pince-nez and large ears. It was a world in which Princesses frequently grew up in total ignorance of the sexual side of love, in courts where every Prince and courtier had his mistress. Marie-Henriette had told Louise nothing, except that she must 'do her duty' as a wife. On the wedding-night, there was the inevitable scene of incredulous horror. 'While all Brussels danced under bright lights and street illuminations,' Louise wrote many years later[1], 'I fell from Heaven into a bed of rocks laced with thorns.' Early in the morning, when Philip had left the bedroom for a moment, Louise bolted into the Park in her nightdress and hid among the camelias in the green-house. Found at last by a servant, she was brought back to the Palace and lectured gently but inexorably by Marie-Henriette on the sin of rebellion. Then she was returned to her husband. Afterwards, Louise would say wildly that her mother must have been Philip's lover, and had only arranged the marriage for the convenience of her own lusts.

Philip took her off to the Coburg palace in Budapest, and in the idiotic but at least lighthearted environment of Hungarian court society, Louise gradually revived. She was fair-haired and

[1] Princess Louise; *'Autour des Trônes Que j'ai Vu Tomber'*; Paris 1921; p. 77.

pretty, in a German way, and her experience of life had been limited to riding-lessons, the rainy park at Laeken, and dull Belgian receptions for five hundred gentlemen in frock-coats. Budapest taught her that she was attractive to men, and that there were consolations in spending money. When they moved to Vienna, Louise unexpectedly became a fashionable person to know: her unsubtle habit of saying what she thought, and her outspoken dislike of the prudery which had made her its victim, attracted young men who found it impossible to talk to the *bien-elevée* girls at Court.

Rudolf, the Crown Prince, liked her and relied upon her to keep his secrets. She did not disapprove of him, and it was partly admiration for Louise which encouraged him into the disastrous marriage with her sister Stephanie in 1881. William II, the future German Emperor, enjoyed her originality and commissioned her to choose hats for his wife Augusta, who, he said, 'always looks like the Ace of Spades'. Ferdinand of Coburg, the peculiar young man who later became Tsar of Bulgaria and a lay figure for British cartooning in the First World War, tried to seduce her. Louise had obliged him by playing the march from *Aïda* while he attempted to summon up the Devil, and had acted as a mourner at the occasional funerals, with Satanist ritual, which Ferdinand organized for his worn-out gloves and cravats.

Her relations with the Austrian family were less good, for although she loved the Empress Elizabeth and feared Franz-Josef, they did not approve of the way she behaved or of the rumours about her in Vienna. Although she had now borne Philip two children, the future Zionist leader Theodore Herzl saw her in a box at the Opera and commented with sentimental relish: 'Eve after the Fall!'

But she had not yet fallen. For twenty years, Louise maintained a dangerous balance, allowing herself the privileges of extravagance and a reputation for daring behaviour, while staying nominally inside the formalities of marriage and the Court. There were probably lovers, but there was no act of open defiance. Then, on a spring morning in 1895, when Louise was thirty-seven, she tripped.

Louise was driving in the Prater in an open carriage when she saw a commotion, and stopped her horses. A young man was struggling to control a black stallion as it stamped and reared on the tan of the riding alley. As other horsemen scattered, the stallion suddenly leapt across into the carriage-way, threatening to collide with the Princess. The rider looked up and met her eyes. She was not frightened, but sat still and watched until he had mastered the horse. Then she drove on. A little later that morning she noticed the young man on the black stallion again, but they said nothing to each other.

The young man was a Lieutenant of the 13th Uhlans, on leave from his regiment, and his name was Count Geza Mattacic-Keglevic. A Croat and a Catholic, from the Varazdin hills north of Zagreb towards Hungary, Mattacic was an extremely simple sort of man. He was brave, he knew a great deal about horses, and he thought that he knew a great deal about how a man of honour should behave. Louise was neurotic and elusive, a woman of strong sexuality who was often almost unrecognizable behind the disguises which her guilt forced upon her. Mattacic, with his stiff moustache and handsome eyes, could be understood at a glance : nothing could ever change him. In the stilted memoirs he wrote to help Louise in the years of disaster which were to follow, he described the moment when he saw Louise : 'I received a kind of electric shock. Something new seemed to have happened to me which I could not understand'[1].

For several months, he went back daily to the Prater in the hope of seeing Louise again, because, as he records shortly, 'it had become necessary to my life'[2]. They did not yet exchange words, but Louise went to the Prater on most mornings, and she was sometimes aware that the young officer was following her about other parts of Vienna. In February she went south to stay on the Kvarner Gulf at Abbazia[3] with Stephanie, now Rudolf's widow, and her own daughter Dora. Mattacic followed her, and managed to arrange an introduction.

He talked to Louise about horses, at first, and dared to tell her that she was a bad rider. He would teach her. They spent a good deal of time together at Abbazia that spring, and it was probably then, although Mattacic denied it in his memoirs, that he made her his mistress. When she returned to Vienna, it was obvious to everybody that she was in love with Mattacic. She put him in

[1] Count Geza Mattacic-Keglevic; *Loca Por Razón de Estado;* Madrid 1904; p. 19.
[2] *Ibid.,* p. 19.
[3] Now the Jugoslav resort of Opatija.

charge of her stables, rode out with him daily, and did not bother
to hide her feelings for this obscure young officer; in conversation, she openly made fun of the Imperial Court and jeered at
her own sister's respect for its etiquette. This situation was
intolerable to the Hofburg, and at the end of 1896 Mattacic was
rusticated from Vienna and Louise herself was forbidden to
appear at Court functions.

With her daughter, Louise went abroad, and in Belgium she
asked her parents for their formal agreement to a divorce from
Philip of Coburg. Leopold refused to listen to her. Mattacic for
his part, went home to face his family in Croatia before rejoin-
ing Louise at Karlsbad, in Bohemia, and travelling on with her
to Merano and Nice.

In Vienna, outraged friends and relations were trying to
awake the dozey Prince Philip to a sense of his wrongs. Geza
Mattacic must be destroyed, they insisted, for the sake of the
honour of the Coburgs and of the Austrian Court. With the
greatest difficulty, they provoked him at last into issuing a
challenge to a man who, as Philip was well aware, was not only
far younger but possessed a formidable skill at arms. He begged
them to have Mattacic arrested and locked up instead, but his
advisers were inflexible, and in early February 1898, two
Austrian gentlemen appeared at the Villa Paradis in Nice to
demand satisfaction for the Prince of Coburg.

Mattacic at once set out for Vienna, and on February 18th, in
the great hall of the Hofburg which forms the *Reitsaal* of the
Spanish Riding-School, he and the miserable Coburg faced each
other with pistols in their hands. Philip fired twice and missed:
Mattacic fired twice in the air. Philip's tireless supporters then
provided the two men with sabres, and they swashed around
uselessly for a certain time until Mattacic, perhaps ashamed of
the whole scenario, nicked the Prince of Coburg in the right
hand and brought the duel to an end.

Three weeks later, the enemies who had failed to get Mattacic
killed in fair fight launched a far more dangerous attack on him.
Bills run up by Louise were produced, totalling over 500,000
florins, which bore the guarantee of her sister Stephanie's signature. Stephanie, it was said, now denied that she had ever signed
these bills, and Philip of Coburg laid a charge against Mattacic
for forgery.

Mattacic went back to Nice, where he found Louise and her household in a state of mounting panic. Dora was now engaged to marry Gunther of Schleswig-Holstein, who had prudently taken her away from her mother and lodged her with his own parents near Dresden. He had warned Louise that the Emperor would probably try to commit her to the accepted equivalent of a dungeon for ladies of the Imperial Court—a lunatic asylum —but he had promised to appeal to the German Emperor on her behalf. Louise had a strong suspicion that once he had got Dora to Germany, Gunther would do nothing more for her mother, and she was right. Mattacic tried to drag her out of her despair, but Louise would only repeat: 'Je m'appèle Louise, et toutes les Louises sont malheureuses.'

Confirmation came from Vienna that Stephanie and two Viennese moneylenders had both testified that the signature guaranteeing Louise's new debts was a false one. Mattacic cabled back that the signature was genuine, and appealed to Stephanie to retract her evidence. Then, in March 1898, he persuaded Louise to set off with him to London, in the grotesque hope that Queen Victoria would lend Louise enough money to pay the disputed bills. Years before, Louise and her husband had in fact stayed with the Queen, and Louise was one of those whose observations convinced her that John Brown was the Queen's lover. But this time her intelligence work was faulty, and their train to the Channel passed the train taking Victoria to the Riviera, a mistake they only discovered when they got to London.

Their desperate lack of money now drove Mattacic to take the fatal step of re-entering Austrian territory. From London, he took Louise to Croatia, at first to the home of a friend and then to his foster-father's castle at Lobor, in the mountains north of Zagreb. There Louise again laid plans to divorce Philip of Coburg. Philip's lawyer, Dr Bachrach, arrived at Lobor and suggested that a settlement might be reached if Mattacic would agree to leave the Princess alone.

Louise refused. But Lobor was already being watched by the police, and Dr Bachrach, apparently with Imperial authority, now closed the trap. Mattacic was summoned to present himself at Zagreb for an Army medical examination and he took Louise with him. One morning the police burst into his hotel room and putting him under close arrest, rushed him to the military prison in Zagreb to begin a captivity which was to last for four years. Meanwhile, other policemen led by Dr Bachrach raided the Princess' room. Disappointed not to find her lover there with her, Bachrach carried out a minute examination of the sheets for traces of sexual intercourse. He offered Louise the choice between going back to her husband and incarceration in a lunatic asylum. She chose the asylum, and was hustled into a special train for Vienna.

In the year 1894, Dr Sigmund Freud of Vienna had advanced in his studies of the release of the subconscious from the technique of hypnosis to the method of the free association of ideas. Four years later, in the same city, Princess Louise was judged to be insane by a special tribunal because 'she was only happy in surroundings of absurd luxury', because 'she seemed totally devoid of love for her parents', and because she had 'no idea of the value of money'. Certified, and thus disqualified from testifying in her own defence in the case of the draft signatures, Louise was committed to an asylum at Purkersdorf for an indefinite term.

She was now beyond the help of law. But Mattacic, who had been shifted to a prison at Müllersdorf, nearer Vienna, was not. He had been stripped of his rank and title and sentenced to six years' cellular confinement, but at least he was legally sane, and his case seemed to the enemies of the Empire to mark him out as a victim of that 'Royalist International' which they were determined to destroy.

His case was raised at last in the Imperial Diet by the Socialist deputy Ignacy Daszynski, a Polish aristocrat who was to become Vice-Premier of free Poland in 1919. Prefacing an attack which opened on February 8, 1902 and lasted intermittently until August, Daszynski observed to the terror of the Speaker that 'we would prefer to let (high society) flounder and be drowned in its own filth', but that the corruption which had been spread through the Austrian Press by Coburg 'hush-money' obliged him to speak. 'This Press has been cowardly enough to pour ordure on the unfortunate Lieutenant Mattacic. He has been coated in slime, thanks to the manoeuvres of the powerful Coburg clique, although he is innocent—I repeat, innocent!'

Daszynski went on to savage the character of Philip of Coburg

—'he is a very miserly man; it runs in the family', he remarked in a clear reference to Leopold II—and of Dr Bachrach, whom, to the noisy delight of the audience he dismissed as 'a little Jew with feudal pretensions'. The insult tarnishes a fine achievement, for the Government gave way under Daszynski's onslaught and freed Mattacic at the end of August.

Louise had been moved to a mental home at Lindenhof, near Dresden, and here Mattacic, after searching the countryside on a bicycle, at last tracked her down. A meeting was arranged through one of her attendants, but the local police became suspicious and Mattacic was forced to leave the district. He finally managed to rescue the Princess by arranging a night escape from a house in Bad Elster in Saxony where she was taking the waters, and getting her aboard the night express for Berlin. From there they went on to the Hotel Westminster in Paris, where Louise told a reporter the usual: 'I plan to live simply and happily in obscurity'.

But this was an ambition which her own extravagance soon frustrated. Marie-Henriette had died in 1902, and in 1904, Louise's creditors had brought an action in Brussels to claim half of Leopold's marriage endowment, asserting that the Belgian system of 'separation of property' was not valid for his marriage to Marie-Henriette and that therefore the Queen's share, calculated as half of all his fortune, should now be divided among his children. Stephanie, who was almost as uncontrolled a spender as her sister, had an obvious interest in this case, and the Radical lawyer and deputy Paul Janson represented them both. The case, however, was lost. Louise remained in the Hotel Westminster running up disastrous charge accounts, and in December 1905 she received a visit from Sam Wiener, who had acted for Leopold in the trial the year before. Wiener, whose visit was kept a close secret, offered her a mansion near Cologne and a pension from her father of £10,000 a year if she would leave Mattacic. She found the courage to throw him out.

Leopold's attitude to Louise had up to now been one of scornful indifference. Almost his only intervention in the years of the Mattacic scandal had been to refuse his sanction to a divorce and, later, to adjure the asylum warders to prevent Louise escaping. Now the matter was more serious for him. Public opinion in Belgium accused him of spending the treasures of the Congo on his own mistresses at the expense of his own children, who were cartooned as pallid beggars crouching in the snow at his doorstep while the King rolled in vicious pleasures in the Palace bedrooms. This lent dangerous force to the attempts to enforce the civil code on the Royal legacy, at a moment when he was still devising ways to keep it intact. Just as Louise and Mattacic had served the Socialist Daszynski as a stick to beat the whole institution of Empire, so the case of Louise and Stephanie became a favourite weapon of the Belgian Socialists in their attack on Leopold himself and on his treatment of the Congo.

Mattacic died young. Louise lived on, shifting nomadically from spa to spa and occasionally whetting the appetite of her creditors with a dribble of cash. In 1907 a special court in Gotha pronounced her divorce from Philip. In 1911, after the death of her father, she and Stephanie undertook on their own behalf the immense and floundering lawsuit against his estate which was to continue intermittently for ten years. The Belgian State had taken over with the Congo certain funds and foundations which the Princesses argued, correctly, to be part of the Royal fortune. Clémentine, Leopold's favourite, refused to sue for her share, but in 1913 the Belgian Government agreed to settle £230,000 on Louise and Stephanie in respect of some of these holdings.

War prevented the payment of this sum to Louise, who was living in Germany and became the target for Belgian charges of collaboration with the enemy. After the war, she was caught in Budapest by the outbreak of Bela Kun's Commune—the Communist officials were entertained to meet a Princess who was poorer than they were—and the money was finally paid over to her in Vienna in the inflated form of 50,000,000 crowns.

CHAPTER XXIV

THE DAUGHTERS:
STEPHANIE AND CLEMENTINE

STEPHANIE'S LIFE was little happier than her sister's. Her recollections of childhood at Laeken were of chilblained fingers, dun clothes worn winter and summer, and the punishment of kneeling for hours on dried peas. Louise was able for a time to understand that their mother was fond of them, in spite of these rigours which she imposed on them because she thought them to constitute a modern upbringing, but Stephanie seems only to have felt the discipline and to have missed the love. Her only friend, she felt, was one of the household servants, a girl who comforted her after punishment, and her idea of her parents was governed by the memory of her father snubbing the mild Count of Flanders at mealtimes.

Her engagement and marriage followed the usual brutal pattern. Rudolf arrived in Brussels in March 1880, accompanied by a mistress, and the plans for her life were broken to the fifteen-year-old Stephanie next day. Leopold told her that both he and her mother were in favour of the marriage, and hoped that she would become in course of time the Empress of Austria and Queen of Hungary. 'You can withdraw now, think over this plan, and give us your answer tomorrow.' The betrothal dinner had already been arranged, but Stephanie dutifully came to her parents next day and gave her consent. Rudolf called that evening to meet her, a handsome young man of twenty-two, and put the engagement ring on her finger before they went in to dinner. They were married a year later, and Rudolf took her off to the dank and draughty castle of Laxenburg for the wedding night. It was the same wretched story that Louise had told, without her sister's disagreeable imagery: '. . . what torments! What horror! I had not had the ghost of a notion of what lay before me, but had been led to the altar an innocent child.'

Rudolf's letters to his wife seem to show that he was fond of her, and interested in finding out what pleased her. Stephanie resented him, and never lost a chance to add detail to her picture of him as a hunt-obsessed dolt. While Rudolf consoled himself with new mistresses or discussed the failings of his marriage with Louise, Stephanie became an expert on the arid details of Court behaviour and shopped for the sort of clothes she considered suitable for a future Empress. She was a cold-hearted young woman, and in accounting for the convictions of cosmic futility which overwhelmed and finally destroyed Rudolf, she has a lot to answer for.

Few people liked Stephanie in Vienna, and this she visited on Rudolf in repetitive scenes. Their marriage, which had pro-duced Princess Elizabeth in 1883, now existed in little but name, and Stephanie records that Rudolf's health began rapidly to collapse from about 1887. He became acutely nervous and rest-less. It is usual to explain this decline in the Archduke as a mental symptom, but a letter to Stephanie (dated March 27, 1887) does mention that he was taking morphine for his per-sistent cough, 'although it's an injurious drug'.

There is no point in once again going over the unexplained aspects of the 'Mayerling Tragedy'. Partners in an apparent suicide pact, Rudolf and his mistress Marie Vetsera were found shot dead in a hunting-lodge on January 29, 1889. He left an affectionate letter to Stephanie, asking her to look after Elisabeth, the 'poor little girl who is all that is left of me', but the Emperor and the Empress never forgave Stephanie for the results of their son's unhappiness. They forbade her to accept an offer from Queen Victoria to stay at Windsor, and she was settled with her four-year-old daughter at Miramar, her rank and privileges withdrawn.

Leopold was angry at this insult to his daughter, and kept up her annuity of £2,000. This may have seemed generous to Leopold, but to Stephanie, wounded very much more deeply in her vanity than anywhere else, it appeared absurdly little. Although she had been staying with him at Ostend, she did not bother to warn her father of her second engagement, which he read about in *The Times* three days after she had left.

Her new husband, whom she married in 1900 in the teeth of Leopold's opposition, was Count Elmer Lonyay, a Hungarian commoner whom Leopold afterwards referred to as 'that shepherd'. The King never forgave Stephanie for this, especially as it made nonsense of his titular control over his children's marriages, and refused to see her again. When he found her at Marie-Henriette's death-bed, he had her put out of the house, to the disgust of the Belgian public.

Stephanie's world collapsed with the fall of the Austrian Empire. In 1921, the Municipal Council of Budapest issued her a licence to open a cinema. Her son-in-law, a Count of the great family of Windischgrätz, was convicted in 1932 of forging French bank-notes.

Marie-Henriette herself had faded quietly out of life, and for a long time before her death had lived a benevolent and obscure life in the provinces. Since about 1895, she had lived permanently at Spa, almost completely separated from Leopold, only occasionally visiting Brussels to attend concerts and the Opera. Her life acquired a faint but pathetic eccentricity. In her garden at Spa, she kept a white llama: within the palace there, two vile 'griffons' yapped about biting the trousers of official visitors and ruining their ladies' skirts. A Mexican parrot talked gaily; a sullen Congolese parrot refused to say a word.

When she died, on September 19, 1902, the King was taking the waters in the Pyrenees with his young mistress, the 'Baroness Vaughan'. The news was broken to him by Xavier Paoli, the Corsican police officer charged with the security of visiting Royalty in France, who was surprised to see tears in the old man's eyes. He left at once for Belgium, but he had sufficiently recovered by the time he got to Spa to refuse to enter the palace while his daughter was in the building, and when the funeral was over, he went briskly back to France.

Only his daughter Clémentine, born in 1872, now remained in Belgium. A quiet, rather cowed personality, she had spent much of her life with her mother at Spa until a quarrel in the year before the Queen's death. For some time, Leopold had allowed her to act as his 'First Lady' in Belgium. She helped him down steps, organized the household at Laeken, and was even allowed to accompany her father on his expensive holidays in the South of France. For one daughter at least, the elderly King had discovered a sort of possessive fondness.

Even this relationship was soon broken. For years, Clémentine had submitted to the proposition that while her parents needed her at home, it was her duty not to marry. The inevitable rumours had circulated, and one of them at least had been turned to good use by Leopold: when it was being said that she might marry the Duke of Aosta, in late 1902, he sent Liebrechts to Italy with instructions to buy arms for the Congo cheaply while the sentimental feeling for Belgium lasted. But after the death of Marie-Henriette, Clémentine at last tried to rebel.

She wanted to marry Prince Victor Napoleon, son of that 'worn-out basso' who had missed so many Royal trains in the great years of Empire, and now an ageing exile in Belgium. Personally harmless, Victor was still the Bonapartist heir, and Leopold refused his consent point-blank. But Clémentine continued to press her father, until in 1904 Leopold retaliated with a full scale campaign of propaganda. Unable, somehow, to go and forbid her again to her face, he tried to argue round her friends, to bribe her by an increased allowance, to persuade Woeste and Smet de Naeyer to write a letter hostile to the marriage, and even to get the Mayor of Brussels to intervene. The newspaper *l'Indépendence Belge* was made to write a leader which observed that 'the King, even if he wished to do so, can hardly consent to the marriage of a Belgian Princess with a Pretender, an exile from his own country who embodies political principles hostile to the present institutions of France'. The Court historian Pierre Daye thought that he could feel the characteristic rasp of Leopold's own style in one at least of the sentences of the article:

'Princess Clémentine, we are utterly convinced, cannot repay the affection of the Belgian people by forgetting her duty towards them, towards her father, and towards the Dynasty which is for ever inseparable from the great Belgian family'[1].

Put in an impossible position, Clémentine surrendered, and returned to her post as Leopold's companion and house-keeper. This was a duty which became harder and harder for her to carry out, as Leopold's relationship with the 'Baroness de Vaughan', his last mistress, became increasingly blatant. In her sheltered life, Clémentine had never met anything like this pugnacious Parisian call-girl, and she had no weapons to use against

[1] Daye; *Léopold II*; p. 462.

her beyond embarrassed and futile appeals to Leopold himself, who only laughed at her. It was a situation only resolved by Leopold's death in 1909. Clémentine and her sisters chased the Baroness out of the country a few days later, and in the following year, she at last married Prince Napoleon and retired to breed more Bonapartes in peace.

As in Britain, the forces of public opinion released by the widening of the franchise gradually affected ideas on the rôle of the Monarchy. Politically, there was a growing dislike of the Royal control of the Executive; sentimentally, it became apparent that the sort of King the Belgians wanted was no longer a remote and glorious Dynast. Instead, there began a hankering for a King who would be the archetypal Belgian, the image of the nation rather than its representative, who would enjoy Belgian beer and a walk down a Belgian street and whose house and family would serve as a comfortable token of security. Leopold's quarrel with his daughters was probably the most potent cause of the rapid decline in his popularity which now began. The Socialist Vandervelde later referred to 'the wretched spectacle offered currently to the nation by a certain divided family, whose daughters are either estranged or expelled from their father's home, and who quarrel with their creditors over the corpse of their mother . . .' and blamed Leopold for his increasingly obvious dislike of the country he ruled. '. . . almost always abroad; a sort of Royal hobo, losing contact increasingly with those he claims to govern.'[1]

For ten years, Leopold's incessant visits to the Riviera, to Paris, or to south German watering-places, had annoyed his subjects. He was one of the founders of the fashionable settlement at Cap Ferrat, where he built a harbour for his yacht 'Alberta' and constructed a series of magnificent villas on adjoining properties which he bought cheaply through his doctor or through his personal firm of architects in Nice. All through the spring and early summer, 'Alberta' would sit at her moorings while the King worked busily in the main cabin at State papers brought to him from Brussels by a succession of couriers. Ashore, the Baroness de Vaughan waited for him in the 'Villa des Cedres', until the moment when Leopold would be helped ashore, settled astride the sputtering motor-tricycle which he always called 'mon animal', and launched noisily off

[1] Speech to the Chamber, December 11, 1907.

along the rough tracks of the headland which led him to his mistress.

Paris remained for him the place of anonymity, the only town in the world in which he could walk the streets in his old clothes, go to the theatres and restaurants he chose, and be sure that no obsequious fuss would be raised to mark his visit. Back in Belgium, opposition newspapers splashed largely imaginary descriptions of his debaucheries across their feature pages, and it is certain that the King, especially on his visit in 1895, seldom went to bed alone. Dancers, singers, demi-virgins and professional call-girls were all fetched round to satisfy his astonishing sexual appetites. As long ago as 1885, the year of the *Pall Mall Gazette* exposures of child prostitution in London, he had been named as a client by Mrs Jeffries when she was charged with procuring pre-pubescent virgins, and the charge, never disproved, had shaken even the Catholic Press in Brussels.

Leopold knew what was being written about him, but even for this sort of abuse he could draw an advantage. His elaborate and incessant affairs with women never for a moment interfered with the routine of his work, and the assumption that he went to Paris to make a tour of the brothels conveniently obscured the political business which he had to transact there. For years, the whole world believed that Leopold had made the dancer Cléo de Mérode his mistress; Belgian politicians thought that the profits of the Congo were being wasted on her entertainment and cartoonists captioned the King 'Cléopold'; the truth was that they had only met once, but that for different reasons both of them found the publicity useful.

Although it remained his favourite playground, Paris was also Leopold's indispensable listening-post[1]. In Parisian society at the end of the nineteenth century, the threads of high finance and of political intrigue could be picked up at most important dinners, even perhaps at a summer lunch at the races. In 1900, Leopold instructed his young equerry de Raymond to make his way into fashionable society and to accumulate useful contacts which could be used to develop the affairs of the Congo; by day, Leopold would wear out the brim of his felt hat with raising it to influential acquaintances, and in the evening he would interrogate de Raymond about the conversation at the latest lunch given by Count Boni de Castellane. But Leopold could

[1] See Count G. de Raymond; *Léopold II à Paris;* Brussels 1950.

also entertain magnificently on his own, and on at least one occasion, he took the entire Cabinet of the Third Republic out to dinner. When he gave a party, he could make himself wickedly amusing, and he always worked hard to convey the feeling that the mere pleasure of their company was all that he wanted from his guests, but Delcassé, as Minister of Foreign Affairs, once noted that 'perhaps his only failing is that he cannot hide his intelligence: one gets suspicious, and afraid of being led up the garden path'.

Leopold's intelligence did not extend to artistic taste. In an age of matchless vulgarity, Leopold was perhaps the most formidable Philistine of them all. Above all, he detested music, which he called 'the most expensive of all noises'; he never went near an opera house or a concert if he could avoid it, and Marie-Henriette had to satisfy her pathetic yearning for melody by rigging up a contrivance called a 'theatrophone' which amplified to her the current production at the Théâtre de la Monnaie. As for poetry, Leopold was only once heard to pass comment: he said, suggestively but obscurely, 'that it reminded him of a mechanical razor'. Visually, he liked whatever would make a Belgian provincial official gasp and feel small. His idea of art's function, and perhaps of the law's function too, is embodied in the Palais de Justice, a black ziggurat approaching the size of Gibraltar which throws the whole city into its cruel shadow; in the Italian renaissance lift which he installed at Laeken; in the green leather upholstery tooled in gold which plumped out the saloon of his private railway coach.

If there was anything more than business and women which brought Leopold to Paris in his later years it was cars. He was one of the earliest and most extravagant of the patrons of the 'Salon de l'Automobile', especially after he had fallen off his tricycle at Cap Ferrat in 1899, and among the cars he possessed was a hundred-horse-power Mercedes in which he drove dangerously and very fast indeed along the roads near Ostend, in the early mornings. Like many Coburgs since, from the ex-King Leopold III to the present Duke of Kent, speed excited him intensely, and he learned to drive himself when he was over seventy, even though he had at least two experienced chauffeurs at his disposal.

One of these men was a French theoretical anarchist, bought in Paris with the cars and addressed by Leopold as 'Citoyen'.

It was noticed by the French that Leopold's narrow, mocking smile grew more frequent as he grew older: perhaps this is partly to be explained by the fact that although he had detested the Second Empire, Leopold never could bring himself to take the Republic very seriously. It was true that in Paris his influence as a visiting monarch was enhanced by the absence of a French Court; the King of the Belgians could make politicians of the Third Republic do things for him to which no official of the Second Empire would ever have consented. But this relative pliability did not affect Leopold's fundamental view of a Republican régime as no more than the débris of a Royal failure. One of his French doctors told him after a medical examination that he would have made a wonderful President of the Republic. Leopold returned: 'What would you say, Doctor, if somebody told you that you would make a wonderful vet?'

CHAPTER XXV

DEFEAT ON THE NILE

H IS FIRST DRIVE towards the Nile had petered out in 1894, leaving Leopold with the enclave of Lado on the left bank. In itself, it was a poor reward for the hard fighting and immense losses of Van Kerckhoven and his men, but it was a foothold on the river from which great strides might be taken to the north and the east. As soon as Leopold had assured himself that the Mérode annexation scheme had been defeated, Leopold set out for Paris to exploit the status of a 'Nile Power' which the precarious occupation of Lado had conferred on him.

This was the most energetic of all Leopold's visits to Paris, although it is hard to define where business exertions ended and pleasure began. In his usual fashion, Leopold took great care to make an attractive impression upon French public opinion, and in the eleven days he spent there, he contrived to be seen at the Comédie Francaise, the Jockey Club, the Opera, the Union Artistique, the Folies Bergère and any number of restaurants. The fact that he enjoyed leg-shows and loathed opera, even perhaps the rumour that his equerries spent a certain amount of their time fixing up assignations with suitable young girls, all helped to present a genial image, the figure of a slyly-smiling old man with a vast white beard, moving patiently through the pavement crowds and peering at shops and ankles like any other elderly tourist. Behind this screen of naïve enjoyment, the real business of his visit could be securely concealed.

It seems certain that in talks with Faure and with Hanotaux, the Foreign Minister, Leopold now improvized an informal and highly secret agreement for common action in the Sudan[1]. In the years immediately following Leopold's visit, the ambitions of France and of the Congo State towards the Upper Nile took

[1] A. J. Wauters; *Histoire Politique du Congo Belge;* Brussels 1911; p. 134.

the form of three converging expeditions which seemed to supplement each other rather than to compete. The best-known of
these expeditions, the French force led by Marchand, borrowed
a steamer from the Governor of the Congo to take it up the
Ubangi on its journey to the north-east. The other French
expedition, which prepared under the doubtful protection of the
Emperor Menelik to advance on the Nile from Addis Ababa,
was the sequel to a number of tentative schemes examined by
Leopold and the French which would have put Leopold forward
as a mediator between Menelik and the Italians after their cata-
strophic defeat by the Ethiopians at Adowa on March 1, 1896.

The third of these apparently concerted movements was the
expedition led by Dhanis, the veteran of the Arab wars, which
left Stanleyville for the north-east in the autumn of 1896 with
instructions to strike the Nile at Redjaf and then head into the
Sudan downstream from the Lado enclave until he arrived at
Fashoda[1]. There he was to open sealed orders for the next phase
of his advance.

It was natural that the new offensive towards the Nile should
excite public opinion in Belgium, and Dhanis had imprudently
encouraged popular interest by saying as early as 1895 that 'our
advance-guard of a thousand well-armed regulars with Krupp
artillery and machine-guns is at Lado or will shortly arrive
there . . . '[2] This was entirely untrue; it was eighteen months
before a force arrived at Lado, and Dhanis himself never got
there at all; but the hyperbole suited Leopold's hectically optimistic mood. He was talking to his friends about the glories of
the Pharaohs—Van Eetvelde complained to the British Ambassador in Brussels that the King's imagination was running away
with him—and in March 1897 the magazine *La Belgique
Coloniale* flew an outrageous kite suggesting that the Nile should
be internationalized and its free navigation placed under the care
of some disinterested Power, neither Britain nor France . . .
But these rather absurd excesses of propaganda cannot in retro-
spect excuse the Congo State from the charge of playing the
hyena's part on the Upper Nile. In 1894, Leopold had trailed the
footsteps of the British in the hope of acquiring scraps which
Britain would not dare to swallow. In 1895-8, he had transferred

[1] Near the modern Kodok.
[2] Wauters; *Histoire Politique;* p. 138.

his loyalty to the French, banking again on the incorrect assumption that France and Britain would rather leave territory to him than face up to each other and risk war for the sake of a permanent settlement. This was not a policy but a mere tactic. It was fortunate for him and for Belgium that the Dhanis expedition collapsed in disaster before it could reach the Nile and become involved in the great confrontation of Fashoda.

The execution of Ngongo Lutete during the Arab wars in 1893 had never been forgiven by the men of the Batetela people who had been his soldiers. But they had been absorbed into the armed forces of the Congo State and disseminated, like an unrecognized poison, throughout the enormous territory. Already, in July 1895, a mutiny of Batetela soldiers stationed at Luluabourg had taken the State administration completely by surprise; the mutineers had won pitched battles against troops commanded by Belgian officers and had overrun large regions of the State in their march back to their homes on the Lomami before they were defeated in October by the experienced generalship of Lothaire and le Marinel. Yet Dhanis had included Batetela troops in his expeditionary force to the Nile, and had allowed them to bring their women and children on the journey from the Upper Congo which Stanley and Van Kerckhoven had shown to be one of the most formidable in Africa. In the circumstances, he was lucky to get as far as the watershed of the Congo and the Nile, in the far north-east, before serious trouble began. But when the outbreak did take place, on February 14, 1897, Dhanis was apparently taken by surprise. A unit in the advance guard massacred its officers, turned about, and headed southwards towards the Lomami, gathering the following battalions to the mutiny as it came down the track; when he tried to hold them at the crossing of the Aruwimi river, Dhanis was totally defeated and had to make his way back to Stanley Falls almost alone. These mutineers fought on in the Manyema for another two years, nor was this the last explosion of Batetela resistance to the Congo State, for in April 1900, a thousand miles from their home, Batetela soldiers manning one of the forts at the Atlantic estuary of the Congo suddenly opened fire with the fortress batteries against an Antwerp liner lying moored in the roadstead. Even as late at 1907, one of the British Vice-Consuls in the Congo found a pocket of Batetela mutineers surviving in a comfortable economy of slaving and gun-running in the south-west corner of the Katanga[1].

The shock of the disaster to the Dhanis expedition was a little offset by the news that Major Chaltin, a Congo officer engaged against the Mahdists in the Bahr-el-Ghazal, had stormed and occupied Redjaf in the very month of the mutiny. But the failure of the two French expeditions eventually destroyed the significance of this victory, too. The party in Ethiopia had already presented Menelik with 100,000 rifles to encourage him to forestall the slow advance of Kitchener and the British by pushing Ethiopia's western frontier up to Fashoda on the Nile. Now two parties led by the Frenchmen Clochette and de Bonchamps set out for the Nile, and after an almost intolerably difficult journey, Bonchamps arrived at the confluence of the Nile and the Sobat on June 22, 1898. However, he was unable to stay there, and left the Nile only a few weeks before Marchand, coming from the west, arrived on the river at Fashoda.

Omdurman was fought on September 2nd. The few Mahdist survivors of that mechanical massacre fled into the wilderness, while Kitchener entered Khartoum and prepared to advance up the Nile towards the French and Ethiopians. He and Marchand met at Fashoda on September 17th, in polite but definite collision, and Europe entered the rapids of the 'Fashoda Incident' which ended, after much talk of war and readying of fleets, in Marchand's withdrawal. France, by the Anglo-French Declaration of March 1899, retired for ever beyond the western watershed of the Nile, while Britain asserted the 'rights of the Khedive' and the Anglo-Egyptian Condominium over both the Bahr-el-Ghazal and the Nile valley. In theory, Leopold and the Congo State continued to assert that the 'rights of the Khedive' no longer covered the Bahr-el-Ghazal and other provinces of the south Sudan. In practice, Leopold was forced once again to withdraw his tiny garrisons south towards the confining borders of the Lado enclave.

If the French stood little chance of maintaining the hold won for them by Marchand on the Nile, the Congo's chances were necessarily thinner still. But in the east, Leopold's quick imagination and his extraordinary skill at the 'concessionaire' technique

[1] British Consular Reports 1908; report of Vice-Consul Beak. The most famous son of the Batetela in modern times was Patrice Lumumba.

of inserting the thin end of the annexationist wedge, nearly brought him a compensating success in Eritrea. Profiting from the effects of the Italian disaster at Adowa, he suggested that he might for a limited time take over the Italian sphere of influence in the coastal lands of Eritrea and in Ethiopia itself. This was not an unwelcome idea to the Italian Government, reluctant to abandon permanently the empire which had been won in Africa and yet faced by a public opinion which had never liked the idea of empire and was now disgusted with it. In a letter written in January 1897, Luzzatti, the Finance Minister reflected:

'I have dreamed of the idea that a friendly King, for example the King of the Belgians, the "Knight of African quests", might take charge of our plateau for a number of years. He's a friend who is not unlikeable and who knows how to make colonies. I wouldn't feel it humiliating'[1].

Leopold's powers of invention were now operating at a pace of fever. An extraordinary document[2] was despatched to William II, offering the Germans a share in various Belgian overseas industrial projects if he would support the plan for an Eritrean lease and suggest to the British that Egypt should give Leopold a similar lease of the Sennar district in the central Sudan. Meanwhile, Sam Wiener was packed off to Rome, and General dal Verme, Leopold's best Italian contact at this period, paid visits to Brussels and prepared for Leopold's own visit to Rome, which took place in April 1897. By the summer, the scheme had taken the shape of a proposed 'Société Congolaise de Colonisation et d'Exploitation' to take lease of Eritrea and also of the Sennar and the town of Kassala, both fertile districts lying towards the Nile, but both within the boundaries which Britain might be expected to claim when the Sudan was reconquered from the Mahdists. The lease was to last for as long as the Congo State remained either independent or as a colony ruled by Leopold and his successors (a clause which recalls the original form of the Anglo-Congolese Agreement of 1894), and its revenues were to be shared equally by Leopold (in the person of the Company) and by the Italian Government. To this vaguely-defined

[1] Letter quoted in L. Ranieri; *Relations entre l'Etat Indépendant du Congo et l'Italie;* ARSC 1959; p. 87.

[2] Quoted in Daye; *Léopold II;* p. 412.

H

cut of Africa, Leopold wanted to add the lease of a corridor to connect the Congo with the Red Sea, by way of the Sennar.

The Italian defeat in Ethiopia had opened a second hole in the tentative patchwork of 'influences' around the Upper Nile, and as he had done repeatedly in the case of the Sudan, Leopold was once more offering the 'neutral' presence of the Congo State as a temporary plug. Unfortunately, the Italian presence in Africa was not strong enough to hold this plug in place. For one thing, the Italian Cabinet was divided, uncertain whether it was worth retaining a foothold in Africa at all; the Government produced a string of proposed amendments to the lease, greatly modifying its length and Italy's military commitment to assist the Company in the event of trouble, and as the Roman Press poked leak after leak into the secrecy which was supposed to be protecting the whole transaction, there was a general loss of nerve, accompanied by a feeling that Luzzatti's connection with Leopold II was too elaborate to be politically healthy.

Another and even more serious flaw in the plan was that Italy, invited to make use of Leopold, was in turn being used by somebody else. The Italian occupation of Kassala on the Atbara tributary of the Nile had driven Salisbury in 1889 to lay down the integrity of the Nile valley as an object of British policy. Now the Italians, besieged by the Mahdists, were trying to get out of Kassala alive, and their danger was made into Salisbury's pretext for launching the campaign to reconquer the Sudan. From 1896 onwards, Salisbury insisted to the unfortunate Italians that they must at all costs hold on to Kassala—if they evacuated the town, there would, of course, be nothing left for him to rescue. This meant that Leopold's plan to lease the 'Italian sphere' depended doubly upon British approval, which he could hardly expect to win. In the first place, the British considered that both Kassala and the Sennar were the rightful properties of the Khedive of Egypt. In the second place, since the British were justifying their advance by the spectacle of the Italians floundering about in a rising tide of Dervishes, Leopold's proposal to get them out of the interior altogether was nothing but a nuisance.

Leopold's only possible tactic was to persuade the Italians to approach Britain on his behalf. This they did with waning enthusiasm. In September 1897, it was arranged that Leopold's friend dal Verme should meet Lord Cromer at Turin station, as his train stopped on its way to the Mediterranean, and hand him certain information which the Foreign Office had requested about the costs of the Kassala garrison. But dal Verme was not content merely to act the part of a messenger-boy, and ignoring Cromer's frigid resentment, he climbed aboard the coach and rode on with him towards Alessandria. Cromer, glacial and just, was at the summit of his career as British Agent in Egypt, and he disliked being asked questions by foreigners without previous notice. He consented to discuss Kassala with dal Verme between stations, but their conversation proved to be little more than a repetition of what had already been said: the Italian pleaded that evacuation could not be postponed much longer and the Englishman insisted that Kassala must be held at least until the Anglo-Egyptian armies under Kitchener had reached the con-fluence of the Atbara and the Nile. Finally sensing the despera-tion of the Italian position, Cromer conceded to dal Verme an assurance that the British would be ready to resume responsi-bility for Kassala by Christmas. It was at this moment that the train began to slow down for Alessandria. Lord Cromer rose to finish the interview, and dal Verme realized with horror that he had forgotten to raise the question of Leopold's plans for Kassala and for a corridor across the Sudan to the Congo. He began to speak, but as soon as it became clear that he was raising the matter of Leopold's concession, Cromer said sharply that it was no concern of his. Now the train was stopping. dal Verme begged him at least to express an opinion. Cromer laughed and said: 'The King of the Belgians is very cunning!' And that was all[1].

Leopold persisted a little longer with the Eritrean scheme, calling at Genoa in his yacht that November to undertake another vain rallying of Italian support. But he was already occupied with a new and quite different project in the same part of the world. In the aftermath of Adowa, he had already taken soundings for what was left of the Italian 'sphere' in Ethiopia. Now, in October 1897, he received in Brussels the optimistic Russian officer whom Menelik had appointed Governor of Ethiopia's southern province, Count Leontiev. It was typical of Leontiev that when asked how large his province really was, he

[1] For this episode, see Ranieri; *Relations entre l'EIC et l'Italie;* pp. 104-5.

defined an area which stretched not only to the Nile on the west but well into what is now Kenya and Uganda to the south[1]. Everything was maximal to Leontiev: to Leopold, he described the enormous harvest of coffee and ivory, the seams of gold, which his province could export for the investment of a few hundred thousand francs, and went on to offer Belgian mining companies a preference in mineral rights. This was enough to rouse Leopold's interest, and although there is no direct evidence that he sought to convert 'Ethiopian Equatoria' into a political concession, the usual crop of 'Sociétés Anonymes' soon sprang up, watered with Royal investments, to take advantage of the situation. A year later, a general commercial company was formed, with Leontiev as chairman; in 1900, a 'Société Anonyme des Mines d'Or' made its appearance, and Leontiev was sitting in the chair of that one too. Two years later, it was discovered that Menelik had never given him the authority to make trading concessions, and both companies collapsed in a wail of lost savings.

British pressure on Lado itself now began to develop, and by 1905 there was talk of offering Leopold a small tract on the Bahr-el-Ghazal in exchange for the enclave. This took notice of Leopold's long-standing interest in the commercial possibilities of the Bahr-el-Ghazal. In 1893, State officers had persuaded a local ruler to concede to their King the right to exploit the copper workings at Hofrat-en-Nahas, far to the north and almost on the latitude of Fashoda. At about the same time, Leopold's men had alarmed France and Britain by their contacts with Rabah, foster-son of the great Zobeir Pasha, whose empire reached from south of Lake Chad in the west to the Bahr-el-Ghazal in the east; the British in Nigeria had once considered an alliance with him for his own purposes[2]. Now Leopold was affecting to believe that the Anglo-French settlement on the Upper Nile in 1899 had cancelled out the humiliating agreement with France which had been forced on him in August 1894, and had restored to life the agreement made in May that year with Britain. In other words, his commercial lease of the Bahr-el-Ghazal was still in force[3]. Acting on this belief, he spawned yet

[1] Quoted in Robinson, Gallagher and Denny; *Africa and the Victorians;* p. 364, Note 4.
[2] See Perham; *Lugard;* Vol. II, p. 8, Note 1.
[3] Wauters; *Histoire Politique;* p. 190.

another brood of 'Société Anonymes', based this time in London, to exploit the wild rubber of the concession. But when the agents of the Anglo-Belgian Africa Company Ltd. and the British Tropical Africa Company Ltd. asked for permission to enter their concession by travelling up the Nile, the British refused to let them through.

It should be said at once that Leopold was quite wrong in his conviction that the Bahr-el-Ghazal was a source of easily-won wealth. The copper mines at Hofrat-en-Nahas were remote from any means of transporting ore, and the Anglo-Egyptian administration of the Sudan, after a period of ill-founded optimism, failed to make a going concern in that region out of either wild or plantation rubber. But Leopold continued to adventure into the region, and a 'scientific' expedition towards Hofrat-en-Nahas, whose real aim was to establish a military post at the mines, was turned back by Anglo-Egyptian forces. Another party, which set out by paddle-steamer from Lado in September 1899, stuck ingloriously in the reed-oceans of the Sudd.

This was a situation which the British could no longer leave unresolved, not least because Leopold was claiming that an Egyptian declaration of 1885, issued by Riaz Pasha, had excluded most of the south Sudan from the lands covered by the 'rights of the Khedive' and in effect transferred the region to the sovereignty of local rulers who were in turn free to cede their rights to the Congo State. Even if, in terms of available force, Leopold did not have a chance of retaining areas of the Sudan which Britain regarded as her own, yet the very persistence and noisiness of his propaganda could in the end provoke fresh international difficulties, probably with the French. To Britain, it now seemed time to end Leopold's career as the dishonest broker of the Upper Nile.

Britain offered him a small slice of the Bahr-el-Ghazal, south of the fifth parallel and west of the Yei river, in exchange for the Lado enclave. This proposal demanded time for reflection, and in the interval, Leopold sent an armed party commanded by Lieutenant Lemaire to examine the value of the goods behind the counter. They had advanced into the Bahr-el-Ghazal as far as six degrees north—well out of bounds by almost any accepted definition—when they were stopped by an Anglo-Sudanese force, but to avoid the absurdity of a clash between Britain and officers seconded from the Belgian Army, a temporary settlement was rigged up in March 1905. It provided for the withdrawal of Anglo-Sudanese troops from the disputed area until a permanent arrangement was made, but Leopold imprudently rushed his own forces forward to occupy the posts evacuated by the Anglo-Sudanese. This was a futile and disastrous outbreak of Leopold's lust for short-term advantages. Its inevitable result was a sharp British order to Congolese forces to retreat southwards, followed by the closing of the Nile to Congolese transport.

Now a settlement was going to be imposed on the Congo State, and it would be a less favourable one. Lado was going to be lost, and little got for it in return. Yet Lado had never been used by Leopold for its own sake: even Van Eetvelde considered it did not pay, and Lord Cromer, travelling up the Nile in 1902, could see few signs of life on the Belgian bank. He suggested:

'The reason of all this is obvious enough. The Belgians are disliked. The people fly from them, and it is no wonder that they should do so, for I am informed that the soldiers are allowed full liberty to plunder, and that payments are rarely made for supplies . . . the Government, so far as I could judge, is conducted almost exclusively on commercial principles, and, even judged by that standard, it would appear that those principles are somewhat short-sighted'[1].

Leopold was ending a Riviera holiday when he heard the terms of the settlement which Van Eetvelde had signed in London on May 9, 1906. The whole enclave had been surrendered, and in return the Congo had gained only the awkward little port of Mahagi, down on the western shore of Lake Albert, and the right to connect it to the Nile by a railway. But even though he must have known how little to expect, Leopold raised a great drama for the benefit of his equerries, crying, 'It's our Fashoda!' and sulking in the train all the way to Paris. The settlement amounted to fair punishment for the turbulence and irresponsibility of his own tactics on the Upper Nile over the past fifteen years, but he preferred to blame Van Eetvelde for its terms.

[1] Letter to Lansdowne; January 21, 1903.

CHAPTER XXVI

LEOPOLD IN CHINA:
THE BELGIAN EXPANSION

THE CONGO was not the only field for Belgian industrial expansion, any more than it was the first. Previous overseas enterprises, by emboldening Belgian business-men to invest their money in remote projects of foreign development, had prepared Belgium for the massive exploitation of the Congo which began at the turn of the century. In a few cases, new inventions made in Belgium had founded the for-tunes of manufacturing empires ruling a domestic market: Ernest Solvay, for example, discoverer of a new process for making soda, was expanding his business into one of the largest chemical groups in Europe. But for the most part, Belgian industry had already satisfied the limited home market, and was now moving out into the undeveloped areas of the world, offering its services to countries without the resources to build their own railways or sink their own mines, in return for long-term exploiting concessions.

Cockerill, the great iron and steel group at Seraing, near Liège, was opening up the South Russian coal deposits with mine-and-steelworks combines. In South America, Belgian interests came to own 3,800 miles of railway track and another 1,500 in China. This type of concession was a variant of a Belgian speciality: the farm of public services, whose most brilliant exponent was the banker Edouard Empain, another of Leopold's accomplices in the Congo and his regular business adviser. A self-made man whose father was a poor schoolmaster, Empain's first major venture was the building of track between Liège and the suburb of Jemeppe, an enterprise which became the model for an extension of small local railways all over the Low Countries. From there, Empain went on to make himself the 'Tramway King', whose streetcars and underground-train services could be encountered all over the world. His most famous achievement was the Paris Métro, opened in 1900, but by 1914 his trams were groaning down the avenues of cities as far apart as Cairo, Boulogne and Astrakhan, and he had railway interests in Russia, Spain and China. As a capitalist, Empain was one of the inventors of the general investment company, a single trust endowed with many holdings in different companies which could use their parent trust as a savings bank. As a town planner, he held a fat portfolio of public concessions for gas, water and electric-light services, and it was Empain who built Heliopolis, designed as a modern satellite town in the desert beside Cairo.

By the year of Leopold's death, in 1909, Belgium was exporting a third of her production, a higher figure than that of Britain. The density of her railway network was more than double that of any other country in the world, and the population had reached 7,500,000. Belgian investment in foreign countries totalled £600,000,000 sterling[1]. This sallying-forth of Belgian enterprise was the object for which Leopold had been working since his travels as Duke of Brabant, and he went on organizing and cadging and bullying and borrowing to clear more ground for the harvests of Belgian industry up to the end of his reign. But as he grew old, his ideas about the technique of exploitation ceased to develop under the impact of experience. Above all, he never grew fully immune to the temptation to expand an economic foothold into one of territorial sovereignty.

In all his complex dealings with China, dependent as they were upon the favour of the existing Chinese Government, Leopold never put aside the hope that his various rights of exploitation would ripen into territorial concessions. Belgium, as a small neutral country which could hardly be regarded as a threat to the Chinese Empire, had an obvious opportunity to do favours for China which would be dangerous if asked of a major European Power: there was everything to be gained by pliant and skilful collaboration with Pekin. But though Leopold at times argued to the Chinese that Belgian investment and concessions could carry no threat to Chinese security, in practice he never hesitated to invoke the support of other Powers in order to force his own terms on Pekin.

From the age of twenty-one, he had been suggesting that a Belgian base should be set up on the China coast and a national

[1] Above figures quoted in de Meeus; *Histoire des Belges;* Brussels 1958; p. 416.

trading corporation formed to open up the inland market. In 1859, he had supported Brialmont's design to acquire an island in the estuary of the Yangtze, and in 1865, he and Banning were cooking up an abortive scheme for the annexation of Formosa. A few years later, however, Leopold adopted less blatant and more effective tactics. At the international congress of ironmasters at Liège in 1873, he had canvassed delegates for the formation of an Anglo-Belgian consortium, possibly with Chinese members, to study the construction of railways in China under concession from the Imperial Government. Nothing came of this, the Chinese being reluctant, but Leopold did not forget the plan. For the first time, he had offered to China the argument that neutral Belgium was the safest contractor for a necessary programme of modernization.

At the time of the Liège Congress, China had at least been strong enough to reject offers of assistance she did not want. Twenty years later, after her defeat by Japan, she was helpless, and the consuls and businessmen of the West crowded in to extort what they could. As the scramble began, the Viceroy Li Hung-Chang, 'China's leading statesman and strongest administrator'[1], set out on a world tour. His main purpose was to improve relations with Russia, then the dominant influence at Pekin, but in Western Europe and the United States he made close studies of military and industrial techniques, and was anxiously courted by Governments and manufacturers brandishing tenders for railway construction. Li took notes, but did not commit himself. However, Leopold determined to scrape an official acquaintance with the Viceroy, and an equerry was despatched to pick him up at Essen, where he was the guest of Krupps at the Villa Hugel, and invite him to Belgium. He accepted, and made an exhaustive tour of Belgian factories, entertained and sometimes escorted by Leopold in person. Belgium gaped at his silk robes and his palanquin, and official bands acclaimed him with a Chinese national anthem which was afterwards discovered to have been composed by the music publisher who sold them the score, but the visit proved in the end to have made good business for Belgium. An Imperial Decree in 1895 had authorized the building of 800 miles of railway to link Pekin in the north with Hankow in central China, and Li, though he gave no promises, was apparently

[1] H. B. Morse; *International Relations of the Chinese Empire*; Vol. 3, p. 104.

impressed by the convenience of granting the construction rights to a Belgian firm.

Leopold sent off Emile Francqui to China in Li's wake, to act as consul, and followed him with a ramshackle 'Congolese' delegation in faked-up uniform. This party achieved little beyond providing Li with a butt for his sense of humour. But while Li Hung-Chang was solemnly pretending not to understand why the delegates were not negroes, Francqui was fixing up the details of the concession with Li's colleague the Viceroy Chang Chih-Tung, in Hankow.

The agreement of 1897 was an extortionate arrangement. It involved forcing the Chinese Government to accept a loan of £4,500,000 at interest originally agreed at four per cent over twenty years. Later the Belgians decided to push the rate up to five per cent, and invoked the diplomatic pressure of France and Russia to dictate the change to China, a tactic which irritated the British and encouraged them to see in the Belgian presence in China a mere tool of Franco-Russian politics. The railway work was carried out by a Franco-Belgian concession company with a Belgian chairman and a solid wad of Congo State money to its credit; the exploitation of the line, once completed, was to be passed on a thirty-year lease to a Belgian company whose shareholding would be divided in three parts, between Belgian and French investors and the Chinese Government. The line was built in less than six years, including a two-mile railway bridge across the Yellow River, by the Belgian engineer Jean Jadot.

As compensation for this remarkable Belgian success, the British extorted from China no less than five other railway concessions, and British resentment at his 'pro-Belgian' attitude contributed to the fall of Li Hung-Chang in 1898. But Leopold felt that his foray into China was still only in its earliest stages: partition was in the air, especially after the Anglo-German agreement of September 1898 over the boundaries of their respective spheres of interest, and he did not intend to be left out of the final spoliation. Comparing the Pekin-Hankow line to a backbone, he asserted: "I shall get the cutlets off it"[1]. But before his butchering could begin, there was another length of backbone to be secured.

[1] Quoted in Lichtervelde; *Léopold II;* p. 284.

The Pekin-Hankow line formed only half of the total plan. A second leg of 700 miles was to connect Hankow with Canton, in the far south, and Leopold felt that his chances for securing this concession were good. But during an absence of Francqui in Europe, an American group approached the Chinese authorities and forestalled the Belgians: the rights to construct the railway were granted to the American China Development Company. All that was left to Leopold's Pekin-Hankow outfit was a right of pre-emption if the Americans should decide to abandon the Hankow-Canton concession, an apparently unlikely case. But Leopold was not disposed to accept defeat, and his emissaries worked hard in the United States to arrange a re-sale. Luck, as well as hard work, brought the American China Development Company round to their offers.

In April 1898, the outbreak of the Spanish-American war alarmed and discouraged the American businessmen who had invested their money across the Pacific, while in China itself, growing nationalist unrest in the provinces of Hunan was making the very districts across which the railway must run unsafe for foreigners. Leopold judged that the growing strength of the British presence in the Yangtse valley made direct pre-emption by his Pekin-Hankow company unwise, but through his American accomplice General Whittier, he successfully acquired a majority of the shares in the American China Development Company. To do so, he scoured the Congo and the Belgian banks for money: it did not deter him that the transaction was blatantly illegal.

The original concession agreement between the Chinese Government and the Americans had 'clearly and definitely stipulated that the interests arising under the contract were non-transferable'[1]. When in early 1904 the Chinese found out that Americans had sold a State concession without even consulting them, they took the step, mild in the circumstances, of refusing to recognise Belgian control. With his usual Protean inventiveness, Leopold set about rigging up a new basis for the Company, distributing the shares between Belgium, France and the great American banker J. Pierpont Morgan.

Morgan, however, was every bit as sharp as Leopold himself, and considerably more direct. The Royal yacht 'Alberta' called

[1] Cheng Lin; *The Chinese Railways, Past and Present;* Shanghai 1937; p. 90.

at Gravesend and brought him aboard by steam-pinnace to lunch and to talk business with the King. Leopold's equerry noted, with well-bred scorn, that Morgan's nose resembled the beak of an enraged turkey; he walked about with his hands in his pockets, and at lunch he spat out food he found hard to swallow[1]. But he stood his ground, holding out for a larger share than a third in the reformed American China Development Company, and the haggling swung sharply his way when the French declined to take up Leopold's offer. Nothing could now prevent Morgan from acquiring half the shares.

The success of the Japanese in the war against Russia strengthened China's hand in bargaining with her European parasites. She did not feel strong enough to revoke the Hankow-Canton concession unilaterally, although the agreement might well have been considered broken and null, but in 1905 she proposed to buy the concession back. Leopold took the lame precaution of letting Morgan's holding rise to fifty-one per cent, but the Chinese were not conciliated by this return to American control. They wished to buy back all the shares of the American China Development Company, adding a large bonus, and the British, to assist in the dislodging of Leopold, advanced China the sum of £1,100,000 towards this enormous expense, guaranteed by the opium revenues of two provinces. Morgan, who was a simple financier and not an empire-builder, was irritated by Leopold's suggestion that he should reject a capital gain approaching two hundred per cent. In vain, Leopold sent his equerry Carton de Wiart to reason with him at Aix les Bains, and in July 1905, once more took him aboard the 'Alberta'. The Chinese raised their offer yet again, and Morgan told Leopold flatly that he did not see why he should be ashamed to realize his original investment at a five-fold profit. This opinion was supported by President Roosevelt, to whom Leopold appealed, and Morgan sold out to the Chinese Government, leaving Leopold with a lump sum of £280,000 for his shares and no Hankow-Canton railway.

This was the furthest penetration into China which Leopold achieved. At Tientsin and near Tsing-Tao, Belgium acquired unimportant territorial concessions, but her stronger competi-

[1] Baron E. Carton de Wiart; *Léopold II, Souvenirs des Dernières Années;* Brussels 1944; p. 84.

tors never intended to allow her a significant share in any eventual partition. At the time of the Boxer Rising, the German Emperor intervened to prevent Belgium from despatching an expeditionary force to help the other Powers. In 1899, Sam Wiener had sounded the Italians on a joint enterprise which would lodge Italy in Chekiang and join China to Genoa by a Belgian shipping line; the following year, Leopold offered Germany Congolese territory in Kivu in exchange for a lease to the Congo of a port in Shantung province and some surrounding territory from the German zone of influence. But none of the territorial ambitions bore fruit, and there remained for Belgium and for the treasury of the Congo only the rich incomes from the various Chinese loans and investments.

Throughout the Chinese episode, Leopold's possession of the Congo had been doubly useful to him: both as a source of investment capital and as a base for 'Congo-law' companies which were more flexible than combinations limited by Belgian company law and which professed to offer services even more strictly neutral than those of Belgian firms. In 1898, Leopold sent his Congolese emissaries on a second commercial sortie against the Philippines. His first attempt to lodge himself on the islands had taken advantage of a period of Spanish weakness; now not only Spain but the United States were involved. Only a few months after the outbreak of the Spanish-American War, United States troops had taken Manila in August 1898, but the preliminary peace arranged the same month in Washington had not settled the future of the Philippines. In both Spain and America, there was controversy. The Spanish still hoped to retain control of the islands, but could see no way to reassert their claim. The American administration, in spite of the imperialist clamours of the Press and a section of public opinion, felt itself too weak politically to undertake a new campaign both against the Spanish and against Anguinaldo's Filipino partisans, who had helped them in the initial campaign. To make things worse, the Germans were interested: there were four German warships in the vicinity, and in Europe informed gossip suggested that William II was going to throw in his weight on the Spanish side, for some price to be exacted in commercial privileges.

Once again, a situation had arisen which suited Leopold's

abilities. A piece of territory was in the market, and a number of Powers, too nervous to seize it and too greedy to let it go to a rival, were hoping for some Providential compromise to be imposed from outside which would allow them all a decent and dignified line of retreat. Where now the United Nations would intervene, with its mandates and expeditionary forces, Leopold rushed forward in the disguise of a neutral and safely unpolitical board of businessmen.

Sam Wiener, who was alarmed by the whole idea, was none the less sent off on a new round of confidential interviews. To the American and Spanish Ambassadors in Brussels, he suggested that all or part of the Philippines might safely be handed over to an uncommitted concession company with sovereign rights, and the company he proposed for the job was the 'Société Générale Africaine', founded in 1897 as the very first of the 'Congo-law' companies with both the brothers Browne de Tiège and Wiener himself on the Board, which had already gone into Far Eastern enterprises by spawning the 'Société Générale Asiatique'. The American ambassador was interested in the plan; the Spanish at first less so. Following up his advantage, Wiener circulated data on the 'Société Générale Africaine' to the American delegates charged to negotiate a formal peace treaty with Spain in Paris, and the Belgian envoy in Washington was assured by Secretary of State Hay that he would discuss the matter with President McKinley. Even in Madrid, opinion became more favourable. Wiener's lobbying among the two sides at the Paris meeting looked as if it was going to bear fruit.

But in November 1898, the Congressional elections gave unexpected reassurance to the McKinley Republicans. A tougher stand was at once adopted by the Americans in Paris. Wiener was pushed aside, as the United States put forward demands for the full cession of the Philippines, and in February 1899 fighting broke out between the insurgents and the US Army. The plan had sunk, and even a hopeful scheme for a joint Belgian-American consortium to exploit the coal resources of Luzon, feverishly carpentered together by Belgian and Congolese representatives in Washington, failed to save anything from the wreck[1].

[1] For this episode, see H. van Leynseele; *Léopold II et les Philippines en 1898*; ARSC II/195616. Also: Daye; *Léopold II*; pp. 445-6.

All over the world, Leopold's little team of financiers was at work, responding to the innumerable minutes which suggested to them some new point of opportunity by injecting doses of Congolese money into railways, fisheries, mining concerns and timber trusts. Shadowy 'Sociétés' rose and fell, and secret emissaries hustled about the world, bribing newspapers, buying lunches for politicians, and filling notebooks with trading figures. Morocco again became a target of Leopold's intelligence services, and Empain prepared an abortive expedition to lay hold of Agadir for a Belgian fishery station[1]. The Congo State, in its official capacity, made Spain an offer for the Canaries[2]. In Mongolia and Manchuria and on the Yenisei in Siberia, the King's agents sought openings for Belgian syndicates in collaboration with Russian capitalists; in Korea, he and Wiener worked with the Americans[3]. Belgian interests were helped forward by Leopold in Persia, where Belgians organized the postal and customs staff, and in Siam, where they worked as lawyers. At different times, Leopold formed ambitions towards Albania; the Baghdad Railway; mining concessions in Greece; Fiji; the New Hebrides; rubber in Bolivia; the Solomon Islands; Mesopotamia; the West Indies.

A part of Leopold's design for monarchy now stood completed. The huge financial resources and the liberty of action which he possessed as sovereign of the Congo State were already altering his position as King of Belgium. In a very real sense, he was the leader of the nation's industrial expansion. He did not merely open industrial fairs and award medals to inventors, he formed the very lance-head of Belgian penetration into remote and well-defended markets. First came the Congolese emissaries, with their portfolios of attractive propositions; then came the Royal investor himself, using to the full his prestige as a reigning monarch to secure the entry of his bewildering menagerie of study-companies and holding-groups; lastly, when the concession was signed and sealed, came the Belgian industrialists to build and carry and sink shafts and sell their tramcars. All this, and a considerable income off such deals, was made possible by the revenues of the Congo. But this was not appreciated by the

[1] E. Carton de Wiart; Léopold II, les dernières années
[2] Daye; Léopold II; p. 446
[3] Ibid., pp. 434-5.

majority of the Belgians. They tended to see in the Congo only the means for the King's increasing absolutism, and intelligent Belgians feared that the Congo would eventually become the object of an international brawl which would involve the safety and the reputation of Belgium herself. As the rumours about Leopold's methods in the exploitation of the Congo grew and united into a running scandal in the Anglo-American Press, this feared seemed to have been fully justified, even though few Belgians, as yet, believed that such reports were true.

CHAPTER XXVII

THE CONGO SCANDAL: THE ATTACK OPENS

NOW IN HIGH GEAR, the Leopoldian machine installed in the Congo was producing the goods at an impressive rate. In the first years of the century, the territory's exports of ivory slackened, as the elephants and the men to carry the tusks grew scarce, but the rubber levy was working wonders. In the peak year of 1903, the State's exports were valued at £2,184,000, of which almost £1,900,000 was in rubber. These figures are drawn from a contemporary Belgian estimate[1], and it should be remembered that it was the gross understatement of such official figures which first convinced the Liverpool shipping clerk Edmund D. Morel that something terrible existed and was being concealed in the Congo, and set him on the course which made him Leopold's most formidable enemy.

The same source, the lawyer Félicien Cattier, estimated that the *Domaine de la Couronne* had made nearly £2,900,000, in clear profit, for Leopold in the ten years between 1896 and 1906. Morel calculated that Leopold had made a personal profit of £2,000,000 in six years[2]. The great concession companies had done well, too. The Anglo-Belgian India-Rubber Company, (ABIR), made a net profit in six years of £720,000 on a paid-up capital of £9,280. Each share had appreciated from its original £4 6s 6d to the price of £35, in the same interval[3]. The reformed Kasai trust, enshrining the dry bones of the free-trading companies, made £750,000 profit in three years, on a capital of £40,000. And Leopold himself drew benefit from their good fortunes: he held at least half the stock in three of the major com-

---

[1] Félicien Cattier; *Etude sur la Situation de l'Etat Independant du Congo;* Brussels 1906; pp. 74-5.

[2] E. D. Morel; *Red Rubber;* London 1906; p. 140.

[3] *Ibid.*, pp. 142-3.

panies, and Morel estimated that his holdings here alone earned him £360,000 in 1904-5[1].

There was a price to be paid in African lives for these results, but in the Congo there were few to see what went on, and fewer still who could afford to report it. The most important of the independent witnesses were naturally the missionaries, in particular the Congo Balolo Mission directed by Grattan Guinness for the Regions Beyond Missionary Union, and the Baptist Missionary Society under George Grenfell[2], but even missionaries faced a problem of conscience in deciding whether to speak out at the price of possible expulsion, leading to the annihilation of the social and evangelical work which had been achieved. However, Guinness laid information about atrocities against Africans before the Aborigines' Protection Society in London as early as 1890, and from then onwards, British, and later Swedish, missionary journals carried a steady succession of such reports. The Baptists were at first rather reluctant to follow this example. Although Grenfell was aware of what was going on around him and very concerned about it, the Baptists had been on good terms with Leopold in the early years of the State, and one of the BMS supporters, the journalist Hugh Gilzean Reid, had become an eloquent apologist for Leopold and the Congo State in Britain.

Stories about the brutal treatment of 'foreign' natives, though they might upset the British public, cut little ice with the official organs of the 'Establishment'. *The Times,* at a low ebb even for that callous newspaper, wrote in a leader in 1895 that 'a system of compulsion closely akin to slavery would be necessary before natives of the Congo Free State could be trained to regular voluntary labour'[3], and there was a weary disdain for 'do-gooders' in the Foreign and Colonial Offices: as late as 1902, the Belgian Ambassador was glad to be able to quote a Foreign Office opinion that the Aborigines' Protection Society was a collection of humanitarian fanatics who had made themselves a serious nuisance to the Government[4]. It was therefore particu-

[1] *Ibid.,* p. 140.

[2] For the history of the part played by British missionaries in the exposure of conditions in the Congo State, I have drawn largely on Dr. Ruth Slade's study, 'English Missionaries and the Beginning of the Anti-Congolese Campaign in England'; *Revue belge de philologie et de l'histoire;* XXXII; 1955.

[3] *The Times;* March 18, 1895.

[4] Quoted in Slade; *English-Speaking Missions.* Leopold was himself at one time a member of the APS.

larly lucky for the anti-Congolese campaigners that the atrocities
came rapidly to affect the persons and property of British subjects, an aspect of the situation which Whitehall could not
ignore. In 1895, at Lindi in the Congo, the Belgian officer
Lothaire arrested Charlie Stokes, an old lay missionary turned
gun-runner who had once helped to rescue Buganda from an
Arab *coup d'état,* and was now nominally in the German service.
Charging Stokes with assisting the enemies of the State by selling
arms to Arab slavers, Lothaire took the law into his own hands
and hanged him on the spot. This act brought strong protests
both from the British Government and from the Germans, but
Lothaire, who had made an outstanding reputation for himself
in the Arab wars, was acquitted both on trial and on appeal.
Another complaint was officially adopted by the British Government in the following year, when reports about the brutal
treatment of 'British' Africans in the Congolese Army induced
Joseph Chamberlain to forbid further recruiting for the 'Force
Publique' in British West Africa.

Evidence continued to accumulate. American and Swedish
missionaries described to the Press the revolting results of the
'rubber system' as it operated in the districts around their
stations, and spoke of the practice of bringing in severed human
hands to testify that a punitive raid against a village slow to
deliver its rubber quota had been thoroughly carried out. British
missionaries maintained their uneasy silence in public, and in
private wrote mild letters of reproach to Leopold, who in
September 1896 set up a 'Commission for the Protection of the
Natives' to report atrocities to the Governor-General. This Commission was composed of missionaries, which for a time
impressed public opinion, but its members were in fact based
far apart, in stations remote from the regions where the 'rubber
system' was operating at full power, and they were allowed no
travelling expenses[1].

In London, humanitarians and radicals suffered from none of
the inhibitions which still gagged British missionaries in Africa:
if their own countrymen would not provide the evidence which
was known to be available, then it would be got from foreigners.
Sir Charles Dilke and H. R. Fox-Bourne, secretary of the
Aborigines' Protection Society, concerted a spring offensive in

[1] Slade; *King Leopold's Congo;* p. 180.

1897. In a parliamentary question put to the Government in April, Dilke laid down the lines of the argument which was to be used by all those who campaigned for British intervention in the scandal of the Congo, and claimed that the British Government, as a signatory of the Berlin Act, was directly obliged by evidence already published to call a new conference of the Powers. On May 14th, *The Times* published a shocking account of Congolese conditions by the Swedish missionary Sjöblom; four days later, Dilke asked the Government if, 'after recent revelations as to the administration of the Congo', it would not be appropriate to revoke Leopold's tenancy of the Lado enclave. None of these questions moved the British Government to action, but pressure was maintained in the House of Commons for the next few years, assisted in 1899-1900 by a new wave of revelations from the American missionaries Morrison and Shepherd, both Presbyterians, who reported that cannibal troops had been used to extort forced labour and taxes in produce from the population along the banks of the Kasai.

The testimony of Morrison and Shepherd was published as the term of Leopold's ten-year arrangement with the Belgian Government drew near, permitting the nation to choose between immediate annexation and the repayment of loans made to the Congo in that period. But it produced little reaction in Belgium; indeed, the Belgian Press wrote such protests off against the 'jealousy' of British missionaries, even though, as Dr Slade has pointed out, no British missionary had yet passed criticism on the administration of the Congo in public. In those years, almost the only Belgian voice raised in humanitarian objection was that of the Liberal deputy Georges Lorand, who questioned the Government in April 1900 about the background to a rising of the Babuja people in the Mongalla region, and asked why Belgian Catholic missionaries had said nothing of the abuses witnessed by foreign Protestants.

The Congo was paying well, and the mass of the Belgian people remained thoroughly hostile to the upsets and expenditures which would be involved in its transfer to the status of a national colony. In such circumstances, Leopold boldly campaigned both to be allowed to keep the Congo and to escape the crippling consequence of paying off his debt to the Belgian treasury. The leader of the Catholic ministry, Smet de Naeyer, did not see why the King should not have his way.

Early in 1901, he laid before the Chamber a bill to allow repayment of the Government loans to the Congo to be indefinitely postponed, and at the same time let it be known that he did not favour immediate annexation. Belgium was thus to sacrifice not only its immediate option on the Congo, but its hard-won control over the fund-raising activities of the Congo exchequer, extorted from Leopold as part of the 1890 'Testament' bargain. To make Smet's position yet more abject, his bill was accompanied by a letter from the Congolese 'minister' Van Eetvelde which suggested that Leopold had acquired the right to decide the moment at which the Belgian Government should be invited to take over the Congo : this was to be done at the King's initiative, while Belgium had lost all rights in the matter of timing.

It was more the insult to Parliament conveyed by Leopold's proposals than concern for the Congo itself which drove Auguste Beernaert, once the King's most loyal minister, to retort with a motion for immediate annexation of the Congo. Socialists and Radical Liberals supported him, and jeered damagingly at the Government's inability to resist Leopold's will and stand on its rights. This was a dangerous situation, and while both bills lay before the Chamber, Leopold fell back on his favourite last-ditch tactic of threatening to scuttle the Congo and leave Belgium with the expense of salvaging it. On June 9, 1901, he wrote to Charles Woeste (for the eyes of the wavering Government): '. . . if annexation is voted now, before the time when the Congo can bring Belgium all the benefits I intend it to confer, the Congo Free State will naturally refuse to carry on with its administration or to take part in a sort of mongrel government . . .'[1] The long letter went on to complain that the Opposition was treating him like a mere plunderer, out for his own profit; Leopold complained, with some justice, that Belgian critics of his financial methods had not understood that the floating of large loans was an indispensable source of investment for under-developed countries.

But, as in 1895, public distaste for annexation rapidly cooled the enthusiasm of the Free State's enemies in Parliament. Smet

[1] Quoted in Daye; *Léopold II;* p. 483.

de Naeyer's bill for the suspension of loan repayments eventually passed through the Chamber with seventy-one Catholic
and Liberal votes against thirty-one Socialists and Radicals. The
'Testament' bargain was now a nullity, and Leopold gained full
financial liberty in the Congo. To this, he added a still more
personal and direct control over the affairs of his State. In
February 1901, Van Eetvelde finally gave in his notice as head
of the administration, after at least one abortive resignation and
a nervous breakdown. A chilly, restrained man, regarded by his
colleagues as having modelled himself on the sort of *gentleman
anglais* he had met in his early years in India and China, he
had never lost the courage to stand up to Leopold when he
thought that a mistake was being made. A year later, the British
Ambassador in Brussels noted that he was the only man who
dared to point out to the King 'the unpopularity he incurs by
his "goings-on", his constant and often mysterious absences from
his own country, and his indifference to public opinion . . . '[1]

Van Eetvelde, although he had left his post, continued to take
work from Leopold until the final surrender of Lado to the
British in 1906, for which Leopold held him to blame. The King
had already used his resignation as the excuse for a recasting of
the Congolese 'cabinet' in Brussels, taking over the departments
of finance, the interior and foreign relations for himself, and
delegating their day-to-day running to three 'secretaries-general',
respectively Droogmans, Liebrechts, and de Cuvelier. A separate
post of Treasurer-General was created for Pochez, a key figure
in Leopold's network of investments and holding companies.

Abroad, the campaign against the running of the Congo State
moved into a new gear with the entry of Edmund Morel into
full polemic action. E. D. Morel, who became through the anti-
Congolese campaign one of the heroes of the great age of
'exposure' journalism, did not come to the affairs of the Congo
as a professional defender of liberty, to whom this was one
crusade among many; his interest in the Congo dated from the
age of seventeen, when he had joined the shipping firm of Elder-
Dempster in Liverpool as a junior clerk. The reports of the
Swedish and American missionaries, collated with studies of
Congo trade figures, made in the course of his work, suggested
to him that such reports were not only likely to be true but that

[1] Quoted in *Biographie Coloniale Belge;* entry: 'Van Eetvelde'.

they were the inevitable result of a system of monopolistic State exploitation conducted without a money economy. The missionaries had seen only a sum of abuses, and had believed that better discipline enforced by Leopold's direct orders could cure them; Morel now declared that the system itself was to blame, and in the first years of the new century he set himself to collect fresh evidence from the British missions and to rouse the country through the Press. He aimed to appeal both to commercial interests, excluded from the Congo market, and to the humanitarian tradition: 'this is a subject,' he wrote, 'on which philanthropy and practicability go hand in hand . . . the link between them is the expert journalist'[1].

But the missionaries were still shy of joining any open attack on their patron. As late as 1904, Grenfell wrote: 'I cannot believe His Majesty is careless of the people so long as the rubber comes in, or I would have to join his accusers'[2]. Meanwhile, Leopold and Gilzean Reid had mounted effective counter-attacks, winning a libel action in 1902 against the publishers of atrocity revelations made by a Captain Burrows, and extracting from a rather witless Baptist delegation to Brussels an address of gratitude for Leopold's bounty towards their missions on the Congo. The other wing of Morel's attack, aimed at British business interests, ran into stout resistance from the Liverpool Chamber of Commerce. One member of the Chamber, John Holt, had accepted and assisted Morel's work, but the other shipping magnates still preferred to follow the leadership of the chairman, Sir Alfred Jones. As head of Elder-Dempster, Morel remembered Jones as 'in many ways a splendid fellow', but he was a close associate of Leopold's, who appointed him consul for the Congo State, and a firm believer in the sincerity of Leopold's humanitarian professions[3]. Like William Mackinnon in Glasgow and Alfred Rabaud in Marseille, Jones was an essential member of Leopold's team of international ship-owners, richly rewarded with trading privileges and Belgian decorations for their services as high-level fixers and propagandists.

In May 1903, the Congo was debated in the House of Com-

---

[1] Quoted in Slade; *English Missionaries and the Beginning of the Anti-Congolese Campaign in England.*

[2] R. Slade; *English-Speaking Missions in the Congo Independent State;* ARSC; Brussels 1959; p. 275, Note 3.

[3] A. H. Milne; *Sir Alfred Jones;* London 1914.

mons, on a motion of Herbert Samuel's that 'the Government of
the Congo Free State having at its inception guaranteed to the
Powers that its native subjects should be governed with
humanity, and that no trading monopoly or privilege should be
permitted within its dominions, and both these guarantees
having been constantly violated, this House requests His
Majesty's Government to confer with the other Powers signatories of the Berlin General Act by virtue of which the Congo
Free State exists, in order that measures may be adopted to
abate the evils prevalent in that State'. In his speech, which
rehearsed the evidence about cannibals in State service and the
baskets of human hands produced at the stations, Samuel
observed: 'Guizot said of the French Republic of 1848 that it
began with Plato and ended with the gendarme. The same might
be said of the Congo Free State'.

In return for the omission of the aggressive phrase about
violation of guarantees, the Government agreed to take action
in two forms. The first was to send a Note to the Berlin Powers,
suggesting that the Congo State might have contravened its
obligations and that a conference should be called to discuss
intervention: this evoked little reaction except from the State
itself, which rejected criticisms and boldly defended the institution of a tax in labour. The French had installed a milder but
still similar economic system in the adjoining French Congo,
and her neighbours were disinclined to risk a European quarrel
over Leopold's colonial methods. But the second action taken by
the British Government was to prove very much more effective.
For some time, the British Consul at Boma, Roger Casement,
had been supplying Whitehall with material about conditions
on the Congo, and he was now ordered to make an extensive
tour of inspection up-river and to prepare a report upon what he
found.

In reply to all this activity, Leopold's tactics were manifold
and subtle. In detail, he went to great trouble to impute ulterior
motives to his accusers; despite Sir Alfred Jones' command of
his Chamber of Commerce, it was put around that a clique of
Liverpool merchants, anxious to sell their gin to the innocent
natives, were trying to destroy the enlightened administration
of the Congo by invented calumnies. The missionaries, similarly,
were represented as bigots prepared to use any means to establish

a monopoly of their own brand of religion. In the same year that Leopold received the Baptist Missionary Society delegation with such polite attention, he cabled the Belgian Minister in the Vatican: 'King requests you before leaving Rome to ask sympathies from Pope for Congo State attacked violently by Protestant missionaries'[1].

After the British Note of 1903, Georges Lorand and Emile Vandervelde, the Socialist, asked more questions of their own in the Chamber. A further group of atrocity reports had resulted in the conviction of a Congolese officer named Tilkens, whose diary had fallen into the hands of the Belgian Socialists and later provided Morel with material for his book *King Leopold's Rule in Africa*[2]. The defence of the Belgian Government, in this period, was to tell such questioners that the Chamber had no right to debate the internal affairs of a foreign State. But Leopold realized that it was inadequate to meet attacks with mere legalisms or with imputations about the motives of his accusers; at all costs, he must prevent Morel's planned union between the trading interests and the philanthropists, and to this end he suggested that the very prosperity of the Congo was proof that internal conditions were satisfactory there. 'We are accused of cruelties,' he wrote to Sam Wiener in January 1902. 'We must quote official figures to show the extent to which deliveries of rubber fall in time of unrest, thus making clear how much it is in our interests to treat the natives well'[3]. A later note goes on: 'To accuse the white man of avarice, and at the same time of maltreating and scattering the negroes, is an absurdity which we are pointing out to the common sense of the public'[4].

Leopold was asking the world to ignore the quality of the atrocity evidence itself, and to make a deduction about its validity on other grounds. But the publication of the Casement Report in February 1904 provided a body of systematic evidence from which no sophistry could divert attention.

[1] Cable of August 16, 1903; Quoted in Slade; *English-Speaking Missions in the Congo State;* p. 299, Note 2.
[2] London 1904.
[3] Quoted in Daye; *Léopold II;* p. 488.
[4] *Ibid.*, p. 489.

CHAPTER XXVIII

THE CASEMENT REPORT

THE STRENGTH of Roger Casement's report did not lie in its direct evidence of atrocities. He did not encounter heaps of dead bodies, nor did he find baskets of human hands; in the few cases where he encountered Africans lacking their hands, the Congolese Government was able to bring formidable, if inconclusive, evidence to suggest that they had been mutilated in accidents. Instead, he saw at work the 'rubber system' itself, the grindings of the drowsy, unsupervised machine of coercion which wore out the people and the land and eventually defeated its object by the destructions caused by its own rapacity.

He saw men and women bolting from their villages at the sight of an European, as his steamer approached the bank, and he saw women with their babies chained in sheds as hostages for the delivery of the rubber quota. At a rubber collection point, he watched Africans being detained or beaten up for failure to produce a sufficient weight of latex. At second-hand, he was told of whole clans who had migrated across the Congo river to escape extortions, of obscene mutilations by punitive raiders, and of mass executions by white officials. He was able to calculate that regions burdened with the delivery of a quarter-ton of copal every year were rewarded with cloth worth eleven-and-a-half francs, the price of a local chicken, for a commodity worth about 350 francs on the open market. In the whole ABIR concession, run by 'sentries' with cap-guns and a few rifles, there was no magistrate to whom any complaint about conditions could be brought. Casement reckoned that between them the concession companies kept about 10,000 men under arms.

How many people died under Leopold's dominion of the Congo? This will never be known, nor could Roger Casement

make any useful estimate[1] even though he had known the
Congo for a good many years as a private citizen, for during
the years between 1895 and about 1908, Central Africa was the
locus of one of the most disastrous plagues recorded in human
history. The sleeping-sickness epidemic of the early twentieth
century, moving slowly east up the Congo to the shores of Lake
Victoria, brought about depopulation upon a scale which only
a major nuclear war might be expected to approach. Whole
communities which Casement had visited on a previous voyage
in 1887 had vanished entirely by 1903. Four years later, the
British Vice-Consul Beak found in Katanga that the distribution
of population had changed so completely that his maps were
useless; villages that remained might have only twenty survivors out of 200, and other communities, infected to the last
man, were waiting to die while unburied corpses stank in the
long grass. There was, at this time, no known cure for sleeping-
sickness[2].

There is no way of extricating from the general catastrophe
a proportion of deaths by massacre or destitution which can be
laid to the responsibility of Leopold's régime. A letter from a
Baptist missionary quoted by Casement in his report records
that the population of Lukolela had fallen from 6,000 to 352 in
twelve years and suggests that the enforcement of the rubber
system had, by weakening the stamina of the local villagers,
destroyed their resistance to the disease. But the reverse was
just as probable: that the disorganization of society caused by

[1] Casement guessed that, from all causes, the population of the Congo fell by
three million in fifteen years. See Lord Monkswell's speech in House of Lords
debate; July 29, 1907.
[2] The struggle of the Congo authorities against sleeping-sickness provided
an instance of the way in which sheer lack of effective control was responsible
for much of the avoidable suffering of the African population. Sir Alfred
Jones, with a generous subsidy from Leopold II, founded the Liverpool School
of Tropical Medicine, where the first useful drug against the disease was devel-
open, and Leopold gave all the assistance he could to Dutton and Todd in
their studies of the transmission of trypanosomes into human bodies by the
bite of certain species of tsetse fly. The pandemic spread of the disease, which
had been known on the West Coast for several hundred years under the name
of 'Gambia fever', was thought to be the result of the movement of large
caravans of porters in State service: Dutton and Todd accordingly developed
a rough system of diagnosis by palpation of the neck glands and urged that
quarantine check points should be set up along the caravan routes. When Beak
visited the Katanga, he found that in spite of specific orders and a flood of
circulars from the Comité Spécial du Katanga, nothing whatever had been
done and infection was spreading everywhere.

the plague left survivors quite unable to meet the State's quotas
of rubber and copal, or to defend themselves against punitive
raiders. What is quite certain—and this emerges much more
clearly from Vice-Consul Beak's report than from Casement's—
is that the combined burden was intolerable. Villagers who had
taken refuge from infection in the bush were saddled with taxes
in food or rubber deliveries or in porterage before they had
cleared the land or built themselves huts. Near Lake Léopold
II, in late 1907, Vice-Consul Armstrong found that Africans
were being obliged to work an average of twenty days a month
solely to meet the rubber tax. Consul Thesiger, describing the
Leopoldville region in the same period, recorded that for rubber
collection 'a nominal forty hours' labour means incessant work
and privation for twenty to twenty-five days each month'[1].

The consular visitations exposed the underlying defects of the
Congo system, and showed a state of affairs which made atrocity
inevitable. It was left for witnesses who spent their working
lives on the upper river—for missionaries, traders, and even
State agents under the influence of fear or remorse—to describe
the atrocities as they took place. A Dane with the American
Baptist Mission, the Rev. E. V. S. Sjöblom, saw men shot before
him for fishing instead of rubber-gathering, and watched a boy
sawing off the hand of a victim who was not yet dead. The hand
was smoked 'before being sent to the commissary'[2]. On Lake
Mantumba, Sjöblom encountered floating bodies lacking their
right hands, and he and a group of other missionaries caught
an entire basket of human hands as it was being carried along
a track for delivery to the local European official. One of these
white agents, this time in the employ of the 'Anversoise', was
recorded in an Antwerp paper as he described a punitive raid
against an 'idle' village. 'We fell upon them all and killed them
without mercy . . . he (a Monsieur X who was in command)
ordered us to cut off the heads of the men and hang them on
village palisades, also their sexual members, and to hang the
women and children on the palisades in the form of a cross'[3].
One Captain Rom, at Stanley Falls, earned a similar note in the
diaries of Mr E. J. Glave for using human heads as 'a decora-

[1] Consular Reports; 1908.
[2] The Aborigines' Friend; July 1897; p. 214.
[3] E. D. Morel; King Leopold's Rule in Africa; New York 1905; p. 129.

tion round a flower-bed in front of his house'[1]. Joseph Conrad, it is now agreed, did not invent the horrors of *The Heart of Darkness,* and it is even possible that he witnessed them. Dozens of sources confirm that such things took place.

The system of 'direct rule', the imposition of Government' officials on tribal society as opposed to the method of co-operation with existing leaders, had broken down. Practically all decisions were supposedly referred to Leopoldville, with the result that little was decided at all. At the village level, there was either a chief who had lost the respect of his people, 'being unable to relieve them of their work or benefit them in any way' (Vice-Consul Armstrong's report), perhaps 'given a putty medal and made a slave-of-all-work" (Vice-Consul Beake), or a soldier with a gun, usually from some other part of Africa, whose only concern was to enforce payment of taxation in produce or labour. The abuses at this level of local government were encouraged by the preoccupation of the rare European officials with the commercial side of their work, to British critics the central vice of the whole apparatus. Lord Cromer, the Jupiter of imperial officials, told the House of Lords[2] that 'the first principle [of good government] is that the duties of admini-stration and the commercial exploitation of the country should not be vested in the same individuals.' Referring to faults in the practice of the East India Company, one of Leopold's earliest studies, he admitted that 'though we had at the head of it many men who were not only merchants but statesmen, the system, if not a failure, was at the best but a limited success'.

Mr Beak commented on the government of Katanga that the time of white staff was 'wholly occupied in pursuits of a com-mercial character and mainly in the collection of revenue, in furnishing the innumerable reports and returns inseparable from a bureaucratic system, and in superintending the transport of imported provisions and merchandise, and export rubber and ivory. In spite of Article II of the Berlin Act[3], no attempt is made either to govern the natives or to assist them in their internal administration'.

By accepting Herbert Samuel's motion in May 1903, the

---

[1] Quoted in *Daily News;* March 29, 1902.
[2] Debate of February 24, 1908.
[3] Mr. Beak appears to have meant Article VI; Article II deals with freedom of commercial access.

British Government had agreed that the sovereignty of the Congo State was not absolute but was conditional upon observance of the terms of the Berlin Act. Casement's report was accordingly sent to the Congolese authorities in Brussels, covered by a sharp Note accusing the State of failing in its obligations. In March 1904, a month after the publication of the Casement Report, Morel founded the Congo Reform Association, which at first put its efforts into lobbying the British Government to set up the 'International Navigational Commission' provided for in Article XVII of the Berlin Act; this body, Morel hoped, would come to supervise and reform not only navigation but the whole administration of the territory. As time went by, however, and especially after Sir Harry Johnston had joined the organizers of the Congo Reform Association, Morel was persuaded that this solution was far-fetched and made bad political sense, and the CRA aligned itself in about 1905 with the growing campaign within Belgium which called for immediate annexation of the Congo by the Belgian Government. If Morel blamed State monopoly and a truck economy for the conditions in the Congo, Johnston was inclined to believe that its international character, especially its employment of white staff from many countries, was responsible for the indifference and incompetence of the administration, and he did not want one supposedly benevolent international body to be replaced by another. As evidence, he reminded the public of the abuses of power committed in the Sudan by internationally-recruited soldiers and officials between 1850 and 1882[1]. Nor did he pay much attention to the possibility of Congolese self-government, for which he thought the African population utterly unready. A practical solution, in the form of a Belgian takeover, was now at hand, and it was up to world opinion and the CRA to encourage the Belgian parliament in its preparations.

In the United States, missionaries were already lobbying President Roosevelt and urging in the Press that, as the first Power to recognise the International Association as a friendly government, the United States now had a special responsibility to demand reforms in the Congo, even though she was not a party to the Berlin Act. Morel himself visited America in 1904,

[1] E. D. Morel; *Red Rubber;* p. xi.

and petitioned Roosevelt to the same effect, and a branch of the CRA was established in 1906, under the leadership of Edwin Mead and Booker T. Washington. A meeting of the Peace Congress at Boston, in December 1904 had already adopted an anti-Congolese resolution against the advice of Cardinal Gibbons.

Leopold fought back with surprising agility. He was, among his other accomplishments, one of the first masters of the modern practice of public relations, and at some moment between 1902 and 1904, he had set up a secret Press Bureau whose job was not only to provide journalists with information favourable to his operations in the Congo, and to emit a stream of public statements of approval from Impartial Travellers, Eminent Economists and Lawyers of Repute[1], but to use very large sums of money from the Fondation de la Couronne for buying the support of prominent men. In the United States, the efforts of Belgian and Congolese consuls to answer criticism were reinforced in 1904 by the operations of Colonel Kowalsky, an emissary from the Press Bureau, who brought the President a personal letter from Leopold begging him not to be fooled by the accusations of jealous Liverpool merchants and expressing the hope that he would not permit Congress to pass formal condemnation on the Congo regime. This letter and the documents it enclosed were accompanied by a photograph of Leopold in a silver frame. Kowalsky and his subsidies to the Press were eventually exposed by the *New York American*, and the whole grimy network of the Press Bureau was uprooted and dangled in public view by the *Patriote Belge* in 1908. This was bound to happen in the long run; newspapers, like Arab maidens, never forgive those who have seduced them; but considering the really forbidding nature of the product the Press Bureau was trying to sell and the evidence available against its hand-outs, it lived an astonishingly successful career.

Nowhere was the Press Bureau more heavily engaged than in Italy, where the Congo State's consul, Signor d'Elia, was using the Bureau's funds to great effect among Italian journalists. This was a country of particular importance to Leopold. It was for the Congo a source not so much of capital as of personnel, and between 1900 and 1907 Italians formed the biggest non-

[1] See Wauters; *Histoire Politique;* p. 262.

Belgian contingent in the State [1]. As early as 1903, the Italian consul at Matadi had embarrassed his Government, on excellent terms with Leopold, by filing a 23-page atrocity report, only a year after Liebrechts had come to Rome to discuss a settlement of Italian colonists in the healthy Kivu region. Italy had already despatched the erratic Captain Baccari to the Congo to report on this scheme and the conditions of Italian staff already employed there, but Baccari's reports, mild at first, rose to a climax of horror at which he finally advised the immediate recall of every Italian official in the State. 'I want to leave,' he told a friend in Africa, 'a trail of hatred along my route, and I want my memory to stay as that of a deadly tempest which fell upon the Congo Free State.' Baccari, who claimed that the State authorities not only opened his mail but tried to poison him, carried on his tempest on his return to Italy. Although the Government refused to publish his report in full, he tried to turn public opinion against Tittoni, the Foreign Minister, who was suspected of acting as Leopold's paid agent.

Consul d'Elia earned his keep in this controversy by fighting a duel with one of Baccari's supporters on May 28, 1905, in which both men were slightly wounded. The damage, however, had been done. In the spring of 1905, questions were asked about the Baccari report in the Senate, while the deputy Santini insisted that in continuing to support Leopold so willingly the Italian Government ran the risk of being drawn into conflict with Britain over Congolese ambitions on the Upper Nile. Surrendering to the opposition, the Italian Government consented to suspend the engagements of officers serving in the Congo.

Leopold was well aware that it was no longer enough merely to rely on the denials and counter-charges of his own propagandists. In 1904, following the publication of the Casement report, he agreed to organize a full Commission of Enquiry, composed of three distinguished lawyers, Janssens from Belgium, Nisco from Italy and Schumacher from Switzerland, which arrived in the Congo that October. The Commission of Enquiry has been criticised, both because it originally included no British member and because its report avoided citing par-

---

[1] In 1906, there were 261 Italians in State employment. See Ranieri; *Les Relations entre l'Etat Indépendant du Congo et l'Italie;* ARSC January 18, 1959, and for the following episodes.

ticular incidents of abuse, but within limits it did its work well. Visiting the western rubber areas, including the ABIR concession, the Commissioners took statements from the foreign mission-aries and tried to verify Casement's findings from copies of his evidence.

The fact that no report appeared until November 1905, although the three investigators returned to Belgium that March, was due more to Leopold's influence than reluctance on the part of the Commission of Enquiry itself. But the delay angered the Radical and Socialist opposition in Belgium, some of whose leaders were now in touch with the Congo Reform Association in London, and they suspected on good grounds that Leopold and the Congo secretaries-general were holding up publication until the Commissioners would agree to put their conclusions in less uncompromising terms.

It was at this moment that the Socialist Emile Vandervelde brought off a parliamentary stroke which went far to make the Government realize that it was becoming a fool's game to stand between the Congo State and its critics. As part of his harassing tactics, Vandervelde asked the Government in March 1905 if bonuses were still being paid to Congo State agents in inverse proportion to the value of goods they paid out to natives for rubber and ivory, a provocative suggestion based on a hint he had received from one of the embittered private businessmen of the Rue de Brederode but for which he had no proof what-ever. As de Favereau, the Foreign Minister, rose to answer, an usher brought Vandervelde an envelope, unmarked and with-out traces of its origin, which he found to contain copies of secret State circulars confirming his question. Now he could not miss. He let de Favereau enter a specific denial, and then read him the circulars. Blows like this one—probably aimed by Albert Thys—drove the Government to consider annexation, with all its dangers, as the only escape from an unbearably pain-ful and humiliating situation[1].

The report of the Enquiry Commission, when it finally emerged, supported almost every one of the hostile analyses already performed on the Congo State. The land laws, 'if applied in abuse, would militate against any development of native life', and were a direct contravention of the Berlin Act. Forced labour, in the Commission's view, was in theory necessary ('mere

[1] The incident is told in Vandervelde; *Souvenirs;* p. 79.

I

persuasion is not enough to oblige them to renounce barbarism . . . '), but in practice was applied by unpardonable sanctions of flogging, raiding and the taking of hostages. The bonus system, concealed under various dishonest disguises, persisted. The powers granted to the concession companies and their exercise were intolerable. The legal system was biased and inadequate. The African population had in many places fled from its homes, 'alarmed by the initial demands and by the methods of certain agents'. Though mildly and sometimes ingratiatingly expressed, the total condemnation implied by the report was plain enough. In two widely-read books, the Jesuit Arthur Vermeersch and, most vigorously, the lawyer Félicien Cattier, drew from the Commission's generalizations the necessary conclusion that there must be immediate and radical reform[1].

For both these writers, annexation by Belgium was the only solution. Vermeersch wrote: 'Although officially we do not have to answer for the treatment meted out to the Congo natives, our honour and the good name of Belgium are at stake if a country which is governed by our King and largely administered by Belgians, is not worthy of the esteem and confidence of civilized humanity'[2].

The Reform Decrees of June 1906, announced by the Congo State, did little to conciliate international opinion. An American consul joined his European colleagues at Boma, and in December Senator Lodge persuaded the Senate to promise approval for any action President Roosevelt might take to bring about a change in the Congo. In a debate in the House of Lords in 1906, Lord Fitzmaurice, Undersecretary of State for Foreign Affairs, derided the probable effect of the Reform Decrees. '. . . While the opportunities of ill-treating the natives are slightly lessened, the chance that the opportunities still left will be made the most of is as great as it ever was, seeing that the State is still the chief trader in the country and that there is still no real guarantee that offenders will be brought to justice'[3].

Year by year, the Lords and the Commons debated the Congo

[1] A. Vermeersch; *La Question Congolaise;* Brussels 1906. F. Cattier; *Etude sur la Situation de l'Etat Independant du Congo;* Brussels 1906.
[2] Vermeersch; *La Question Congolaise;* pp. 360-64; as quoted in Slade; *King Leopold's Congo;* p. 203.
[3] Debate of July 3, 1906.

question with such unanimity of moral disgust that the fixture finally became a bore and emptied the benches. Even after the Belgian Government had begun the long political struggle which ended in annexation, Parliament in Britain continued to complain about each delay and to demand that any definition of the Congo's new colonial status should include guarantees against continuance of the old abuses. The Archbishop of Canterbury and the Lord Mayor of London put their weight behind Morel and the Congo Reform Association. In the Speech from the Throne, on January 29, 1908, King Edward VII hoped on behalf of his Government that the negotiations in progress between Belgium and the Congo State would ensure that the Congo was 'humanely administered in the spirit of the Berlin Act'.

Men like Edmund Morel and John Holt had done the hard work of hammering the Congo situation into the British public consciousness. Their lonely chariot now became a bandwagon. Fruity voices vibrated with concern on public places and from the best pulpits. Sir Edward Grey announced that 'no external question for at least thirty years has moved the country so strongly and so vehemently as this in regard to the Congo'[1]. Lord Cromer boasted: 'In the report of the Belgian Commission, I heard a statement to the effect that the triumph of the law was to make the black man work. In Egypt, we thought that whilst giving every inducement to the Egyptian to work, the triumph of the law consisted in preventing him from being flogged for voluntarily choosing to remain idle'[2].

In the clamour of all this indignation, there could be distinguished a self-congratulatory piping of hypocrisy; a note specially galling to men who represented victims nearer home. The connection between the Irish party in the Commons and Leopold's Press Bureau has yet to be studied, but members were astonished to hear Mr McKean, from Monaghan South, telling them furiously that it was 'no wonder they were called Pharisees and Philistines all over the civilized world', that the pains of Ireland under English rule by far outdid the sufferings of the Congolese, and that to listen to some pious speeches 'one would have thought that the British Colonies were little paradises . . .' He added 'Give me the autocracy and the despotism

[1] House of Commons; February 26, 1906.
[2] House of Lords; February 24, 1908.

of King Leopold in Ireland a dozen times before your boasted constitutional government!'[1]

Keir Hardie said bitterly that what he saw in the Congo was only an image of the whole past of the human race; 'the rich and strong oppressing and robbing the weak and unfortunate'. Mr Nolan (Louth, South) asked the House to spare attention for conditions in India and in London.

Some of these outbursts were less than fair; others may even have been paid for. Taken in its time, the anti-Congolese campaign was one of the noblest manifestations of British liberal altruism. It expressed the belief that exploitation of the weak by the strong was not only unChristian but involved all human beings in a moral imperative to protect the victims. Despite the trading interests of a minority in the Liverpool Chamber of Commerce, the motives of Morel and Casement, Dilke and Samuel, were not material, and attempts by Belgian historians to prove that the leaders of the anti-Congolese campaign were hypocritical or corrupt read very badly now[2].

Without the campaign, the rubber system of the Congo might have lasted longer than it did, although Leopold's death in 1909 would almost certainly have led to annexation and reform. Its fault—a serious one—was that its tone was unpalatable to a Belgian Government. Already ashamed of their long surrender to Leopold's manipulation, Belgian parliamentarians were now fighting to win back their self-respect and their proper dignity under the Constitution. Sermons from foreign Powers exasperated them, and helped Leopold to play on their patriotism. Their task was more painful than Britain realized.

[1] House of Commons; July 5, 1906. It was in this debate that McKean convulsed the House with laughter by exclaiming, in perhaps half-intentional Irishism, 'What an impossible position! No, those who ask for intervention have not, to use a popular phrase, a leg to stand on . . .'

[2] None of them read more ironically today than the remarks of Pierre Daye in his biography of Leopold II (Paris 1934; p. 492, footnote): 'We may note that during the 1914-18 war, John (sic) Morel was imprisoned, while Roger Casement was condemned to death for high treason and hanged by the British. That is enough to suggest the moral worth of the two principal architects of the anti-Congolese campaign.' After the second world war, Pierre Daye himself was arraigned as one of the most prominent of Belgian collaborators, and condemned to death in his absence: he now lives in Spain or the Argentine.

CHAPTER XXIX

PARLIAMENT DEMANDS THE CONGO

T HE GREAT CONTEST over the Congo which was now joined between successive Belgian Governments and their King marked something of a national coming-of-age. But for the Belgian public, the vices or virtues of the way the Congo was being administered were not supremely important. The battle was fought, not for the Bantu rubber-tappers of Lake Tumba, but for the defence of the Belgian Constitution. As Lord Mayo later warned the House of Lords, 'if we imagine that the state of public opinion in Belgium on the Congo question is anything approaching the public opinion in this country, we are deceiving ourselves most grossly . . . the Belgian people know nothing whatever about the Congo, and I do not think they care to know'[1]. Thus is was possible for most Socialists to want to detach the Congo from Leopold, but to oppose a Belgian takeover—even to improve conditions there. For them, the Congo was a plague-hulk which should be cast adrift.

The Congo had to be taken away from the Belgian Crown. At last, though still obscurely, Belgian politicians began to see the extra-constitutional power which Leopold had built up through his possession of a personal estate in Central Africa. In the financial and political life of the nation, Congolese money played an impressive but alarming part, and in Brussels itself the anti-Congolese uproar in the outside world was forcing the Catholic administration into an uncomfortable solidarity with the King, which he was not slow to use to his advantage. The time had come when those who believed in the Constitution and those who regarded it as an instrument of class domination could unite against the apparent danger of royal dictatorship, and in the course of the *reprise* debates of 1906-8, the Belgian Parliament learnt, by standing up to its King, to accept sovereign res-

[1] House of Lords; February 24, 1908.

ponsibility. 'It must be remembered,' Lord Mayo told the House of Lords, 'that this is the first time since Belgium obtained her independence that her Parliament has been called upon to decide a question of international importance'[1].

The next move in the attack on Leopold came from Emile Vandervelde, who renewed his questioning of the Government in February 1906. He chose a moment when a committee selected by the Congo State authorities was studying the Reform Decrees which were published in June of that year; as one of the handful of Socialists to whom the Congo presented a moral challenge rather than a bourgeois entanglement, he concentrated on producing evidence to confirm and supplement the report of the Commission of Enquiry. In the Chamber, Vandervelde's offensive stirred an increasing number of Radicals and 'Left' Catholics, who could not accept the assertions of Smet de Naeyer, the head of the Government, that the shocking stories about the semi-enslavement of African labour which continued to come out of the Congo were just individual cases and not the inevitable results of a system.

Vandervelde's courage was quickly rewarded. In March, Auguste Beernaert returned to the attack, proclaiming his confidence in those who were preparing reforms and calling for the immediate revival of the annexation bill which had been shelved in 1901[2]. Plainly, this disregarded Leopold's arrogant letter to Parliament of 1901, which claimed for the Congo State the right to choose the moment for the hand-over of power. But now it was no longer possible to evoke in the Chamber the docility which had let Leopold name his own terms five years before. With the Government refusing to oppose it, Beernaert's motion was passed.

Leopold knew at once that something decisive had happened. The hostility of world opinion and of the Belgian parties, various enough in its motives, was now too strong to be conciliated by the skills of the Press Bureau or suffocated by hectoring private letters to the Cabinet. In this year, 1906, Leopold made the last major reappraisal of his life.

He was going to lose the Congo. At the best, if he did not lose it entirely, he would be forced to share its administration

[1] *Ibid.*
[2] See p. 245.

prematurely with Belgium and to dismantle the apparatus of monopoly which was producing so much wealth. Accordingly, he set about the construction of a series of defences in depth. Annexation itself would be resisted. That position once overrun, he would fight to restrict the effects of annexation to the purely political level and to keep the reformers off the substructure of Domaines and trusts. As a third line of defence, the millions of his capital, untidily invested in dozens of different structures and under dozens of different titles throughout the Congo, would be reorganized, concentrated, and prepared for a stealthy and gradual removal from Congolese and even Belgian jurisdiction.

At the age of seventy-one, Leopold was able to summon up the ability of a young man to distinguish, ruthlessly and without fondness, the essentials of his plan from its details. The essential was to make and to retain great wealth for the independent use of the Belgian Crown; to this end, the Congo was ultimately no more than the means. It had served its purpose; cleared of its essential installations, it could be left to Belgium as an empty house is left to a new landlord.

Early in the year, Leopold went down to the Riviera, and settled himself and his suite around the bay of Villefranche, where the 'Alberta' lay at her moorings. For three months, the old King worked and planned to prepare for the decisive struggle which lay immediately ahead of him, a brief period astonishingly fertile in results. Life on board the royal yacht, where Leopold preferred to live, was intense, regular and, for the King, happy. At eight, he began the day with a breakfast sufficient for three younger men, disposing of five or six eggs and a whole pot of marmalade. After working for most of the day aboard the 'Alberta', his young equerry Carton de Wiart would ferry him ashore and accompany him as he toured the various building schemes he owned on Cap Ferrat. It was a peaceful existence, in a Mediterranean spring, and Leopold had at this time another cause for content. In the Villa des Cèdres on Cap Ferrat, his young mistress Caroline Lacroix was looking after their son, born in February and christened Lucien Delacroix, later named Duke of Tervueren when Caroline became the Baroness de Vaughan.

From his labours aboard the 'Alberta', Leopold emerged at last with two portfolios of documents. For immediate issue, there was the assorted group of papers which have come to be known as 'The Documents of the Third of June'. For the autumn, completed in outline but not yet arranged in detail, Leopold held back 'The Great Mining Plan of 1906'.

The documents of June 3rd represented the sudden release of a barrage from all three of Leopold's defence lines. Their language, as addressed indirectly to Parliament, was insulting and showed absolutely no signs of a wish to conciliate the enemies of the Congo State. Their content, however, showed clearly that Leopold was preparing for an orderly retreat behind a rearguard action.

The first document in the series was a letter addressed to the three Secretaries-General of the State[1] but intended for public consumption. On the front line of defence, it sharply re-asserted Leopold's claim to control the timing of a *reprise* by Belgium. After a certain number of ostentatious congratulations to the Secretaries-General on their achievements for native welfare, and exhortations to make the Congo even more delightful for its African inhabitants[2], the letter warned that 'the Congo's adversaries are pressing for immediate annexation. These people no doubt hope that a change of régime would capsize the work in progress and allow them to salvage rich fragments of plunder'.

In a passage of the letter particularly resented by Parliament, Leopold proclaimed : 'I consider myself morally bound to warn the country when, without prejudice, I consider that the moment for examining the annexation question is near and is propitious. At present, I have nothing to say.'

The second part of the Documents took the form of a codicil to the 'Will' of 1889, by which he had made Belgium his heir in the Congo. Now he claimed that the 1889 Testament had been a free, unilateral gesture on his part, revocable and alterable as he pleased. 'Belgium's claims to possess the Congo arise from my own two-fold initiative, from the rights which I acquired for myself in Africa and from the way in which I have used those

---

[1] Droogmans, de Cuvelier, Liebrechts.

[2] Commenting on the Reform Decrees, also part of the documents of June 3rd, Lord Fitzmaurice observed in the House of Lords debate of July 3, 1906, that to read them, 'the position of the native in the Congo Free State might really be regarded as so idyllic that some of your Lordships on leaving this House might almost be disposed to take a ticket immediately for the Congo.'

rights to the benefit of my country. This situation imposes upon
me the duty to ensure effectively, and in a manner consistent
with my original and enduring idea, that my legacy should
remain useful in the future both to civilization and to Belgium.'

The way in which that 'ensuring' should be carried out formed
the nucleus of the Codicil. 'When taking possession of the
sovereignty of the Congo, with all its goods, rights and privileges, my heir will take over, as is just and necessary, the duty
to respect all the State's engagements to third parties, and to
respect all the instruments by which I have arranged that land
will be reserved for the natives (sic), for the endowment of
philanthropic and religious projects, for the foundation of the
Domaine de la Couronne, and for the establishment of the
Domaine National; he will also respect the duty not to diminish
in any way the integrity of these various institutions without
assuring them at the same time of an equivalent compensation . . . ' Here, then, was the second line of defence in action.
If there should indeed be an act of annexation, then Leopold's
own financial structure would be left intact. The *Domaine
National*, according to A. J. Wauters, administered lands covering a quarter of the Congo's surface and, from lands and mines,
raised money equivalent to half the Congo's normal revenue[1].
The 1889 Testament had been stripped of its meaning, and Belgium would inherit a husk.

The next item in the Documents was the result of the Congolese commission's work, the Reform Decrees of June 1906. The
reforms, which reorganized native occupation rights and modified the powers of the local administration, did not affect the
original Leopoldian doctrine of State rights to unoccupied land.
Nor did they impress international opinion. 'Every man in the
House except one[2] agrees,' Lord Percy claimed in the House of
Commons debate of July 5th, 'that the Decrees which have been
announced are hopelessly inadequate to secure radical and real
reform, even if they are carried out in Congo Free State territory,
which is doubtful.'

A fourth enclosure in the Documents was a decree proposing
a new increase of the public debt by the floating of a railway-
construction loan. (One of these lines was the sensible Congo-

[1] A. J. Wauters; *Histoire Politique;* p. 287.
[2] Mr McKean.

Katanga project, which is not a reality even yet; another would have connected Lado on the Upper Nile to the Congo border; a third, and shadier, offered magniloquent prospects of a railway linking the upper Congo to the Algerian coast by a trans-Saharan track.) The last item of the Documents was a proclamation by the Secretaries-General affirming their belief that the *Domaine* system was the only practical means of exploitation in the Congo, and by implication rejecting arguments for a restoration of free trade.

Before discussing the consequences of this arrogant clutch of proclamations, it is worth moving ahead of narrative for a few months to give an account of the second group of documents, the so-called 'Great Mining Plan'. Although they were not made public until late October or November 1906, these provisions formed an essential part of Leopold's new strategy. The 'Documents' had attacked the whole suggestion of an immediate *reprise* by Belgium, and had taken steps to limit the effects of annexation to keep intact the King's personal estate. The 'Mining Plan' formed part of the third line of resistance, a mobilization and relocation of funds to escape the effects of a more ruthless and complete take-over.

Apart from the 32,000,000 acres over which the *Domaine de la Couronne* had mineral rights, most of the mining and prospecting titles of the Congo would have passed at annexation under the control of a Belgian colonial administration. This Leopold now attempted to forestall. Mining rights for the unassigned regions were distributed between three great new trusts, whose capital had already been arranged by Leopold through his incomparable network of international financial contacts.

On October 26, 1906, the 'Union Minière du Haut-Katanga' came into being. The 'Comité Spécial du Katanga' conceded to its offspring the monopoly of copper, tin, gold, coal and iron in the 17,500,000 acres of the Haut-Katanga until 1990, and passed its proportion of the share capital over to the 'Société Générale' in Belgium. Half the capital for 'Union Minière' was subscribed by 'Tanks'[1].

Three days later appeared the 'Compagnie du Chemin de Fer du Bas-Congo au Katanga'; a group which, as recorded above,

[1] This description follows that of A. J. Wauters; *Histoire Politique*.

was partly financed from the new loans in the Documents of the Third of June, and which was to act as a mining group rather than as the railway company its name implied. Half its capital was provided by the Société Générale, half by the 'Banque de l'Union Parisienne'. It was granted a ninety-nine-year concession of mining rights over the Kasai basin (52,000,000 acres).

The third group, founded on November 6th, was the 'Société Internationale Forestière et Minière du Congo', now better known as FORMINIERE, granted a twelve-year prospecting concession and a ninety-nine-year exploiting concession over a whole empire of loosely connected regions covering 347,000,000 acres. Most of its capital was subscribed by the Fondation de la Couronne (Leopold also made over the Fondation's mining rights to FORMINIERE), and by the American group of Ryan, Page and Whiteley[1].

The effect of this arrangement was to put all the unassigned mineral wealth of the Congo into arrangements falling under the description of 'the State's engagements to third parties'. In all three cases, foreign interests were deliberately engaged through British, French and American capital. An additional and most effective deterrent to interference by a subsequent Belgian régime in the Congo was the heavy participation of the Société Générale in the new companies[2]. Few Belgian politicians would dare to tamper with the holdings of that golden monster; and in the event, much of this new structure was left intact after Belgium ultimately achieved annexation. The survival of the 'Union Minière' as a practically autonomous—and immensely arrogant—force in the Congo, defended in Belgium by the might of a bank which no Government dared to defy, was the rock on which the lost ship of Congolese independence struck in 1960.

Nobody was more horrified by the tone and the implications of these documents than the Belgian Government. They were intended, at least partly, to act as a deterrent, threatening presumptious Belgium with every kind of Royal and international disapproval if she dared to claim more than the bare walls of the Congo and asked for a few sticks of the furniture. But they did not act as a deterrent. Instead, they made it quite clear that

---

[1] A last move in this game was the attachment of the new gold mines at Kilo, on the Aruwimi, to the *Domaine de la Couronne* on December 21, 1906.

[2] The Governor of the Société Générale was Chairman of all three companies.

the authority of the Belgian Parliament under the Constitution could not submit to these conditions and survive.

All through the summer, British and American speakers fulminated against the Codicil and ridiculed the Reform Decrees. In Belgium, the parliamentary battle did not open until the late autumn, when the deputies reassembled. At first, the wretched Smet de Naeyer tried again to stand on his old position of non-interference in Congolese internal affairs, but volleys of angry questions from the Socialists, the Radicals and the Left Catholics of his own party forced him to express an opinion on the Documents of the Third of June. In a passionate Chamber, on December 14th, the Liberal deputy Paul Hymans demanded: 'I want an answer: Yes or No. Do the royal wishes expressed in the letter of June 3rd set conditions to which the King means to attach the annexation of the Congo by Belgium? Is it accepted that Belgian law, not the terms of some bargain, will set up the colony's institutions?' Auguste Beernaert followed Hymans with a challenge to the Government to declare whether or not it intended to set about the formalities of annexation at once.

This moment was the end of the road for Smet de Naeyer. Considered by his enemies as no more than the most flexible of Leopold's tools, Smet was a clever and attractive man who was not without a will of his own. His mind was usually thronged with over-subtle ideas, as his desk was thronged with a hopeless chaff of disorganized official papers, and his evasive manner led acquaintances to suppose that he lacked consistency. But it had been out of conviction that he had supported Leopold over the Congo, as he had supported him in the controversy over national defence in 1905; Leopold, however, had from the beginning taken advantage of Smet's sympathy to dictate to him[1], and it was all the more courageous of Smet to have defied Leopold in private over the Congo as the 1906 debates began. By early December, he had realized that some further gesture must be made at once to satisfy the really threatening elements which were beginning to appear in the tumult of international protest. Germany and France had now both moved to the point of demanding minor territorial concessions from the Congo State,

[1] He used to instruct Smet in detail not only on what arguments he was to use in debate, but on what his Cabinet colleagues were to say. See Carton de Wiart; *passim.*

taking advantage of President Roosevelt's appeal for a fresh International Conference on the Congo, and Smet sent his Foreign Minister de Favereau to Leopold on December 6th to tell the King that he would have to give ground.

'You want to give in this time: that means you'll always be giving in,' Leopold objected. De Favereau replied that ' . . . this policy of holding on to what one conceives to be one's rights, without discussing them, has produced no good results. It has prevented nothing'. At the end of a long and painful interview, Leopold retreated and let de Favereau know that he would do as he asked, complaining 'I have been reigning for forty-two years. It's too long; they're all sick of me; they don't want me any more. They don't understand the country's real interests'.

Back in Brussels, Leopold was following the debates from Laeken by telephone. But Smet de Naeyer had already in effect given his notice; after the token resistance of the first weeks, he now surrendered almost unconditionally to the attack mounted by Hymans and Beernaert.

To Hymans, Smet stated that the declarations made in the letter of June 3rd were 'solemn recommendations', no more. In other words, his Government did not regard them as valid additions to the Testament or as binding in any other way. He added that the proposed treaty of annexation would only cover the details of the transfer of power: beyond that, the Belgian Parliament would retain full liberty to set up whatever form of colonial administration it chose. To Beernaert, Smet replied simply: 'The Government will press forward, with all its strength, the discussion of the Colonial Law bill, and once it has been voted, it will lose not a day in preparing the transfer agreement, which will allow the Chambers to give their verdict on the colonial problem before them in full knowledge of the circumstances.'

As he listened to the jubilation of his opponents, Smet de Naeyer no doubt realized that his own career was close to its end. The old King, considering himself betrayed, did all he could to hinder Smet's work on the preparation for *reprise,* in particular by withholding the information about Congo finances which was now indispensable to the Government, and in March 1907, the frustrated Cabinet resigned. Meanwhile, the Chamber approved by 128 to two (and twenty-nine Socialist abstentions) a motion to hasten the preparation of the annexation and colonial-law bills, and on December 17th a committee of seventeen members, under the chairmanship of Frans Schollaert, was appointed to study the project, collect the necessary data, and draft texts.

Smet's sacrifice achieved two things. It breached Leopold's first line of defence by rejecting his claim to hold the initiative of *reprise* and by setting in motion the machinery for immediate annexation. It pierced his second rampart as well by denying his right to set conditions affecting the colonial administration of the Congo. In March, Leopold had written: 'If Belgium . . . wishes to take over the Congo, she must make an agreement with the Donor . . . This agreement must at the least include the obligation for Belgium to take on all the contracts undertaken by the Free State; to respect the Foundations set up by the Donor, the decrees which he has classified as constitutional, and the procedure for the ultimate revision of those decrees. If Belgium wishes to take possession of the Congo after my death, it will be the terms of my recorded last wishes which will govern the manner in which she makes use of the legacy'[1]. It was Leopold's right to impose such limitations—symbolized by his use of the typical term *donateur*—which Smet had flatly refused to accept.

[1] Quoted in Lichtervelde; *Léopold II;* pp. 350-51.

CHAPTER XXX

THE LAST BATTLE: THE DYNAST AND HIS 'FONDATION'

SINCE 1905, the Congo Reform Association and its allies in the British Parliament had been pressing for Belgian annexation of the Congo as the most practical solution. But the policies of the Congo's international critics remained disjointed from the policies followed by the Belgian enemies of the Free State. The Catholic party and the 'doctrinaire' right-wing Liberals now advocated *reprise* by Belgium, while the Left Liberals and the Socialists, once seen as the Belgian allies of the CRA, attacked the annexation project and preferred the sort of 'internationalisation' for the Congo which Sir Harry Johnston had condemned two years before. Vandervelde, almost alone in his party, held on for annexation and took pains to maintain solidarity with Edmund Morel[1]. Most Socialists regarded the acquisition of the Congo, especially of a reformed and therefore less profitable Congo, as a drain on resources which ought to be used on welfare at home; they might still have agreed with their newspaper *Le Peuple,* which had asked on January 15, 1895, at the time of a previous suggestion of annexation: 'What is one to say about the criminal folly of our governors who are light-heartedly preparing to attach to Belgium a gigantic territory, when they are still unable to ensure the safety and well-being of the children of the Motherland?'

The outlook for annexation in Parliament, though signalled clear, could still be a stormy one. Leopold, back at Cap Ferrat, regained his courage, and in wordy, evasive telegrams to Brussels, made it evident that he was not going to allow the drafting Committee of Seventeen to examine the financial struc-

---

[1] He was one of the few Belgians who accepted Morel's motives on their face value. In his *Souvenirs*, he wrote that Morel 'inspired me with sympathy and admiration for his marvellous qualities as a "fighting man" ' (English phrase in the original).

ture or current accounts of the Congo State. This refusal, as will become clear, arose from good reasons. Leopold preferred to let it be understood that he was standing on his pride—'I will give them my Congo, but they have no right to know what I have done there!' he told an orderly about this time[1]—but his more urgent motive was to avoid the exposure of the tangle of gimcrack frauds and illegal short-circuits which stood service for a Congo treasury. In keeping this dark for the moment, he did both himself and his Belgian heirs a considerable service.

In April, Smet de Naeyer's Cabinet was defeated over a bill defining hours of work in the mines, and gratefully resigned. Leopold took the train for Brussels, pleased that Smet had fallen, but apprehensive about his successor, Jules de Trooz. 'To think they are accusing me of tyranny,' he complained to an equerry on the train, 'of personal power! At my age, the only personal power one means to keep is the power to reserve oneself a good place in the cemetery'[2] Those who knew him well were not deceived by this tactic of affecting a maudlin senility.

Early in May 1907, de Trooz declared that he would pursue Smet's policy of immediate *reprise*; in June, after some ominous delays, he proposed to the Congo State authorities that a cession treaty should be negotiated with the Belgian Government; in July, the 'Congolese' accepted. Four negotiators were appointed for each party. Those for the Belgian Government, it was noticed, included at least two men very close to Leopold: the lawyer van Maldeghem, who had served many useful years in Congo State service, and Baron Joostens, who had been Belgian Minister in China. Five months later, the negotiators signed a draft treaty, which was laid before the Chamber by de Trooz on December 3rd. Its contents created a major sensation.

Once again, Leopold had brought victory out of apparent defeat. The first article of the treaty, in direct contradiction of the principles laid down by Smet de Naeyer the previous year, stated: ' . . . the Belgian State pledges itself to respect the Foundations existing in the Congo'. By profuse and continual intervention in the work of negotiators (a body adequately packed with men he could control), the King had worked them round to the point of view that the Fondation de la Couronne

[1] G. Stinglhamber and P. Dresse; *Léopold II au travail;* Brussels 1945; p. 52.
[2] Carton de Wiart; *Léopold II, Souvenirs des dernières années;* p. 160.

was a genuinely philanthropic institution, as dedicated to the improvement of Belgian life as the 'Institut Solvay'[1].

But this success, for which Leopold had made several important concessions, could only be temporary and he knew it. The Chamber was outraged, and the Fondation de la Couronne would not be allowed to escape its critics a second time. All that had been gained was time, which Leopold used to pump the money out of the doomed Fondation into certain secret reservoirs of his own, prepared in Europe.

It is not easy for governments to define the precise border between property which is 'personal' and property which is 'charitable' through being set at the disposition of some benevolent foundation. The status of 'foundation' can be no more than a label to avoid property laws, and this was true enough of Leopold's 'Fondation de la Couronne'. The title, first used in the June Documents of 1906, covered the complicated reality of Leopold's personal estate. It might be argued that the 'Fondation' was a genuine charitable foundation, in that its purpose was at least largely to undertake public works in Belgium, but any charitable foundation must be based on a deed of gift and be self-governing: the 'Fondation de la Couronne' was Protean in form and activity, and it was the instrument of Leopold's unfettered will.

The nucleus of the 'Fondation' was the *Domaine de la Couronne,* the tract of land which covered one-tenth of the surface of the Congo. It soon became as well an enormous portfolio of property deeds, shares and holdings, and the receptacle for most of Leopold's personal cash fortune when that was not masquerading as the official treasury reserves of the Congo State. Almost all real estate bought in secret for the 'Fondation' was in Belgium, and in his book published in 1906[2], Félicien Cattier calculated that it held property worth 18,250,000 Belgian francs in the districts of Brussels and Ostend alone[3].

Later, the 'Fondation' acquired various villa properties round Villefranche and Cap Ferrat. Stengers, in his study of Congolese finances, made a rough estimate of 40,000,000 francs (about

[1] Later founded in commemoration of the great industrialist Ernest Solvay, himself one of the negotiators on the Congo side.

[2] *Etude sur la situation de l'Etat Independant du Congo.*

[3] It was typical of Leopold's taste for multiple personality that items for 5,000,000 francs had been bought from 'His Majesty Leopold II, King of the Belgians'. (Cattier; *Etude;* pp. 220-39.)

£1,750,000 at contemporary rates of exchange) for the income which Leopold received off the real estate and shareholdings of the 'Fondation' between 1900 and 1907[1].

What was the function of the 'Fondation' in practice? It was threefold, if one accepts the original text of the unpublished decree of December 23, 1901, which set up the *Domaine,* but only the third of the objects was generally known before Leopold's death. It was intended, in the first place, to produce revenue to pay a number of annuities to members of the Royal Family. Secondly, a provision of £20,000 was made for the yearly maintenance of the superb glasshouses and tropical collections at Laeken. Thirdly, and of course much the most important, the surplus was to be used 'according to the directive of the Sovereign-Founder': in short, on public works.

Extracted from the Congo, these huge sums of money were to be spent in Belgium. Millions were spent on Ostend, which Leopold wanted to become the world's most important resort, endowed with museums, exhibition halls, new hotels, and improved streets. At Tervueren, while a choir sang the Congo anthem 'Vers l'Avenir', Leopold laid the foundation-stone of a 'World College' for overseas colonial administrators (it was never completed). In Brussels, over £1,000,000 was put into improvements of the Royal palaces. The park at Laeken was adorned with a Chinese restaurant; a Japanese pagoda, which the King had admired at the 1900 Paris Exhibition, was re-erected at Laeken at a cost of £80,000, illuminated by 2,000 light-bulbs in the evenings. On the fabric of Laeken itself, over 700 masons worked with seven steam cranes[2]: Leopold's eventual aim was to transform the palace into a national place of assembly for world congresses, served by underground railway from central Brussels. Grandiose designs for the expansion of Laeken provided for items like a Royal bed of malachite and Katanga copper. When Albert, the heir to the throne, was shown over the Laeken works, he commented to Leopold: 'But, uncle, it will be a little Versailles!' The old King growled: 'Little . . . ?'

In the capital itself, parks, avenues and monuments were built to bring Brussels nearer to Leopold's conception of an imperial city's proper appearance. At Ixelles, as well as an agree-

[1] J. Stengers; *Combien le Congo a-t-il coûté à la Belgique ?;* ARSC 1957; p. 170.
[2] Quoted in Stengers; *Combien le Congo a-t-il coûté . . . ?;* p. 201.

able district of parks and restaurants, Leopold planned to erect
something which he described vaguely as a 'Walhalla', to commemorate the gigantic dead of Belgium's heroic past. Luckily
for Brussels, this was never built. But perhaps the most spectacular monument erected by the King in his lifetime was the
enormous 'Arcade de la Cinquantenaire' at the end of the Rue
de la Loi, and the story of its construction was an illuminating
instance of Leopold's relationship to his subjects.

The Arcade, as its name suggests, was to have been erected
in time for the fiftieth anniversary of Belgian independence in
1880. Money, however, ran low, and for years the monument
remained half-finished while successive Belgian governments
refused to make themselves unpopular with the middle classes
by allotting the project further public funds. Leopold looked
on in agonies of rage and humiliation until, unable to restrain
himself any longer, he resolved to intervene. But to have paid
openly for the completing of the Arcade would have offended
the Government of the day, and brought on him charges of
extravagance with Congo gold. Accordingly, his equerry Carton
de Wiart was sent round to sign up a list of rich benefactors,
who put their names to a letter proclaiming that public spirit
obliged them to pay for the building of the Arcade, on the
understanding that Leopold would privately reimburse them
for the sums they spent. At the inauguration in 1905, these
'benefactors' stood in the place of honour looking as foolish as
they felt, while the King prowled about the monument grinning
maliciously, affecting great surprise at the design (which he had
helped to draw), and congratulating them on their generosity.

Other allotments from the 'Fondation' went towards the
establishment of a Belgian merchant navy, towards the building of harbour-works, racecourses and casinos, and even on a
marble stairway from the 'Alberta's' jetty at Cap Ferrat. But an
important flow of its money maintained a further series of
public gifts, known as the 'Donation Royale'. This was a
massive transfer of Royal estates and residences to the care of
the Belgian nation, to take place after Leopold's death. The
Belgian Government gingerly accepted this present, made on
the occasion of the King's 65th birthday, but by subsequently
destroying the 'Fondation de la Couronne', cut off the income
which was designed to supply the very large costs of maintaining the properties (the status of the 'Donation' was not sorted

out until 1930, when King Albert established it as a public corporation under the Minister of Finance).

The 'Donation Royale', like most of Leopold's presents, served a practical as well as a generous purpose. His unhappy daughters were once again the target of the operation. By Article 913 of the Civil Code, the father of two or more children was forbidden to leave more than a quarter of his fortune in free gifts: the 'Donation' represented that quarter, the most that he could legally put out of the reach of Louise, Stephanie and Clémentine. It was significant that the contents of the 'Donation' were almost all inherited royal properties, family houses and estates which he was known to possess, as opposed to the secret holdings of the 'Fondation de la Couronne' which he could dispose of freely enough as long as details of their value remained a mystery. Even so, Leopold resorted to gross illegality to extort the Ciergnon properties from the estate of his insane sister Charlotte and throw them into the safety of the 'Donation', anticipating a right of purchase which was only supposed to operate at her death and paying her estate in unsold Congo shares. This was one of many Leopoldian deals which the Belgian Government had to unsew after his funeral.

Nothing was more bewildering about the 'Fondation' than its financing. Leopold, like Almighty God, existed in at least three persons. The King's personal estate was Leopold; the 'Fondation de la Couronne' was Leopold too; the Congolese Treasury was Leopold once more. All three persons were consubstantial: the money belonged to each of them and to all of them: it was a single fortune playing three rôles at once. The relationship between the Congo and the 'Fondation', as revealed by Professor Stengers in his study *Combien le Congo a-t-il coûté à la Belgique?*, was particularly curious.

The 'fonds special', the nucleus of Leopold's monies, used the Congo State as a sort of milch cow. The proceeds of the various loan issues which the State was obliged to make went in large part to the 'fonds special'. In other words, the savings lent to the Congo by hopeful investors passed straight into Leopold's personal wallet. The way in which he used Congo investments to pay off debts to Rothschilds has already been described[1]. A more subtle procedure was Leopold's practice of keeping part of the stock of the Congo loan issues; he tore the share coupons

[1] See p. 193 above.

off the counterfoil, before they went on the market, and kept
them to use as a sort of personal currency. Some he used to pay
for 'Fondation' expenses (the builders of the Arcade received
12,000,000 francs worth of unsold Congo stock), and some he
paid into accounts of his own against various debts. He was,
almost literally, printing his own money.

In the negotiations with the Belgian Government which led
up to annexation, it was discovered that a sum of slightly over
£1,000,000 advanced to the Congo State by Belgium was miss-
ing. After a tactful interval provided by the Government to
allow some rapid cooking of the Congo books, the Congolese
authorities offered fresh accounts to show that the sum had
been advanced in turn to the 'Fondation de la Couronne'. It
was never recovered. Professor Stengers suggests that it corres-
ponded to the amount which Leopold levied off the Congo's
revenue and share capital.

After Leopold's death, an even odder transaction came to
light in scattered, tantalizing fragments when Leopold's orderly
Auguste Goffinet, in charge of the 'fonds special', came under
the scrutiny of the lawyers representing the Princesses. The
daughters hoped to prove that the contents of the 'fonds special'
formed part of their rightful inheritance. But Goffinet replied
that the 'fonds special' had ceased to become the King's exclusively personal property: there had been mixed into it 'sums
entrusted to him by third parties'. This remark has never been
fully elucidated, but Professor Stengers suggests with some
evidence that the 'sums' amounted to the £16,000 subscribed by
the Belgian public for the old 'Association Internationale Africaine'. Leopold spent that money within a few years, and only
recalled it to mind when he came to lay another of his innumerable plans to evade the Civil Code. If the 'fonds special' could
be shown after his death to belong in some way to the nation,
then it was safe from the claims of his daughters and could be
spent on more Basilicas, cenotaphs and pseudo-Trajanic boulevards. Congo shares to the sum of £16,000 were then, it seems,
torn off their stubs and put into the 'fonds' pigeon-holes under
the title of the debt owed to Belgium for the AIA.

Little of all this was unearthed at the time of Belgian annexation. The Committee of Seventeen was sufficiently embarrassed
by what it did discover in its search for information, and the
Government, preparing Leopold's report of the 'Fondation's'

activities for study by the Committee, tried to alter its emphasis
and to exaggerate the medical and educational work which had
been paid for in the Congo itself. The Government, conscious
of what most other imperial powers thought of Leopold's ideas
on colonial budgets, wanted to show that at least some of the
Congo's wealth had been ploughed back into Africa. So it had,
but partly in a way which the horrified Belgian negotiators
realized they must at all costs conceal. On behalf of the Congo
Treasury, Leopold had bought through anonymous 'men of
straw' major and even dominant shareholdings in two of the
concession companies running the French Congo. His Congo
owned much of France's Congo, and France did not know it.
The papers of this transaction were suppressed by the Government and secretly destroyed in 1926[1].

The Chamber was not aware of all the details of these scan-
dals. But the deputies, although conscious of what the 'Fondation' had achieved for Belgium, were now determined that it
must go; some because they regarded it as the central installation in the Congo's atrocious machine of exploitation, most
because they considered to be a violation of the Constitution's
spirit and a threat to the supremacy of Parliament. Jules de
Trooz had died on the last day of 1907, but the new leader of
the Government, the same Frans Schollaert who had presided
over the investigating Committee of Seventeen, insisted that
the 'Fondation' should be excluded from the annexation agreements.

In February, rather to the Government's surprise, Leopold
gave way: unknown to them, he had completed the last and
most secret caches for his fortune, and he was ready to let the
'Fondation' go. However, he made sure that he did not let it go
cheaply. While holding out for better terms from the Government, he did not see any inconsistency in threatening Belgium
with the probable consequences of delay, and he told his young
equerry Carton de Wiart: 'Belgium will lose the Congo, you'll
see! The other Powers will share it out. It will be shameful, but
perhaps better that way.'

Carton de Wiart, probably angry at being addressed as if he
were a gullible deputy in the Chamber, dared to retort that
Leopold had no right to say such things. 'It would indeed be

[1] Stengers; *Combien le Congo a-t-il couté . . . ?*; p. 278.

shameful, but not only to Belgium—there would be jeers of a particularly hateful kind . . .' At this point the King put him out of the room and slammed the door in his face[1]. But his orderly was correct in his forecast. The delay and the terms which Leopold was trying to extract from Schollaert were already raising a fresh wave of international indignation, and within Belgium itself the King's unpopularity seemed to be bringing into danger the very future of the Belgian monarchy. The popular opposition Press equated Leopold's greed for money with the exigences of his young mistress, and each new uproar over the Congo released another flow of incredible gossip about the King's sexual tastes.

This situation was confirmed by the publication of the terms for the abandon of the 'Fondation' on May 5, 1908. This 'Acte Additionel', a postscript to the annexation agreement, made the Belgian Government look as if it had allowed Leopold to name his terms. At a cost of about £2,000,000, the Government agreed to complete the 'Fondation' works at Laeken and Ostend, and to pay off outstanding debts on various other building projects. The goods and movable assets of the 'Fondation', which Belgium might well have kept to pay off these expenses, were returned to Leopold's disposition. To Belgium, he gave the empty lands in the Congo within the area of the *Domaine de la Couronne*, the mines on the rivers Aruwimi and Uele, the shareholding of the 'Fondation' in 'Forminière' and the 'Société du lac Léopold II', and a number of buildings in Belgium, including the Pagoda at Laeken, the grandstand at the Ostend race-course and a golf course at Coq-sur-mer, not all of which were given freehold. A group of annuities to various zoos, botanical gardens, and missions, and to the retiring administrators of the 'Fondation' was guaranteed. Finally, 'in recognition of national gratitude', Leopold himself received a present of £2,000,000, to be paid in instalments out of the future colonial budget[2].

When the 'Acte Additionel' appeared, the main annexation debates had already begun on the 'Loi Coloniale' bill produced at last by the Committee of Seventeen. In June, discussions were interrupted by a general election, preceded by a difficult and bitter campaign in which the Socialists especially urged the country to reject the annexation of the Congo as a burden

[1] Carton de Wiart; *Léopold II; Souvenirs des dernières années;* p. 188.
[2] Wauters; *Histoire Politique;* p. 344.

which the King plotted to deposit on the Belgian taxpayer
because it had grown too heavy for him to carry alone. However, with a reduced majority, the Catholics retained their
dominance, and the debates on annexation reopened on June
18th.

During the recess, Schollaert and Jules Renkin, who was to
be the first Colonial Minister of Belgium, had sought out the
King at Wiesbaden, where he was taking the waters for his
swollen leg, and begged him to soften the terms of the 'Acte
Additionel'[1]. Leopold refused, but the Government's prospects
were now rapidly improving, following the publication of fresh
evidence on Congolese conditions. After more than two months
of discussion, the annexation treaty (with the 'Acte Additionel')
and the colonial law bill were at last put to the vote on August
20, 1908.

The treaty passed by eighty-three votes to fifty-four, with
nine abstentions. The colonial law, less controversial, passed by
ninety to forty-eight, with seven abstentions. A few deputies
clapped: a few hissed. The battle was won, but few in Belgium
had wanted to begin it. There was little elation. The nation had
acquired an enormous African colony, under-administered and
apparently saddled with debts, which was already the subject
of fierce international controversy. Belgium had annexed the
Congo, not because she wanted it, but because it had to be taken
away from the King.

Nor was this the end of trouble. Since the beginning of the
year, British Notes had arrived regularly to insist that annexation must include some guarantees for the protection of the
African population. Grey's Note of March 27th had demanded
yet again that the Belgian Government should make clear their
intention to obey the provisions of the Berlin Act in their spirit
and their letter, adding specifically that this implied the relief
of the natives from excessive taxation, the grant to them of
sufficient land both for food crops and cash crops, the intro-

[1] Leopold, whose real purpose at Wiesbaden was to talk to the Emperor
William II, was not pleased to see the Belgian ministers and treated them like
intruding schoolboys. His equerry Stinglhamber was told to serve them only
the wine at twelve marks a bottle —'that's good enough for ministers'— but,
pleasantly enough for Schollaert and Renkin, he bungled the arrangement and
throughout their stay they drank the reserve of Steinberger laid in for the
Emperor at 70 marks a bottle. Leopold did buy the ministers tickets for a
performance by Isadora Duncan, but whether this was a gesture of appreciation
or contempt was not recorded.

duction of monetary currency and free trading rights for merchants of all nationalities. Commenting on the draft annexation treaty, Grey observed that his Government 'learned with some apprehension' that Belgium intended to respect the rights of the notorious concession companies 'in their entirety'[1].

The Leopoldian system was dismantled only gradually by Belgium. Severe reports continued to arrive in London from the corps of consuls now assembled in the Congo; there were further angry debates in the Commons; more Notes; more meetings of the Congo Reform Association, which did not dissolve until 1913. Region by region, the new Belgian colonial administration slowly abolished the State monopoly of the products of the 'empty lands'[2], but Belgium remained sufficiently defensive about international interference to tell the United States in 1909 that she did not consider that she had inherited the treaty obligations of the Free State. Gradually, however, conditions improved. The visit of Albert, the heir to the throne, to the country which Leopold had never seen was an encouragement to the reformers, and British recognition of the transfer of power, withheld long after it had been accorded by the rest of the world, was granted at last in June 1913.

On November 15, 1908, the starred flag of the Free State was hauled down in the Congo for the last time. In Belgium, Leopold published a rather querulous document of self-justification after the final vote for *reprise*, describing how he had tried to 'open the darkness of Africa to a ray of light', and claiming with an impudence which his enemies were too weary to reproach that he had never made a penny out of the Congo.

He was now very much alone; his splendid health was failing at last; and the great work of his reign—the erection of the 'Fondation de la Couronne' on the pedestal of the Congo State—had been destroyed. Yet life rose again; he was not quite

---

[1] After the Enquiry Commission of 1906, the 'Anversoise' company surrendered its concession to the Free State, which exploited the area but contracted to deliver to the company at Antwerp the ivory and rubber from the concession, at agreed prices, until 1952. A similar agreement was applied to the 'ABIR' company. In 1908, fresh talks began, resulting in the agreement of May 23, 1911 which annulled the 1906 arrangement and granted the two companies restricted areas of land in their old concessions; at the same time, the Congo administration returned the shares it had held in the companies. In November that year, they fused into the modern 'Compagnie du Congo Belge'. See *Biographie Coloniale Belge*.

[2] Slade; *King Leopold's Congo;* p. 211.

finished. As Jules Renkin left to see the Congo, in April 1909, he wrote him a letter in which he spoke about his father's model agricultural estates in Belgium, and added: 'I would be grateful if, while you are in the Congo, you would be good enough to let me know about any fertile lands which I might acquire in order to do what the late King did in Belgium . . .'[1]. And in a speech at Antwerp in June that year, he frightened the Government very much by suggesting that 'certain lands or certain mines (in the Congo) could be granted to the founders of banks in the Far East or of Belgian shipping lines . . .'[2]. The old King's optimism, like his sly virility, could only be extinguished by his death.

[1] Letter of April 3, 1909.
[2] Wauters; *Histoire Politique;* p. 388.

CHAPTER XXXI

THE OLD KING AND THE DEFENCE
OF BELGIUM

FRANTICALLY ABUSED by his own subjects and regarded abroad as some sort of hybrid of Pluto and Priapus, Leopold nevertheless achieved in the last years of his life the most important service he was able to perform for Belgium. The great defence controversy broke out again, and by a tireless campaign of propaganda which ended in victory only a few hours before his death, he contrived to endow Belgium with at least the essentials of a modern military system. Belgium was not able to hold her ground against the German invasion five years later, but the army fought well and was able to retain to the end of the war a corner of Belgium territory beyond the Yser. The survival of a Belgian Government and King on Belgian soil, with the glory which the army won by its refusal to be driven over the frontier, saved the national self-respect and acted as a certain unifying force in politics for the first years after the war.

Leopold resumed his defence campaign after a disastrous and even grotesque meeting with the Kaiser in Berlin, in January 1904. The Anglo-French *Entente* was in obvious preparation, and France was working hard to detach Italy from the Triple Alliance with Germany and Austria: although the German Chancellor, von Bülow, was keeping deliberately calm about these operations, his master was not. William II disliked Leopold in any case, jealous of his colonial achievement and perhaps sympathizing with his wife's disgust at the Belgian King's private life[1], but on the occasion of Leopold's state visit to Berlin he tried to drag him by main force away from the influence of France and Britain.

The visit began reasonably well. Leopold, privately convinced

---

[1] After the 1904 visit, the Empress Augusta was said to have sent the court chaplain to exorcise the rooms Leopold had been staying in.

that whatever dangers Belgium now had to fear came from the
direction of Germany, nevertheless pumped up agreeable plati-
tudes about the unreliable nature of France and tried to suggest
that the progress of the Flemish cultural movement within Belgium represented a national turn towards the Teutonic. In spite
of the enduring tension between the Congo State and Berlin
over the Congo-German East Africa frontier in the Kivu, he and
von Bülow liked each other and enjoyed their conversations.

William II saved his powder until the last day of the visit.
Then he took Leopold into his study and launched out into a
strange quasi-historical exhortation about the 'Burgundian'
lands between France and Germany. He reminded Leopold that
previous leaders of the Belgians had been Dukes of Burgundy.
Why should Leopold not revive that old empire, and annex
districts like French Flanders, Artois, and the southern
Ardennes?

As he realized the implications of this wild suggestion, Leopold became, for once in his life, genuinely frightened by
another human being. His eyes bulged in their sockets, and he
giggled nervously. All he could find to say was that the Belgian
Cabinet and Parliament would never stand for such an idea. The
Kaiser, infuriated by this feeble reply, flew into a rage and told
him that he could have 'no regard for a monarch who considered
that he was responsible before deputies and ministers, and not
merely before the Lord who reigns in Heaven'[1].

He said—as Leopold had feared that he had for a long time
wanted to say—that he was a soldier in the tradition of Frederick
the Great and Napoleon: that just as Frederick had set off the
Seven Years' War by attacking Saxony and as Napoleon had
destroyed his enemies by the sheer rapidity of his assault, so he
would 'allow himself to be guided by strategic considerations
alone' if Belgium did not join him in the event of war.

Silence followed. The Kaiser had stated, in as many words,
that he no longer considered Belgium's neutrality to engage him;
he would act as if it did not exist. Seventy-five years of Belgian
foreign policy, dedicated to renewing and maintaining the
guarantee of neutrality from the Powers of Europe, ended at
this moment in failure.

[1]The scene is described in von Bülow's memoirs; quoted in Daye; *Léopold II*;
pp. 466-7.

The farewell dinner for Leopold which followed this interview was a gruesome business. The King had sufficient presence of mind to let von Bülow know that there had been a disastrous quarrel and to beg him to do what he could to mitigate its effects, but at the military review at the station, Leopold distractedly put on his ceremonial dragoon helmet back to front and stood there brooding while the crowds laughed at him.

At the German end, some of the damage was repaired by von Bülow in a conversation with the Emperor the same evening, after Leopold's departure. It was too late for any diplomat to erase the impression made upon Leopold himself, who at once set about reviving the defence plans which he had earlier laid down in despair. After the rejection of 'personal', non-transferable military service by the Chamber in 1887, political interest in projects of army reform had waned rapidly. Leopold had continued to preach his theme to the unwilling ears of successive governments, but with little success. In 1897, Brialmont had organized an ex-servicemen's demonstration, of suspect spontaneity, which petitioned the King in favour of 'personal' service; Leopold used his right of reply to issue another sermon in favour of the reform. But this was no more that a charade: the nation was hostile to further discussions of compulsory military service, and Smet de Naeyer's Government, surrendering to public opinion, announced in June 1901 that the duration of military service would be cut and that it favoured the voluntary-militia system to that of conscription. For once, Leopold accepted his defeat, and wrote gloomily to Brialmont in November that 'the volunteer experiment is being tried out, and it must be tried out in good faith . . . '

The quarrel in Berlin brought him sharply back to the unresolved problem of defence. Smet and the King prepared plans for extending Belgian fortifications: to Leopold, however, it was illogical to build more casemates without at the same time providing an effective recruiting system to man them, and on his demand that 'personal' military service should once again be thrust at Parliament, he and his Government returned to their quarrels. In the following year, Leopold took advantage of the series of national fetes arranged to celebrate the seventy-fifth anniversary of Belgian independence to argue before the Belgian people that defence was the first duty of a patriot. His tour of the Belgian cities was transformed, to the alarm of his ministers, into a Royal whistle-stop tour to rouse enthusiasm for the cause of personal military service. At Ghent, on June 18, 1905, he spoke of the defence bills then before the Chamber and ended: 'I hope that Belgium has before her long years of prosperity. It is up to her to make sure she gets them.' A month later, at the culminating anniversary ceremony in Brussels, and in the presence of leaders of the Government, he was even more precise. Banging on the platform with his walking-stick, he called for action: the sort of action which had been taken by the 'men of 1830' to create Belgium in the first place.

In a characteristic (and necessary) appeal to considerations of thrift, he called the defence bills 'the most useful measures introduced since the law setting up our railway system, the first in Europe, in 1834. This scheme will give our commercial prosperity modern foundations and will guarantee our safety without raising taxes by a "centime" or increasing the draft by one man. May God protect the Belgians, and may the Belgians, by their deeds, successfully consolidate their independence and increase their prosperity!'

The King had practised this speech for hours in his cabin aboard the 'Alberta', and it was greeted with loud cheers by the crowds: the Government winced. Immediately afterwards, Leopold sent for Auguste Beernaert, whom he regarded as the ringleader of the pacifist movement in Belgium, and launched into a furious quarrel with him beside the platform, while embarrassed ministers and fascinated spectators peered at them both. Beernaert considered that the King had spoken out of place, and put unfair pressure on the decisions of Parliament; Leopold, then and at a second meeting later the same day in the Palace, practically ordered Beernaert to vote in favour of the new forts at Antwerp. The two old men, the ex-minister as obstinate as the King, failed to budge each other. It was their last dispute: their arguments were taken up by next day's newspapers, but they did not meet again. Undeterred, Leopold spoke yet again a few days later in Antwerp itself, site of the planned forts and capital of Belgian anti-militarism.

'Do you wish,' he challenged the audience, 'to be led, perhaps against your will, down the fatal path to decadence? I am asking you, and I demand an answer from you!' (Yells of 'No! No!').

'You do not wish it; very well, then, it is simple. Let us vow ourselves, by the solemn oath of free citizens, to support the bill
advanced by my Government which would make Antwerp into
the greatest port in the world . . . ' He ended, to the delight of
his listeners, by using his unsuspected Flemish to shout
'Antwerpen boven! Voor Antwerpen en, bovenal, voor Belgen-
land!'[1]

Such speeches excited the Press, but ultimately did little to
affect opinion in Parliament. The Government, well aware of
the risk it was running in putting forward any kind of programme for rearmament, did not particularly wish to seem the
instrument of a profoundly unpopular King; Smet de Naeyer
disliked Leopold's crude implications that those who opposed
the Antwerp forts were bad patriots, while the arguments about
the cheapness of the works and the commercial prosperity they
would bring were simply mountebank's patter. If the left-wing
Liberals called for personal military service when the debates
opened at the end of 1905, it was because they were beginning
to understand that Belgian neutrality would be worth little in
a new European war.

The debates were hard enough; Leopold made them harder
for Smet by his incessant notes and instructions. Their contents
were often sensible enough, but it was intolerable that the King
should tell the leader of the Government the order of his
speakers in the Chamber, or whom in the Opposition he should
lobby. By early 1906, Leopold had retreated in disgust to a
country house; as the debate dragged on, he complained to
Smet: 'The Chamber is no longer fulfilling its duty under the
Constitution: it has made a mess of everything, and managed
to bring discredit on itself. I shall stay on here, where it's
pleasant enough; I have no wish to be in Brussels presiding over
scenes of national impotence'[2].

At Karlsruhe, in September that year, Leopold cautiously
renewed contact with the Kaiser. Perhaps regretting his outright
horror at William's suggestions for a Belgium expansion southwards towards the historic Burgundy, he was once again
intriguing against Luxemburg, and he needed and obtained
German approval for certain plans which subsequently came to

[1] Long live Antwerp. For Antwerp, and above all, for Belgium!
[2] Quoted in Carton de Wiart; *Souvenirs des dernières années;* p. 122.

nothing[1]. But a more personal reconciliation was made in the spring of 1908 at Wiesbaden, where the two monarchs exchanged formal visits; Leopold, now dangerously fat, cramming his body into German ceremonial uniforms which had fitted him a decade ago but now would scarcely button, and the Kaiser taking care to call unexpectedly so that the old King was caught at a disadvantage with his feet up, reading the Belgian papers in his hotel bedroom. This time, the Kaiser was quite cordial. He had some reason to be grateful to Leopold, who had ingratiated himself in the past year by suggesting to other Powers (without success) that Germany should be granted certain trading privileges in the South American market. However, this access of warmth did not reassure Leopold very far, and he continued to canvass the friendship of his other guarantors, in particular that of France in the person of Georges Clémenceau.

A last and ultimately successful assault on the practice of *remplacement* opened at the end of 1908. The volunteer experiment, accepted glumly but loyally by Leopold in 1902, was now acknowledged even by the Minister of War to have been a failure, and Schollaert, leader of the Government, prepared to challenge the right wing of his own party and its Nestor, Charles Woeste. After almost a year of hard parliamentary fighting, supported by the King's customary barrage of personal letters to his allies and opponents, Schollaert carried through the abolition of *remplacement* and the institution of personal military service for one son in each family, a victory only achieved by a deliberate alliance with the Socialists against Woeste and his 'Ligue Antimilitariste'.

It was December 1909. Suddenly, Leopold was taken ill, and there was talk of a serious abdominal operation. The bills had passed the Chamber but there remained the obstacle of the Senate. Leopold told his doctors: ' . . . you must above all keep me alive till next Tuesday, because that is the day of the final vote on the military law, and I want to be able to sign it before I die'. On December 14th, the operation was carried out, and the

---

[1] The Grand-Duke who had six daughters and no sons, had fallen seriously ill. Leopold proposed that the Belgian heir, his nephew Albert, should become Grand Duke as well as King of the Belgians, leaving Luxemburg with internal autonomy. At least one influential Luxemburger favoured this idea, but the Duke recovered and lived to 1912, leaving his title to his eldest daughter. See Carton de Wiart; *Souvenirs des dernières années;* p. 150.

bill, which the Senate had passed, was brought to Leopold to sign. At 6.30 in the evening, still under the effects of chloroform, he traced his last shivering signature on the bill. Early in the morning of the 17th, he was dead.

CHAPTER XXXII

LEOPOLD: HIS MISTRESS AND HIS DEATH

LEOPOLD in his last years was a figure of European notoriety. Wherever the rich and the elegant gathered, he was to be found, enjoying to the full the almost painful elaboration of 'Edwardian' luxury—the chairs specially constructed to be straddled facing backwards, the liverish cuisine of rich meat and game reduced to a cream by pestle and mortar—without succumbing to the moods of cosmic doubt which affected some of his contemporaries. Leopold was confident. His Biblical beard was snowy; his little fingernails were grown as long as boars' tusks; he was very rich, and he did not care very greatly what people thought of him. In his seventies, he could still beget children and, not without strain, deal with the tempers of a spoiled and uneducated mistress in her twenties.

Like many highly-sexed men, he was sensitive about his health to the point of hypochondria. On wet days, his great fan-shaped beard was stowed away in a Russian leather bag, in case it became sodden with rainwater and gave him a cold. He feared a cold almost more than any other disease; all doors had to remain shut, and visitors who sniffed ominously were at once shown out of the Palace. Germs were kept away by the process of boiling the table-cloths daily, by frequent eau-de-cologne rubs, and by other measures ranging from patent underclothing to the ironing of *The Times* already described. His bowels also preoccupied him, and throughout the day he would repeat at intervals (he always spoke of himself in the third person before servants) 'Donnez-lui la boule', and be handed his carafe of warm water to drink. At Wiesbaden in 1908, it was noticed that he carried his own glass, bulging out of his pocket, to sip 'the waters'. But he remained remarkably healthy until the year before he died, when his defective leg became suddenly worse and he began rapidly to put on weight.

As a young man, Leopold had been quite humourless; late in his life, he developed a facility of wit and was often to be seen grinning to himself. He acquired an *alter ego* in the person of the financier Valère Mabille, who resembled Leopold closely and who was always accused by the King of having committed the various sins and excesses ascribed by the Press to himself. Irritated by the way in which certain European monarchs avoided him as morally unclean, he became more tolerant towards the moral lapses of others[1].

Edward VII was one of those who found Leopold intolerable, perhaps seeing in him some distorted reflection of his own tastes. Victoria, on the other hand, though she never liked him, seems to have forgiven him much for his father's sake, and this tolerance Leopold found curiously embarrassing. 'The King of the Belgians came to dinner one night,' noted Sir Frederick Ponsonby in about 1898. 'He seemed very nervous and frightened of her (Victoria) and sat twisting his hands like a schoolboy. It was curious that she should like him, because his morals were notorious, but the Queen seemed to overlook this'[2]. At Victoria's funeral, however, Leopold was not allowed to walk in the cortège behind the hearse and was confined to a state carriage, and the new King deliberately omitted to follow the convention of sending him greetings on his birthday. Occasionally their paths crossed accidentally, as in Paris in 1905, when Edward VII and Leopold found themselves in the same theatre. 'When we entered our box,' Ponsonby recalled, 'I caught sight of King Leopold, who sank as low as he could in the stalls, like a hare in a field when shooting is going on.' The Press assumed they must have had dinner together, which 'annoyed King Edward quite enormously'[3].

Much more serious, from Leopold's point of view as a member of a ruling dynasty which must soon undergo a succession, was his unpopularity in Belgium itself. The resentment at his

---

[1] A fuss was made by Belgian officials when Leopold proposed to decorate Caruso. Leopold noted to his secretary : 'Kindly point out to the Minister of Foreign Affairs that it is not at all certain that Caruso pinched a lady at the Zoo. It was near the monkey-house. Caruso asserts that the lady went too near and was pinched by a monkey, not by him. The facts remain obscure. What is not obscure is that Caruso, a foreigner, gave a free concert for the poor Belgians of Paris and raised 110,000 francs for them . . . We are not concerned with whether Caruso did or did not pinch a lady in another hemisphere.' (Quoted in Carton de Wiart; *Souvenirs des dernières années;* p. 209.)

[2] Sir Frederick Ponsonby; *Recollections of Three Reigns;* 1951; p. 55.

[3] *Ibid.*, p. 222. He does not mention that Leopold had his mistress, the Baroness Vaughan, beside him in the next seat.

Congo policy and his views on conscription found expression in attacks of astonishing fury on his private life, and there was a distinct resurgence of Republicanism among the Socialists and their mass support. The Socialist morning paper *Le Peuple* ran from about 1906 a daily item or more or less fictional scandal entitled 'Résidence Royale', but only an extended quotation can give the Knoxian flavour of these articles.

In the first article of a series for *Le Peuple*, Jules Lekeu wrote on July 19, 1906: 'Up to these last years, Leopold seemed to be a monstrous business tycoon who relaxed from the cares of his fabulous enterprises in the arms of any passing houri who took his changing fancy, in the manner of our middle-class merchants and speculators: actresses and good-time girls provided him with a harem . . . Today, the situation has changed: the King no longer stoops to prostitution, like his associates, in wild outbursts of sensuality and lasciviousness: prostitution climbs to meet the King . . .

'Public opinion now unanimously charges Leopold the African (who has also been known as Leopold the Asiatic) with taking on not only the attitudes but the habits of his new rôle as exotic potentate. The King has lost all notion of the rights and duties of constitutional monarchy . . . We accuse this gloomy Sire of throwing away a fantastic number of millions in the degrading company with which he is not afraid to surround himself and to foul his old age, and we protest in fury when we recall that those millions were made from the blood of wretched Africans slaughtered in the jungles of the Congo as they harvested rubber—without counting the vast total of other millions, mentioned today only with disgust, which were levied on the Treasury and savings of our country: that is to say, on the labour of our proletariat! To megalomaniac financing and building, the King now adds megalomaniac debauchery, and this debauchery is founded on plunder and on crime.'

Whatever damage Leopold might have done to constitutional liberties, Lekeu could have paused to reflect, he had certainly done little to impair liberty of speech in the Belgian Press. Six more long articles in the same vein followed, referring to 'obsessive senile passion', to 'legions of bastards' (Leopold I was under fire at this point), and finally defining the King as 'the living symbol of public immorality', but there was no prosecution. The Press was as free as in those days when Napoleon III had almost threatened war to stifle Belgian journalism. Anyway, too much of what was being said was true.

When Lekeu spoke of 'prostitution climbing to meet the King', he was speaking of the Baroness de Vaughan. He did not exaggerate. Her real name was Caroline Lacroix, and Leopold first saw her in 1900 in a corridor of the Elysée-Palace Hotel in Paris, where, at the age of about sixteen, she was operating under the control of a young man called Emmanuel Durrieux. At once, the discreet business of 'assignation' was begun by Leopold, and a few days later, Caroline was summond to a private house in the Rue Lord-Byron, ignorant (according to her own story) of the identity of the client she was to meet.

After a long wait, the door opened to admit 'two silent gentlemen, one of venerable aspect with a long white beard . . .'[1]. For some time, Leopold and his equerry were content to sit and stare at her, while her nerves frayed under their inspection. They took in her chestnut hair, her touchingly plump figure, and the rather childish directness of her expression. Leopold approved of what he saw; later, *Le Peuple* explained to its readers that 'nothing stimulates or reawakes the exhausted vices (of old debauchees) more than a smooth virginal face topping the gorgeous body of an Aphrodite; thus they can keep the greedy illusion that their caresses amount to a sort of rape'. Perhaps this was Caroline's original appeal to Leopold, but she soon became very much more important to him than the instrument of a passing experiment in lust. In spite of her bad temper, her vulgarity and her disloyalty, it was possible for a contemporary to write that their relationship was 'a solid and genuine attachment which was for his last active years a real consolation for all the misfortunes he had endured'[2].

When he had stared enough, Leopold sent the equerry out of the room, and began to talk to Caroline, gently holding her hands between his own. Did she know who he was? She thought he looked like pictures of the King of Sweden. Leopold laughed, and suggested that he looked more like the King of the Belgians. Then he became more practical. Back at the hotel, she would find all she needed for a journey to meet him at Bad Gastein, a

[1] Baroness de Vaughan; *Souvenirs*.
[2] G. de Raymond; *Léopold II à Paris*; Brussels 1950; p. 63

few days later. She was to travel under the name of the Countess Rienzi, posing as Leopold's god-daughter. Apart from the question of whether she wished to come—which was not even mentioned—all had been arranged.

In due time, Caroline gave her pimp Durrieux the slip and caught the Orient Express to join Leopold at Bad Gastein. Now began a partnership which was to last until his death and to involve both of them in depths of emotion which they had not expected to visit. After many transient mistresses, Leopold discovered at last that there was a woman with whom, by and large, he could bear to live. They quarrelled loudly and often in public, but observers came away with the impression that Leopold enjoyed these scenes and, even when he was over seventy, drew a sort of vigour from them. For her part, Caroline at first grudgingly and later more willingly put up with the public abuse which came her way, for none of Leopold's ruses to keep their relationship secret had any effect, and the Royal family in Brussels knew about her within a few days of her arrival at Bad Gastein. Inevitably, she became more dependent upon the King than a more experienced courtesan would have been, grateful to him for his advice and his protection.

At first, Leopold kept her as much as possible out of Belgium. Once a week, she would make the journey from Paris to Laeken, to be entertained by Leopold in an improbable bedroom decorated with false books and desks to look like a study. They took holidays together abroad, and he was with her at Luchon in the Pyrenees when he heard of Marie-Henriette's death. After this, he felt less inhibited about having Caroline near him in his own kingdom, and he moved her into the Villa van der Borght, connected to the Laeken grounds by an ornamental covered bridge.

In 1902, when she was eighteen and the King was sixty-seven, Caroline became pregnant and was installed in the Villa des Cèdres at Cap Ferrat, where a boy baptized as Lucien Delacroix was born. For this boy, and for his brother Philippe, born eighteen months later, Leopold rediscovered the affection cut off by the death of the young Count of Hainaut thirty-three years before. The dynast was again the father of sons, and immediately after Lucien's birth, he began to press for some measure of legitimization. But the Belgian Government would not hear of it, and it was then that Leopold gave Caroline the title of 'Baroness de Vaughan' and her first son that of 'Duke of Tervueren'. Some sort of family life was arranged for the two boys at the Chateau de Balincourt, near Paris, which Leopold decorated in his usual taste with silver baths and porphyry walls, and here he spent many months of his last years playing with the boys and their pony in the park, and helping Caroline to ignore the wads of abusive mail which arrived daily from the outside world.

He wanted to legitimize the children: the rest of the Royal family fought with every weapon to frustrate him. In this they were assisted by the Brussels public and Press, who mobbed the Baroness when she appeared in public and relished every new 'revelation' about her supposed sexual tastes. It was assumed that Philippe, the second son, was not Leopold's, and when Caroline committed the absurd indiscretion of renewing contact with Durrieux and inviting him to the Villa at Laeken, it was suggested that he was the child's father and played a part in a Royal *ménage à trois*. Other articles gave imaginative descriptions of secret rooms with obscenely-placed mirrors and curiously-equipped couches. Inevitably, the day came when the Baroness was stoned in the street, but when Leopold summoned the leader of the Government, Frans Schollaert, and demanded guarantees that this would not be allowed to occur again, Schollaert asked outright that he should send his mistress away from Brussels for a time.

In private, a succession of obscure but violent scenes centred on the Baroness. In her memoirs, she claimed that a member of Princess Clémentine's household planned to compromise her by seducing her aboard the 'Alberta' and letting the news get to the King. On this occasion, Leopold chose to believe her version of events, but they quarrelled severely over the reappearance of Durrieux and even over Leopold's treatment of his equerries.

The family attack on the Baroness was led by Clémentine and her two sisters; neither they nor the Belgian public thought it just that the patrimony which would have rescued them from their debts should be spent on villas and jewellery for a Parisian call-girl. The Princesses, acting through Cardinal Mercier, made an approach to the Pope, and extracted from him a pronouncement that Leopold must either give up his mistress or marry her. This tactic miscarried: to the horror of his daughters, Leopold prepared to accept the second alternative. He would marry his mistress, but, as he told the Baroness, not yet. 'Let the storm die down a little . . . but there's one thing which must be done without delay: legitimize the children.' Unable to circumvent the Belgian constitution, Leopold ultimately arrived at a compromise: he recognized his sons as Princes of Saxe-Coburg-Gotha, of German nationality.

On December 1, 1909, Leopold arrived in Brussels from Balincourt. He looked unwell to the courtiers who met him at the station, and he asked to have his bed made up in the tropical palm-house at Laeken, instead of in the Palace. Four days later, he was showing signs of paralysis. Leopold went on working at his state papers, in the stifling greenhouse heat, but he took his condition seriously, and sent for the Baroness Vaughan. Arriving in Brussels in the late afternoon, she found a reassuring note from the King, enclosing tickets for the evening performance at the Théâtre de la Monnaie. Puzzled, she went obediently to the theatre, and afterwards came round to see Leopold at supper in the palm-house. During the evening, he had been examined by his own physician, the ubiquitous Professor Thiriar, who had helped to deliver Lucien at Cap Ferrat and who had posed willingly as a 'man of straw' for the King in various directorships.

Now Leopold told his mistress that he was going to die: Thiriar had given him a ten per cent chance of surviving a major and necessary intestinal operation. Caroline began to cry, while the King commented gloomily that too many doctors had been called in to his case. 'They will put in too much work and kill me. If it didn't mean shaving my beard off, I would go disguised as a poor tramp to some panel clinic, and have a chance of surviving'. Then, quite unexpectedly, he added that they would be married the following day.

Still wearing the black silk dress she had worn to come from Balincourt, the Baroness was married next morning by the Laeken chaplain to a King in a white flannel dressing-gown. When the ceremony was over, Leopold called Auguste Goffinet, who had acted as one of the witnesses, and said to him, not without dramatic relish: 'Let me introduce you to my widow. I place her under your protection for the few days which she must spend in Belgium after my death.'

If this version is accepted—it is that of the Baroness, but others dispute the exact day of the marriage—Leopold married his mistress on the morning of December 13th. He spent the rest of the day working feverishly, unwilling to be interrupted by politicians or relations, and later that same morning he instructed his lawyer to transfer a mass of his personal possessions, decorations, silverware, footmen's liveries, even the fittings of the 'Alberta', to the last and most secret of his Foundations. For the Baroness, he arranged that six deed-boxes containing a small fortune in Congo stock should be brought to her early next morning, before his operation. Towards evening, he took the Last Sacrament, and consented to see Clémentine, who was in an agony of embarrassment in case she ran across the Baroness in the confusion of the few small rooms in the palm-house; Albert, heir to the throne, called, and was succeeded by the Prime Minister, Frans Schollaert, to whom Leopold essayed a few tired remarks about the transience of popularity: 'It comes and it goes, and it's not worth the scum it leaves behind it.'

The operation began at ten o'clock on the morning of Monday the 14th, and lasted for four hours. By the evening, Leopold was conscious and able to sign the Personal Service Act brought to him from the Senate. His doctors were optimistic. On Tuesday and Wednesday, he held his ground, while the Baroness screamed and wept outside his door at the crowds of officials and well-wishers who tried to push past her into the sickroom. He seemed to be gaining strength. Then, early on Thursday morning, gasping sounds came from his bedroom: the Baroness and the doctors rushed to him and found him clutching his throat, attempting to get out of bed. They held him back, his head fell sideways, and after a few moments, he died.

CHAPTER XXXIII

SOWING SALT IN THE FURROWS

THERE were many aftermaths to the death of the King. Immediately, the Baroness was thrown out of the Palace by the Royal family. She found the doors of the Villa van der Borght locked, and seals affixed by Louise's lawyers to the boxes of Congo stock, and only the assistance of the old Governor of the Société Générale, Baron Baeyens, enabled her to get them away to France.

As for Leopold, who had demanded a private funeral attended only by Albert and his closest relations, his wishes were ignored: crowds of chattering foreign princes followed his coffin through the streets of Brussels, and the procession was held up by people trying to get a glimpse of Louise and Stephanie or buying satirical pamphlets about the dead King.

But in a more significant way, Leopold's intentions were still being carried out. In 1910, the inquisitiveness of the Princesses' lawyers at last wore down the resistance of Baron Auguste Goffinet, one of the twins who had served Leopold as aides-de-camp since 1875, and he revealed the existence of an unsuspected network of 'Sociétés Anonymes' and trusts which the late King had established as the last hiding-place for the Royal fortune. In the summer of 1907, while the Government was pressing him to abandon the 'Fondation de la Couronne', Leopold had sent for a German lawyer from the dynasty's home town of Coburg, and with his assistance had set up a secret and entirely illegal body into which he poured the wealth of the 'Fondation' and the rest of his assorted holdings and properties. It was into this 'Foundation of Niederfüllbach', housed in a castle near Coburg, that he had confided even the valuables of the Laeken dining-rooms and his personal jewellery, a few days before his death. The Foundation of Niederfüllbach, composed partly of German lands and forests and partly of the assorted fortunes of the Congo, had a triple purpose. After Leopold's death, its income was to be divided into three equal shares: a third to be redivided among certain male members of the house of Saxe-Coburg-Gotha; a third to be ploughed back as additional capital into the Foundation; and a third to be spent 'according to the directions left by the Founder', in other words, on the familiar programmes of Belgian public works and monuments.

But Niederfüllbach did not stand alone. Goffinet now admitted that eighteen buildings in Brussels which were thought to be his own property in fact formed part of another Leopoldian foundation, and investigations brought to light two more large holding companies. One of these was the French 'Société immobiliere de séjour et d'exploitation horticole de la Côte d'Azur', into which Leopold had transferred his properties on the Riviera in 1909. Its purposes, again, were a mixture of the dynastic and the benevolent. The eldest male of the Belgian line of the Saxe-Coburg-Gothas was to be chairman of the company, and to have the use of the various estates and villas on the Mediterranean, as a sort of permanent summer retreat for the Belgian Kings. At the same time, the company was to finance sanatoria on the Riviera for the use of officials employed in the Congo. A second company, whose equally grandiloquent name is usually shortened to the 'Société des Sites', had been set up in Brussels a month before the King's death; far richer in capital than the 'Société de la Côte d'Azur', it contained Leopold's real estate in the Brussels region, and the books, paintings and furniture from the Royal palaces. Both companies were partly dependent upon the Foundation of Niederfüllbach. The Belgian Government discovered 'Côte d'Azur' stock at Niederfüllbach, and the various directors and trustees, including Dr Thiriar, formed in effect a single body of men devoted to carrying through Leopold's purposes beyond the grave.

Lawsuits over the property of these three bodies continued for decades. The action brought by Louise to claim the wealth of Niederfüllbach failed, but a settlement was arranged between the Belgian Government and the Princesses shortly before the outbreak of war[1]. The other two trusts were finally dismantled in 1921, the Ministry of Finance taking over the 'Sites' property, and the Colonial Ministry taking the shares of the 'Côte d'Azur' on behalf of the Congo.

[1] See page 212.

With the discovery and uprooting of this last group of companies, Leopold's great plan for emancipating the Belgian Kings finally came to nothing. He had wanted his dynasty to be, not unconstitutional, but capable of acts of national leadership above the day-to-day relations between Crown and Parliament which the Constitution existed to define. This power could most easily be founded upon money, and that money must flow from private sources which were not dependent on Parliament and Civil List. To achieve this end, he mastered and used with unique skill the techniques of colonial exploitation and trust capitalism.

He failed. Albert soon regained for the Monarchy the popularity which Leopold II had lost, but the future of the Belgian Kings was set in the twentieth century towards a domesticated rather than an imperial image, and the most successful Kings and Queens have been those who interfered least in politics and could show a contented and ordinary family life. Leopold was defeated by the growth of democratic politics in his reign, and by the scepticism of the mass of Belgian people towards expensive and glorious projects of national aggrandisement. He once said of his subjects that 'one has to lash the Belgians constantly to obtain any progress at all; they dislike that and kick back'[1]. Leopold offered the Belgians nothing that they really wanted, and in the end they showed that they could kick harder than any King could lash.

[1] Liebrechts; *Léopold II, Fondateur d'Empire;* p. 340.

SHORT BIBLIOGRAPHY

ANSTEY, R. T. *Britain and the Congo in the Nineteenth Century.* London. 1962.

L'Assiette au Beurre. (French illustrated satirical magazine.) Paris. 1901-7.

BANNING, EMILE. *Mémoires Politiques et Diplomatiques.* Brussels. 1927.
    Reflexions Morales et Politiques. Brussels. 1899.

BATAILLE, HENRI. *Les Dernières Années de Léopold II.* Paris. 1911.

BAUER, LUDWIG. *Leopold The Unloved.* London. 1934.

BAUNARD, MGR. *Le Cardinal Lavigerie.* Paris. 1894.

BIEBUYCK and DOUGLAS. *Congo Tribes and Parties.* London. 1961.

BIOGRAPHIE COLONIALE BELGE.

BRAUSCH, GEORGES. *Belgian Administration in the Congo.* London. Institute of Race Relations. 1961.

CAMMAERTS, EMILE. *The Keystone of Europe.* London. 1939.
    The Prisoner at Laeken. London. 1941.

CARTON DE WIART, COUNT. *Léopold II; Souvenirs des Dernières Années.* Brussels. 1944.

CATTIER, FELICIEN. *Etude sur la Situation de l'Etat Indépendant du Congo.* Brussels. 1906.

CEULEMANS, FATHER P. *La Question Arabe et le Congo.* Brussels. Académie Royale des Sciences Coloniales; Vol. 22. 1959.

CHAMBRUN, GENERAL DE. *de Brazza.* Paris. 1930.

CHENG-LIN. *The Chinese Railways, Past and Present.* Shanghai. 1937.

CORNET, R. J. *La Bataille du Rail.* Brussels. 1953.

CROKAERT, PAUL. *Brialmont.* Brussels. 1928.

CROWE, S. E. *The Berlin West African Conference.* London. 1942.

DAYE, PIERRE. *Léopold II.* Paris. 1934.
    L'Empire Coloniale Belge. Brussels. 1923.

DELEPINNE, BERTHE. *Elisabeth, Reine des Belges.* Brussels. 1955.

DELSINNE, ARMAND. *Le Parti Ouvrier Belge.* Brussels. 1955.

DICTIONARY OF NATIONAL BIOGRAPHY.

ERRERA, PAUL. *Léopold II et Beernaert.* Brussels. 1920.

FABRI, J. *Les Belges au Guatemala.* Académie Royale des Sciences Coloniales. 1955.

FANE, P. A. W. (Countess Westmorland). *Correspondence.* London. 1909.

LE FEBVE DE VIVY, L. *Documents d'histoire précoloniale belge.* Académie Royale des Sciences Coloniales. 1955.

FREDDY, G. *Léopold II Intime.* Paris. 1905.

GRAND-CARTERET, JOHN. *Popold II, Roi des Belges et des Belles* (cartoons). Paris. 1908.

HUBNER, COUNT. *Neuf Ans de Souvenirs d'un Ambassadeur d'Autriche à Paris.* Paris. 1904.

HYDE, H. MONTGOMERY. *The Mexican Empire.* London, 1946.

HYMANS, PAUL. *Frère-Orban.* Brussels, 1905.
Mémoires. Brussels. 1958.

LEGUM, COLIN. *The Congo Disaster.* London (Penguin). 1961.

LICHTERVELDE, COUNT L. DE. *Léopold II.* Brussels. 1926.

LIEBRECHTS, C. A. M. *Léopold II, Fondateur d'Empire.* Brussels. 1932.

LOUISA, MARY AMELIA (Princess Louise of Belgium). *Autour des Trônes que j'ai vu tomber.* Paris. 1921.

LUGARD, LORD. *The Diaries of Lord Lugard.* Edited by Margery Perham. London, 1959.

MANNONI, O. *Prospero and Caliban.* London. 1956.

MATTICIC-KEGLEVIC, COUNT GEZA. *Loca Por Razón de Estado.* Madrid. 1904.

DE MEEUS, ADRIEN. *Histoire de Belgique.* Brussels. 1958.

MERLIER, MICHEL. *Le Congo de la Colonisation Belge à l'Indépendence.* Paris. 1962.

MILNE, A. H. *Sir Alfred Jones. A Story of Energy and Success.* London. 1914.

MOOREHEAD, ALAN. *The White Nile.* London. 1960.

MOREL, E. D. *King Leopold's Rule in Africa.* New York. 1905.
Red Rubber. London. 1906.

MORLEY, JOHN. *Life of Gladstone.* London, 1903.

MORSE, H. B. *The International Relations of the Chinese Empire.* London. 1910-18.

OLIVER, ROLAND. *The Missionary Factor in East Africa.* London. 1952.
Sir Harry Johnston and the Scramble for Africa. London. 1959.

PIRENNE, HENRI. *Histoire de Belgique.* Brussels. 1929.

RANIERI. *Les Relations entre l'Etat Indépendant du Congo et l'Italie.* Académie Royale des Sciences Coloniales. 1959.

RAYMOND, G. DE. *Léopold II a Paris.* Brussels. 1950.

RESZOHAZY. *Origines et Formation du Catholicism Social.* Brussels. 1958.

RICHARDS, CHARLES. *Some Historical Journeys in East Africa.* London. 1961.

RICHARDSON, JOANNA. *My Dearest Uncle. Leopold I of the Belgians.* London. 1961.

RIDDER, A. DE. *Le Mariage de Léopold II.* Brussels. 1925.

ROBINSON, R., GALLAGHER, J., and DENNY, A. *Africa and the Victorians.* London. 1961.

ROEYKENS, FATHER. *Léopold II et l'Afrique.* 1855-80. Académie Royale des Sciences Coloniales.
Les Débuts de l'Oeuvre Africaine de Léopold II. 1875-9. Académie Royale des Sciences Coloniales. 1955.

SCHREIBER, MARC. *Belgium.* London. 1945.

SINGLETON-GATES, P., and GIRODIAS, M. *The Black Diaries.* Paris. 1959.

SLADE, RUTH. *The Belgian Congo. Some Recent Changes.* London (Institute of Race Relations). 1960.
English-Speaking Missions in the Congo Independent State. Académie Royale des Sciences Coloniales. 1959.
English Missionaries and the Beginning of the Anti-Congolese Campaign in England. Revue Belge de Philologie et d'Histoire. No. 33. 1955.
King Leopold's Congo. London. 1962.

SONIS, COUNT DE. *Lettres du Comte et Comtesse de Ficquelmont.* Paris. 1911.

STANLEY, HENRY MORTON. *The Congo and the Founding of its Free State.* London. 1885.
The Exploration Diaries. Edited by Richard Stanley and Alan Neame. London. 1961.
Unpublished Letters. London, 1957.

STENGERS, JEAN. *La Place de Léopold II dans l'Histoire de la Colonisation.* Brussels. La Nouvelle Clio. October 1950.
Combien le Congo a-t-il coûté à la Belgique? Brussels. Académie Royale des Sciences Coloniales. 1957.
La Première Tentative de Reprise par la Belgique.

STENMANS, ALAIN. *La Reprise du Congo par la Belgique.* Brussels. 1949.

STEPHANIE DE BELGIQUE (Princess Stephanie). *I was to be Empress.* London.

STINGLHAMBER, G., and DRESSE, P. *Lèopold II au Travail.* Brussels. 1945.

TALLEYRAND-PERIGORD, DOROTHEE DE (Duchess of Dino). *Memoirs.* London. 1909.

TAYLOR, A. J. P. *Bismarck. The Man and the Statesman.* London. 1955.
Prelude to Fashoda. English Historical Review. January 1950.

THOMSON, R. S. *Fondation de l'Etat Indépendant du Congo.* Brussels. 1933.

TRANNOY, BARON DE. *Jules Malou.* Brussels. 1905.

URSEL, COUNT HIPPOLYTE D'. *La Cour de Belgique et la Cour de France.* Paris. 1933.

VAN DER ELST, BARON. *Léopold II et la Chine.*

VAN DER SMISSEN, E. *Léopold II et Beernaert*. Brussels. 1920.

VANDERVELDE, EMILE. *Souvenirs d'un militant socialiste*. Paris. 1939.

VAN LEYNSEELE, H. *Léopold II et les Philippines en 1898*. Brussels.

VAN ZUYLEN, BARON P. *L'Echiquer Congolais*. Brussels. 1959.

VERBEKEN, A. *La Révolte des Batetela*. Académie Royale des Sciences Coloniales. 1958.

VERMEERSCH, FATHER A. *La Question Congolaise*. Brussels. 1906.

VON WISSMAN, H. W. *My Second Journey* . . . London. 1891.

WAUTERS, A. J. *L'Etat Independant du Congo*. Brussels. 1899.
Histoire Politique du Congo. Brussels. 1911.

WOESTE, CHARLES. *Echos des Luttes*. Brussels. 1906.

INDEX

Aborigines' Protection Society, 242, 243
'Acte Additionel', 279, 280
Adowa, battle of, 222, 225, 227
'Affair of the Horses', 43-4
Afrikaansche Handelsvereeniging, 110, 116
Albert of England, Prince, 24, 39-40, 69
Albert, heir to Belgian throne, 152, 274, 281, 297
American China Development Co., 235, 236
d'Anethan, 77, 80, 81
Anglo-Belgian India-Rubber Corporation, 189, 201, 241, 250, 257
Anglo-Congolese Treaty, 162, 170, 171, 225
Anglo-Egyptian Condominium, 224
Anglo-French Declaration, 224, 228
Anglo-French *Entente*, 283
Anglo-German Agreement, 167, 169, 170, 234
Anglo-Portuguese convention, 161
Anglo-Portuguese Treaty, 126, 129, 132
Angola, 86, 124, 159, 163
Antwerp, 49, 50, 62-3, 78, 80, 143, 282, 286-7
'Antwerp programme', 150
'Anversoise', the, 193, 200-201, 252
Arab Wars, 159, 171-6, 222-3
Arcade de la Cinquantenaire, 275
aristocratico-metalliques, the, 22, 65, 137
Aruwimi River, 128, 159, 223, 279
Armstrong, Vice-Consul, 252-3
Association Democratique, 65-6
Association Internationale Africaine, 95-101, 103, 105-7, 109-10, 113, 117, 120, 123, 130, 142, 277
Association Internationale du Congo, 117-9, 121-7, 129-35, 143, 179, 254
Association of Militant Democracy, see *Peuple, Le*
Austria, 29, 31-4, 37, 40, 67, 72, 93, 156; and Triple Alliance, 283
Austro-Prussian War, 18

Bachrach, Dr, 209-11
Bagamoyo, 86, 95, 166
Bahr-el-Ghazal, 124, 159, 166-70, 174, 181-2, 192, 224, 228-9

Banning, Emile, 71-2, 92, 108, 132, 136, 144, 156, 181-5, 189, 197, 233
Banque Nationale de Belgique, 63, 78, 147
Batetela people, 176, 223-4
Beak, Vice-Consul, 251-3
Becker, Jerome, 167, 174
Beernaert, Auguste, 142-8, 151-3, 156-8, 174, 186-8, 195-6, 198, 245, 262, 268-9, 286
Belgian cooperatives, 150
Belgian court, 28-9, 101
Belgian labour movement, 150-2, 154-5, 158
Belgian Left, 11, 23, 100, 144, 153, 186. See also Socialism
Belgian Press, 31, 32, 38, 40-1, 71, 100, 116, 146, 244, 292-3, 295
Belgian trades unions, 150-1
Belgians Abroad, 58
Benedetti, 69, 70, 78
Berlin Act, 134-5, 145, 149, 159, 161, 174, 176, 181-3, 186, 196-7, 244, 248, 253-4, 257, 259
Berlin Conference, 132-5, 143, 145-7, 163
Bismarck, 68-70, 73, 78, 126, 132-3, 135, 156, 157, 166
Blondeel, 39
'Boerenpond', 155
Boma, 103, 105, 114, 124, 125, 136, 146, 196, 201, 248, 258
Borchgrave, Baron de, 89-91
Boulanger, General, 148, 156
Brabant, Duke of, see Leopold II
Brazza, Count Savorgnan de, 87, 89, 115-6, 119-22, 125
Brederode, rue de, see Companies of rue de Brederode
Brialmont, Alexis, 46, 48-52, 54, 57-8, 62, 156, 233, 285
Brooke dynasty, 55
Browne de Tiège, Alexandre, 190, 192-4, 200, 238
Browne de Tiège, Constant, 193, 200, 238
Browne de Tiège Loan, 188-9, 190, 192-4
Brussels Anti-Slavery Act, 183, 187
Brussels Anti-Slavery Conference, 174, 178-9, 180-4

*For further information about Granta Books
and a full list of titles, please write to us at*

Granta Books

2/3 HANOVER YARD

NOEL ROAD

LONDON

N1 8BE

enclosing a stamped, addressed envelope

———————————

You can visit our website at

http://www.granta.com